THE END IS THE BEGINNING

Also by Jill Bialosky

Prose

Poetry Will Save Your Life

History of a Suicide: My Sister's Unfinished Life

Poetry

*Asylum: A Personal, Historical,
Natural Inquiry in 103 Lyric Sections*
The Players
The Skiers: Selected Poems
Intruder
Subterranean
The End of Desire

Fiction

The Deceptions
The Prize
The Life Room
House Under Snow

Anthology

Wanting a Child (edited with Helen Schulman)

THE END IS THE BEGINNING

A PERSONAL HISTORY OF MY MOTHER

JILL BIALOSKY

WASHINGTON SQUARE PRESS

ATRIA

New York Amsterdam/Antwerp London
Toronto Sydney/Melbourne New Delhi

WASHINGTON SQUARE PRESS

ATRIA

An Imprint of Simon & Schuster, LLC
1230 Avenue of the Americas
New York, NY 10020

First Washington Square Press/Atria Books hardcover edition May 2025

WASHINGTON SQUARE PRESS / ATRIA BOOKS and colophon are trademarks of Simon & Schuster, LLC

Some of the text has been adapted from "What It's Like to Lose a Mother While the World Is Mourning," Oprah Daily; "For My Mother's FaceTime Burial, Lipstick and Howling Winds," New York Times; "How to Say Goodbye," Real Simple.

The events and experiences detailed here are rendered as the author has remembered them to the best of her ability. Some names, identities, and circumstances have been changed.

For information about special discounts for bulk purchases, please contact Simon & Schuster Special Sales at 1-866-506-1949 or business@simonandschuster.com.

The Simon & Schuster Speakers Bureau can bring authors to your live event. For more information or to book an event, contact the Simon & Schuster Speakers Bureau at 1-866-248-3049 or visit our website at www.simonspeakers.com.

Interior design by Davina Mock-Maniscalco

Manufactured in the United States of America

1 3 5 7 9 10 8 6 4 2

Library of Congress Cataloging-in-Publication Data has been applied for.

ISBN 978-1-4516-7792-8
ISBN 978-1-4516-7794-2 (ebook)

In memory of my mother, Iris Yvonne Bialosky (1933-2020)

For my beloved sisters, Laura, Cindy, and Kim
(in memoriam, 1968-1990)

What we call the beginning is often the end.
And to make an end is to make a beginning.
The end is where we start from.
— T. S. Eliot, *Four Quartets*, Part IV *Little Gidding*

It is love, not reason, that is stronger than death.
—Thomas Mann, *The Magic Mountain*

Note to the reader

This is a book made of impressions, memories, and stories, some my own, others told to me. In recounting the early years of my mother's history, I depended on photos, intuition, research, and my own imaginings. This is not a biography of my mother. It is one daughter's rendering informed by observation and bearing witness. In writing this book I'm aware of the uncomfortable experience of intruding on someone else's private life. I am also cognizant that there are things I will never know about my mother. All of us hold our private worlds close. I have not attempted to capture the whole of my mother's life, having chosen to write only about certain pivotal moments. I may have gotten things wrong, including some of the family history I have pieced together. Though I have struggled with whether to tell this story, I found myself unable to refrain, such is my belief that my mother's experience of profound loss, heartbreak, and endurance will be inspiring to others.

I.

My mother has just died. It's March 29, 2020. A cold, brutal late afternoon. No sun. Only a white lifeless sky. We're on Long Island. We left the city for our weekend house two weeks ago and then Covid struck and with no end in sight to the pandemic, we've been isolating here. I think of Camus's famous opening line in *The Stranger*. "My mother died today. Or maybe yesterday, I don't know." I, too, feel this strange distortion of time. Maybe because of Covid and because not only am I trapped on Long Island, but I'm far away from Cleveland where I grew up, where my mother died, and lived all eighty-six years of her life.

Outside, two construction workers are demolishing the old deck attached to our house. Everything feels out of whack. Through the window I watch workers, with masks on, strip down the floorboards of the deck, and like pallbearers, carry the warped strips of wood to the dumpster. We had planned for a new deck before Covid hit, hired an architect and a contractor, but now with the pandemic blazing it seems unnecessary and indulgent. There's too much change, but it's too late. We've already made the investment.

March is cold. I'm always cold. There's a catch in my throat that won't clear. A heavy weight that won't lift. Part of me is in denial. How could my mother be dead? My son Lucas is with us when we receive the phone call. He's twenty-five. "I'm sorry, Mom," he says. "I can't believe Mimi's gone." My youthful mother refused to be called Grandma. My husband, David, hugs me, and I cry into his T-shirt. This is my family. My tiny world David and I built brick by brick. We've had this house since Lucas was two years old and memories of his coming of age are everywhere. I know why some people think houses are haunted. It's because a house takes on the personality of its owners. Even the old deck with its once flapping dark blue awning, sometimes holding up five or six inches of snow, torrents of rain, faded by sun, carries memories.

It's a strange time to mourn the loss of one's mother, when the entire world is mourning the crushing fatalities from the pandemic. It's unreal. Soaking vegetables and fruit in the sink, wiping down cans, milk bottles, and groceries from the store before putting them away, wearing plastic gloves and masks. Straight out of a dystopian novel, the streets empty, everyone existing in a bizarre world of mourning and need for protection.

I pace the floors, I lie down. I take a long walk. I don't know what to do with myself. How to calm down. Again, it's the feeling of being estranged from my mother's dying. If I was with her, perhaps the reality would sink in and I wouldn't feel so disconnected. There's a tight pang in my chest. My eyes burn. Sometimes I can't catch my breath. Has it really happened? When I learned she was failing, I'd been in New York in lockdown. I wanted to be with my mother as she passed. The care home where she has lived for the last few years quarantined all visitors. If I want, I can pretend it hasn't happened. I can close my eyes on death, try to go back to normal but then I'm brought back by its stark reality. My mother could be inscrutable, irrational, impulsive, willful, demanding. Certainly not a PTA-joining and cupcake-baking mother, rather a single mother who raised four daughters on her own. She was never ordinary.

It seems blasphemous. Preposterous, not to be allowed to attend my own mother's funeral. Another devastation of Covid. I think of all the others mourning the deaths of their loved ones and not being able to bid them farewell, and it is as if we are travelers together on the River Styx in a weird state of limbo. I'm crying inside but tears won't come. I fight with myself about whether I can still figure out a way to travel to Cleveland in the first month of a deadly pandemic. David's judgment is less clouded by emotion. I speak to the rabbi on the phone who will preside over the funeral. In Jewish tradition the body must be buried within twenty-four hours. This is to give comfort to the soul of the deceased and quicken the journey to the next world. It also allows the mourners to begin the grieving process. He wants it to happen tomorrow.

For dust you are and to dust you shall return, from Genesis. The body must go into the ground and the mourners must help bury the body. But I won't be there to take the cold visceral earth in my hands and throw it onto her casket, a ritual that symbolizes the body going back to nature and to its final resting place.

I ask the rabbi if, under the circumstances, we could wait a few days. I want to be there. The rabbi expresses his condolences and tells me what I already know but don't want to accept, that it's impossible without first being quarantined. He says he knows it's hard for me not to be at my mother's funeral, but there's no choice. The virus is too contagious and dangerous. He's the rabbi affiliated with the care home in which my mother resided, and he says that he knew my mother, that she was a sweet and lovely person. He briefly outlines the plan for her interment. No funeral service. Only a graveside burial. Only ten people are permitted. Everyone must stand six feet apart. The ritual of Kriah, the tearing of the cloth, a symbol of pain and grief; throwing dirt on the coffin, a mark of closure. Afterward the seven-day shiva candle.

In Judaism the period of Nisan is the first month of the Jewish calendar, and since Passover is the spring festival of liberation, it is a special time for our mother to pass over, the rabbi informs me. Ordinarily, when someone dies, there's a thirty-day mourning period following shiva, but Passover cancels it to commemorate the month of rebirth. It's days before the beginning of Passover. The story in the book of Exodus, of the ten biblical plagues where God commanded the Egyptians to suffer so that they knew who was in charge, comes to me. History repeats itself. A virus permeates the globe. Sooner or later, we, too, those of us whose lives will be spared, if we are vigilant in our seclusion or quarantine, or are lucky, will eventually be delivered, just as the Israelites were eventually delivered from slavery more than 3,000 years ago. But we are only slaves to a disease. Is it really a special time for my mother to die? I don't know.

The rabbi asks me more about my mother and her life for the brief eulogy he is planning to deliver. He's spoken to my other two sisters as well. The youngest of the four of us has been gone for years. I tell the rabbi that my mother was a loving mother. That she raised us girls on her own. That she lost her first husband, my father, when she was only twenty-five and then a daughter when she was in her fifties. As I speak to the rabbi, I realize there is so much I don't really know about my mother, so much that I've never fully understood. She was monumental in my life. It was as if there were a cord from her heart to mine that was never fully severed. Who was she before she had me? What had she sacrificed to raise us? Born in 1933, what was it like to come of age in the forties and fifties, when so little was expected of women save to be wives and mothers? Suddenly there are no more words that I can say.

———

THE DAY OF the funeral I wake up. I'm confused. Foggy. We've been in lockdown. Day 20, or maybe 21. Days blur. Rituals are important. Especially during Covid. I crawl out of bed, dress, grab my coffee. Outside the workers have shown up again. I can see them from the windowed doors that open out to the deck from the main room of our barn-style house, in masks and thick long beige worker pants and coats covered with white sheetrock dust. In the early morning fog, they could be mistaken for ghosts. I wonder if their hands are cold. I hear the vibration of wood being stripped from the floorboards. It's like the sound of a breaking heart.

———

I EAT A small bowl of granola, a boiled egg. I take a walk— walks have become essential during lockdown. I'm wearing my old and ratty winter jacket, long pants, boots, and a scarf around my neck. My lockdown outerwear. The ground is hard from the cold. The wind stings my eyes and face. A morning thrush calls its timeless sorrow. A screech and then a pause for two or three seconds and another screech, as if making the sound requires enormous strength. I hold on to it.

I walk down the long quarter mile road that leads to our house and is abutted by a horse farm—put in my earbuds, and an audiobook lifts me momentarily from a mournful world where people by the thousands are dying and others are living in quarantine or seclusion, losing livelihoods, loved ones, like I have lost my mother. Black birds rest on the wooden fence. The horses in their large pens I can see from one side of the road are wearing red wool blankets as they graze. Occasionally one will sigh or neigh and from our house I can hear their cries, carried by the wind. They, too, have become my companions.

This week I've been listening to *Howards End*, a novel by E. M. Forster about the privileged lives of siblings Margaret, Helen, and Tibby Schlegel; where they'll reside once their lease is up is the crux of its plot. I'm at the part in the novel where Margaret has just learned of the death of her friend Ruth Wilcox and, through a letter from the care home where she spent her last days, discovers that Ruth has bequeathed her country house, Howards End, a symbol of the Eden of the past, to Margaret. I will be receiving no bequeathment. At the end, my mother had so little, her possessions long distributed or given away. Did my mother ever experience an Eden in which she was cast out? I want to stop time. To stop the funeral that awaits at eleven this morning. The sky is gray, the air cool and full of moisture. The wind picks up. Soon it will rain. I tie my scarf more tightly around my neck, walk a few more laps up and down the long road. Each day in lockdown I try to walk at least four or five rounds for exercise, then make my way back home.

———

IT'S SO QUIET in the house. Lucas is on the computer in his room. David is in his study working. When he hears the door open, he comes out and gives me a hug. He's sad, too. We don't speak. There are no words. I go into the bathroom to wash my face and dry my eyes. I must look pretty for Mom.

I dress for the virtual graveside burial in a black flowing blouse my mother would love, put on the sapphire earrings she gave me, lipstick—my mother never left the house without it. David changes from his now-that-we're-in-lockdown sweats into a crisp blue button-down shirt and dark khaki pants. Lucas wears a pullover sweater. In Cleveland, a driver in a sedan arrives to pick up Laura, the only sister in Cleveland. Cindy is in lockdown in Connecticut. We sisters group-text (and occasionally Laura snaps us a photo) as the car drives through mostly empty roads to Mount Olive Cemetery in the Cleveland suburbs where my youngest sister, Kim, is also buried.

We switch from text to FaceTime, watching the burial on a 4.7-inch screen. In Cleveland, a pearl-gray morning of howling winds. Laura shows off her new sunglasses. We blow kisses. The sedan pulls up the long drive to the cemetery. It is one of the grayest days I remember. At 11 a.m. the service begins. Along with my sister are my paternal aunts, uncles,

and cousins, all standing six feet apart and wearing masks. My
mother's maternal relatives—her parents, aunts, and uncles
have already departed from the earth. Her younger brother
is quarantined in Minneapolis. Through the window of my
phone, a jerky kaleidoscope of cloudy sky, a small blue tent
flapping in the wind, underneath a podium where the rabbi
presides, a quick flash to the mahogany coffin soon to be lowered into the ground. It seems impossible that my mother's
frail body is inside it. Hundreds of gravestones like dominoes
stand in the background, a few bare trees just beginning to
bud. A bluebird skims the weighted sky. I look up from the
tiny screen on my phone and out my own window in Long
Island at a family of trees in the yard; their crippled, arthritic
branches form a chorus of joining arms.

The rabbi, in his long black coat and black top hat, a white
mask strapped over his face, speaks loudly, head dramatically
raised to the sky over the demented wind. As a child I believed
God was watching over me. I went to temple, and I listened
to the rabbi and the rabbi spoke of God and throughout my
childhood I spoke to God in my head, especially in times of
anxiety and stress. God help me pass my math test. Make
me as beautiful as my mother. Please God make so-and-so
like me. Make Mom happy. The things girls say. The places
we hurt.

As a child, I saw God as a replacement for my father who
died when I was two. Now I still pray to God when I'm in crisis,
scared. Prayer is a way to forestall anxiety. Jewish doctrine has,
in my experience, been vague about the afterlife. My mother
believed in reunion, that when she died her soul would be
reunited with loved ones. In this moment, watching the rabbi

pray to the sky as he says the Kaddish, this is a consolation. And though I do not have the imagination for that belief any longer, I will give it to her. It soothes me to think that in her dying, she was anticipating reclamation.

The rabbi conveys to the small gathering that Iris's daughters, Cindy who lives in Connecticut and I in New York, have saved many hundreds, maybe thousands of lives by not traveling. I'm not so sure, but nevertheless, I'm briefly comforted. He recites an incantation of prayers and blessings in Hebrew over the relentless wind before he offers a more personal eulogy. Iris Yvonne Bialosky was a loving mother of four daughters, he says. He remembers the other central figures in my mother's life, from her aunts, parents, and brother, along with her two sisters-in-law, her nieces, and nephews. He mentions that she worked in real estate and retail, and that she was loved by many, and then abruptly his eulogy concludes. I want more to be done and said for my mother, exactly what I don't know, the end of a life—it's too short, more should be said but it's Covid and raining and there are no more words. What about my mother's early years before I knew her, her marriage to my father, the loss of her mother when she was a child. How she was not financially secure or mature enough to take on the care of her daughters. How, as a woman coming of age in the early 1950s, she was ill-equipped for what befell her. Suddenly, as the rain is pouring on my roof in New York and on the black umbrellas in Cleveland and slapping the thousands of headstones, for all she has endured, my mother feels heroic and noble. Perhaps this is the moment when it occurs to me that I must write about my mother, make my own eulogy, and go on a quest to understand and capture the woman behind the mother who was often so unknowable to me. Motherhood is deep. We all must mourn our mothers. We must travel from the end to the beginning.

———

LAURA RISES FROM her fold-up chair and throws handfuls of earth on the top of the coffin, the first handful is for her, and then she takes a handful for me and throws it on the coffin lid, and then another handful for Cindy and the last for our sister Kimmy before the casket is lowered into the ground. Tears burn my eyes. "The Lord is my shepherd. I shall not want. He maketh me to lie down in green pastures . . ." the rabbi begins. "He maketh me to lie down in green pastures," I repeat in my bedroom holding my phone in my hand, grateful for the psalm's command, its authority. Yes, I, too, must lie down. Rain continues to fall as if the angels are weeping. I wonder, is she already an angel.

———

AFTER THE VIRTUAL burial, I say the blessing and light the seven-day shiva candle to begin the mourning period. I retrieved it with gloved hands the day before—the Jewish Center kindly left it in a plastic baggie outside on their porch. Later in the day, I take another walk. Put in my earphones. *Howards End*, chapter 12, Margaret privately mourns Mrs. Wilcox: "A funeral is not death, any more than baptism is birth or marriage union. All three are the clumsy devices, coming now too late, now too early, by which Society would register the quick motions of man." The rain has stopped. I look up at the sliver of light parting the darkening sky.

———

DAYS AFTER THE funeral grief comes in waves. Mostly when I'm not expecting it, in the shower, setting the table, where I remember my mother telling me where the knife goes, and the wineglasses always above the knife. Day by day, as the workers tear down the deck, first taking away the metal poles and railing, I'm unsettled. Memories of my mother are still swirling; how the rewards of living were diminished by worries, regret about my mother's difficult life, the push-pull of wanting to forget her, the need for my own freedom to build my own family, and my inability to let go. I'm nostalgic for all that has passed. I'm afraid of forgetting. My mother was hard to capture fully. I suppose all mothers are. Larger than life, they leave their shadows and absence. She was beautiful. She liked to laugh. She liked men. She loved her daughters. She was the mother I fought against and the mother whose history shaped every aspect of my life. In my mind, I picture my mother's latching eyes. She's still working her way inside me.

———

LUCAS GOES BACK to the city to quarantine in our apartment with his girlfriend. It's hard to let him go.

———

DURING THE WORKDAY, David and I go to our separate quarters. Like John Cheever—who every morning dressed in his suit and tie, rode the elevator of his apartment building down to the lobby, and then took the stairs to his workspace in the basement, like clockwork—I go to my own newly formed study in Lucas's bedroom, bookshelves packed with video games, trophies from sports, a few stuffed animals I'm not yet able to part with. I turn on my computer. Look out the window at the bare trees that have not yet begun to bud. What am I doing?

I'm grateful for the hours of tunneling in and distraction. But at night, my dreams are dark, complex, as if I haven't really slept, my unconscious swimming in the sea of memory, bringing my mother to the surface as if my dreams are an underwater theater for my desire not to let her go. She's obstinate. Has always been obstinate. There is a tear in the sky that I don't know how to mend. What will the world look like without my mother to care for? My sisters and I have always been her safety net. As we moved through adolescence, we kept each other afloat. Then later, after we left for college, the roles slowly shifted, and we became our mother's caretaker.

She passed on to me her delight in flowers, beauty, her voracious appetite for good food, art, and dreams for romance that sustained her through her many losses. Why, for so long, did her despair and sadness overwhelm me? Did she want to die? Had she had enough, finally unmoored from her suffering? How much does a daughter owe her mother? Did I do enough? These questions plague and distract me.

It's the first time I am free from my mother's dependence. There should be release, but I don't feel it yet. I come outside Lucas's bedroom to take a break. Watching the construction workers from the living room is good distraction. They toss the molded wood and remnants from the old deck into the dumpster in our driveway. David masks up and goes outside to talk to them. I offer them coffee or cold water. We chat about the weather and the pandemic; small talk keeps us afloat. The buzz of the drill and the saw cutting the wood for the new floorboards offer strange comfort. Perhaps because of the buzz of the drill I think of Emily Dickinson's poem, "I heard a Fly buzz—when I died."

> I heard a Fly buzz – when I died –
> The Stillness in the Room
> Was like the Stillness in the Air –
> Between the Heaves of Storm –
>
> The Eyes around – had wrung them dry –
> And Breaths were gathering firm
> For that last Onset – when the King
> Be witnessed – in the Room –
>
> I willed my Keepsakes – Signed away
> What portions of me be
> Assignable – and then it was
> There interposed a Fly –
>
> With Blue – uncertain stumbling Buzz –
> Between the light – and me –
> And then the Windows failed – and then
> I could not see to see –

Iris, too, willed her keepsakes, and signed away her assignables by putting her children in charge of her care. There was no other choice once she became sick and lost her independence. Did she meet her King? Did she feel the stillness in the room? Was she ready to let go?

Like a spy, I watch from the window glass the construction workers cart away the dumpster, like a deep casket that holds the bones of the deck, and the new construction begins. The construction is like a grand theater. I succumb to the sounds of the cutting of wood, the punch of a staple gun, the drill and churn of the cement mixer; leveling and measuring, the miraculous hum of a new structure being built. The two workers lay out the string line to mark the frame, dig holes for the steel posts, pour in concrete, cover the holes with plywood, cut and fasten 4 x 4 posts. I'm amazed by the care, artfulness, and precision it takes to construct the deck. I imagine if my mother were here, she'd be ordering them around like she used to do when she remodeled our house.

When bad weather keeps the workers away, David and I grow anxious for them to return. They offer not only distraction, but our only physical contact in this strange new world, though we must stand six feet apart and wear masks to speak to each other. While so much is falling apart, people losing jobs, dying, it seems indulgent to build a new deck, but at the same time life affirming. We must go on.

———

THE SCAFFOLDING FOR the new deck begins to take hold. I'm used to the banging, the buzzing of saws, the odd comfort of the drill. Now I'm looking forward to the new deck, a place to read or work in quiet; to listen to the rain fall. Sophia, our golden mix, curled in her outdoor chair, her chin resting on the cushion, eyes transfixed by mine. I'll observe the stand of trees coming to blossom in spring shedding their rain of pollen. Witness the birth of green leaves in summer, watch as they lose their bond to the branch and cover the ground in the fall. In winter the skeletal branches reach to the sky like arms stretched overhead as if in praise. In the background it is the cacophonic sound of bird and insect life (the crispy music of cicadas, the buzz of bees and wasps) that offers company. It's amazing how the world goes on, regardless of those we've lost. There was a tree in my neighbor's front yard. It toppled over during a storm and was cut down, leaving a thick four- or five-foot trunk where a few healthy branches jutted out. Over time, the branches grew and spurred new ones. I, too, am waiting for new growth.

————

EVENTUALLY, THE FLOORBOARDS are laid, the roof that stands on pillars built (we decide on an open wooden high ceiling instead of an awning), and the smell of fresh cedar in the air we breathe, as if the deck has taken on its own life and miraculously finds harmony and equilibrium in its setting. Blue birds and red cardinals take a moment of sanctuary landing on the beams that hold its railing. Bees and wasps join the chorus. Spring turns to early summer and the lavender and hydrangeas slowly bloom, etching away the haunted ghosts of winter. The nature of grief. Some days you don't feel it. No pain. No sudden weeping. It works its way silently.

I stand on the sturdy new deck, three times bigger than the old one, and watch the tree branches swaying in an orchestration conducted by summer wind. Through the brush I witness a deer and her fawn nuzzling against her, pheasants weighed down by their size, flapping their wings to rise and escape our barking dog. Sophia is on the hunt. It's her nature. She sniffs for the scent of moles underground, when she finds one, she rolls her head side to side in the mud, listening, then begins to frantically dig, catches one in her mouth and doesn't want to let it go. We have to pry open her mouth to release it. Cruelty from beauty. I can't blame her. I look up to the sky. Some days it is vast, others the clouds hang low almost to the ground. My mother's spirit won't leave. Is she telling me to immortalize her life, from the end to the very beginning? The tear won't yet mend. Like Emily Dickinson, *I hear a fly buzz by.*

2.

A call from the hospice nurse early on Saturday morning, March 28, 2020. Iris is eighty-six years old. She has a 102-degree fever. Restless, uncomfortable. Morphine. Further decline. A restriction has been lifted from the visitor ban from two weeks ago. Laura, my older sister, has been living in Cleveland for a year and is allowed into the care home as long as she wears a mask and doesn't go anywhere other than my mother's room. My other sister, Cindy, and I are furloughed respectively in Connecticut and New York in lockdown. Laura group-texts once she enters our mother's room, its walls covered in framed photographs of her family and the floral paintings she created in the arts and crafts room when she was still in assisted living. Mom looks terrible, Laura texts.

The care home tests Iris for Covid and tells us the test results are negative. I don't believe them. Covid has struck other patients at the care home. The pandemic is raging. Why my mother's sudden fever? The nurse tells us she is dying. It's only a matter of time. Hospice is with her. I always imagined that when my mother's time came, I would be by her side, as she slipped away. I think she would have wanted all three of her daughters surrounding her to ease her departure. Now it sinks in that this won't be possible.

There are things I want to say to my mother. I want to tell her that I'm sorry that her last years have been unpleasant and compromised. I want her to forgive me for not living closer to her in the last years of her slow dying. I want assurance from her that she knows I have done my best. For her to give me a sign that she is ready. This is magical thinking because now she can't articulate her thoughts into full sentences. Only a word or two, a nod.

Covid prevents my travel. Flights are restricted. If I drive, I'll have to quarantine for fourteen days before I can enter the care home. By then, my mother will be gone. I pace my bedroom to quell my anxiety and distress. I'm still searching for other alternatives before resigning myself to the inevitable.

Laura will have to be the lone Charon guiding my mother toward the River Styx. During the hours of limbo, waiting for her to pass, I recline on the chaise lounge in my bedroom with my phone next to me, waiting for further news and listening to the rain fall on the roof. I knit my Covid poncho, allowing the reality of my mother's dying to slowly slip in. I don't fear for my mother to die, for her body to leave us; I want her to go, to be at peace—she is frail, uncomfortable, and unable in the last weeks to eat or drink because swallowing causes pain. It is time for her to pass to the Elysian Fields. I want her to be in tranquility, to no longer suffer from bodily and spiritual discomfort and to no longer be lonely. I'm not afraid for my mother. But I'm afraid of who I will be without her. Only later will I understand that she hasn't left me. She's more a part of me than I comprehend.

Outside daffodils have shot up, waving their crowns;

forsythias in their crude and blinding crimps of yellow burst forth, as they did every spring in the yard of my childhood home. I'm not ready. Grief crawls up my throat.

FaceTime: my mother under a white blanket, white thinning hair pulled back, hollowed eyes, sculpted cheekbones, the flannel blanket tucked over her body in her room at the care home. Her face reminds me of a painting I can't recall, maybe by Rembrandt. Lucas and David briefly join the FaceTime with us three sisters. We reminisce. How she stood over me to make sure I meticulously dried every piece of lettuce for the salad for her elaborate holiday dinners. Never put bottled condiments on the table. Kept a suitcase of antique toy cars and trucks she collected at flea markets in her house for when my toddler son and nephew came to visit. We sisters remember Laura's teenage bedroom with posters of Marilyn Monroe, John Kennedy, Herman's Hermits, The Beatles, and other celebrities my mother curated as wallpaper (as an adolescent I used to stare lustfully at the poster of the young Marlon Brando on a motorcycle), instructing the painter for hours on where to plaster each poster because she was prone to change her mind, a quirk I sadly inherited. Now I remember more, Paul Newman with those soulful eyes, sexy Brigitte Bardot, *The Mona Lisa* with a bouquet of colored flowers in her lap (the only color on the black and white walls). My mother's beautiful kitchen with the copper pots hanging over the sink and her Fiestaware from her flea market days. Lucas tells Mom that he remembers how when we came to visit in Cleveland, my mother would take him to the playground where I played as a child. "I love you, Mimi," he says. Tears swell. My throat catches. I tell my mother I love her, too, that she's been a wonderful mother. What I mean is, under the circumstances in which life presented itself to her, but that I don't say. I did not always think she was wonderful. I don't know what else to say. Laura says she thinks she can hear us.

Last text from Laura a few hours later.

Five p.m., March 29. Mom is gone.

Laura sends us a photo. My mother's white, thin hair falls to her neck, her skin is gray, her mouth open as if caught in a sigh. She is dead but she won't leave me.

The white flannel blanket covers my mother's frail body. At least she's warm, I irrationally think. I can no longer look at the photo of my mother's gray haunting face. The photo of death. Of a body whose soul has passed. I want to remember her vivid eyes before she got sick. I wonder if they washed her before they took her. I wonder who dressed her. I wonder if she would want to wear her wedding ring when she is entombed underground, but we want to keep it to remember her. There were so few things that she owned. I am mad that I was not with her to hold her hand as she took her last breath. After the FaceTime I go into the bedroom and lie down. I'm weighted to the bed. I can't move.

I try to hold my mother's passing soul in my body. Or perhaps her spirit has not quite left us. In Judaism the Kabbalah states that the soul is granted a glimpse of God's Divine presence before death. The soul experiences a deep sense of peace and serenity as if it is preparing to return home. The Talmud says that we run to the world to come. Those great rabbis, before they died, declared out loud the souls of the dead that would accompany them to the heavens. Because my mother is a believer, I imagine my father, my sister, my great aunt Harriet, my mother's mother, and her father, ready to receive her.

3.

Iris is eighty-five when the social worker calls my office in New York City at the publishing house where I'm employed as an editor to tell me they're transferring her to a new unit. It is winter of 2019. For the last seven years Iris has been living on the Menorah Park Campus. When she first moved to Menorah Park, she dwelled in one of the campus's assisted living facilities called Stone Gardens in her own apartment. When she could no longer manage her daily care, she was moved to the Weinberg Unit for skilled nursing care. And now, as her disease has progressed further, the nursing facility is deploying Iris from the Weinberg Unit to the Fairmount Unit. "It's the place where they send the residents to die," Fran, my mother's private aide, tells me over the phone when I give her the news. My mother is in the last stages of Alzheimer's.

I plead with the social worker not to send her to Fairmount. After years in Weinberg, she's finally comfortable there. The social worker explains that now she requires two aides to lift her from her wheelchair to the toilet, to shower, to get her out of bed (her body goes limp), and the Weinberg Unit is not staffed for the care required. She's no longer able to hold herself up. If she slumps in her wheelchair, someone must sit her upright. She's lost control of her legs to stand. I understand the need to move my mother to another unit where she can get better care, but I don't want to accept her condition, nor do I want to disrupt her since she has settled into the routine of life in Weinberg.

———

TO HELP MY mother adjust, Cindy and I travel to Cleveland. From our respective homes, we both catch early Saturday morning flights; sometimes mine is so early that I fall asleep in the Uber on the way to the airport. We have our own ritual. We've been traveling back and forth to Cleveland for years, more often since she's been sick, and as her health continues to diminish, we go once a month. After check-in, we meet at the Delta Sky Club, picking at toasted English muffins with peanut butter, slices of fruit, a slippery hard-boiled egg, bracing for the visit. How will she look this time? Will she remember us? Be more diminished? Will her hair be washed, her nails manicured?

After the plane touches down in Cleveland, we wheel our overnight bags to the food court at the airport to search for fresh bagels or pastries to surprise her with, stop at the kiosk for a bag of peppermint patties, Mom's favorite, some almonds for sustenance, then take the airport shuttle to the rental car park. With Cindy as the designated driver, we begin the forty-five-minute journey to the care home, bracing ourselves for what's to come. We've traveled to Cleveland so many times during the ten years that my mother has been ill that we could navigate through Cleveland Hopkins Airport blindfolded.

Once we enter the sliding glass doors of Menorah Park, the stench—a combination of urine and warmed-over cafeteria food, or is it the smell of decay—makes me gag. I've always been sensitive to smells. To the left of the foyer is a desk where a security guard stands, and then an information desk. Behind an open window sits the receptionist, closely observing what visitors bring in since Menorah Park is a kosher institution. Once we got busted for taking in a non-kosher pizza (we figured out how to bring it back in by putting the pizza box in a tote bag). I am still getting used to my mother living in an institution with restrictions. Her life has already become restricted enough, and I want some small privileges for her.

———

WHEN YOU ENTER Menorah Park's building, you'll find a medium-sized lobby with a row of synthetic dark purple couches, a room that is meant to make one feel comfortable, where family members can sit, relax, wait for a driver. Tucked in the corner of the lobby are a few empty and broken wheelchairs. On one side a security station. The floor is covered with a purple-burgundy smash of carpet that belongs more on the floor of a disco than the vestibule of one's last resting home. The vibe is outdated, ready for a re-do. Along one side of the room stands a fake player piano. A stuffed dummy of a musical maestro in a tuxedo is flopped over the keys. It reminds me of an image out of a Fellini movie, life as mere circus and charade. Look, it's the jester of the dead playing

his last sonata. Is it meant to be funny? Cute? A joke to entertain the grandchildren? How to describe the ambience.
It's not like a country club or a cozy living room like some
other nursing facilities—it's a touch kitsch. We look at each
other, shake our heads. We try to lift the mood, push our
happy buttons, knowing our mother will be thrilled to see
us, but it's hard.

We walk through the foyer to the ladies' room to make use
of its facility, apply a touch of lipstick, brush our hair, to look
pretty for Mom. I see women my mother's age in their eighties
leading independent lives, still able to converse, to be active, to
be the leading ladies in their own world. Why did my mother
get this terrible disease? There are no sure answers. I'm still
perplexed by how we got here, how we assigned our mother
to a care home. How we didn't realize when she moved into
assisted living seven or eight years ago, able to walk, converse,
and have her meals in the dining room, just how much the
disease's slow progression would steal from her. Denial is a
powerful coping mechanism.

———

ENTERING THE FAIRMOUNT Unit is like entering a horror movie or a dark painting by Blake or Goya. Residents
are hunched over their chairs, some fallen onto the table in
the main dining hall. Others with their ghostly heads down
and mouths hanging open. There is a special room for the
residents on feeding tubes. They recline in stretchers with a
flexible tube connected to their nose or belly. Stroke victims
live here, too; one is a young man, maybe he's fifty, with brown

skin and unbearably sad, dark, penetrating eyes—they are his only mode of communication—he's unable to feed himself or speak, his arms are contorted, and his head rests on one side of his wheelchair. Others wear mitten-like open-toed slippers on their feet and terry cloth mittens on their hands so that they don't injure themselves. My mother refuses them when offered. She'll only wear the soft black shoes with the Maryjane straps that I have brought for her. Dignity is still important to her. She won't see herself like the others. But surely dignity must also be important to my mother's fellow travelers on this unit, and my heart breaks to see these dwindled lives where the life force has weakened.

In the main room of the unit the nurse stands at attention at her rolling station doling out meds and typing data— weight, food intake, body temperature—into her computer. She's tall and stern, with an Eastern European accent, maybe from Poland or the Ukraine. Stoic. If I ask her a question about my mother, how she's been doing, if she's eating, if she still cries—one of her aides told me that sometimes my mother cries out of sadness or loneliness or despair (it is hard to know) and asks for her daughters—her replies are cool, quick, emotionless, and then it's back to the computer. I'm reminded of Dante's *Divine Comedy*, of the inevitability of death. Of the strength required to be a passenger as souls begin their journey toward God. Perhaps because the nurse is surrounded all day by people who are sick and dying, and by their difficult and critical relatives, she needs to steel herself, focus on doling out meds and taking temperatures. We call her Nurse Ratched in homage to the character from *One*

Flew Over the Cuckoo's Nest. Thinking of the film, Cindy wonders what would happen if we gave the residents some gummies. Humor helps us to keep a distance from the suffering around us.

———

THE RESIDENTS ARE parked in the main dining room, the more lucid watch television, some are asleep, others nearly comatose, as if they are ghosts already roaming in the realm of the shades. I tell Cindy that it's like entering hell's first circle, the state of limbo in Dante's *Inferno*, a holding place before death:

> No tortured wailing rose to greet us here
> but sounds of sighing rose from every side,
> sending a tremor through the timeless air,
> a grief breathed out of untormented sadness,
> the passive state of those who dwelled apart,
> men, women, children—a dim and endless congress.

We laugh uncomfortably and then take a deep breath. It's hard to believe our mother's life has come to this.

At lunchtime, aides serve the meals, some residents are spoon fed. After their duties are complete, the staff might be grouped at one table, texting on their phones or talking about what they did the night before, running a play-by-play of a Cavaliers' game—Clevelanders are passionate about the Cavs. The TV, always on, scrolls through game shows, Lifetime movies, news, and sports. For the residents of the Fairmount Unit, time is "a silent sister . . . a column of mercury without a scale," as Thomas Mann wrote in *The Magic Mountain*, his 1924 novel about life in a sanitarium in the Swiss mountains for those suffering from tuberculosis.

As I began writing this book, by coincidence I was listening to the audio version of *The Magic Mountain*—all thirty-seven hours and twenty-seven minutes of it—one of the classic novels on my to-be-read list, not realizing how it would become a lens for me to consider the nature of my mother's life in an institution. The novel is about what it's like to live institutionalized in a place where life exists in its own separate reality.

Like the sanitarium in Mann's novel, there is eccentricity among patrons of the Fairmount Unit. One woman holds a doll and combs her hair. Another scribbles with crayons on a coloring book and continually attempts to get the aides' attention. A hunched-over man occasionally bursts into song.

The residents appear to be in a state of melancholy. My mother is, too.

———

I FIND IRIS among the others in her wheelchair, her head slightly lowered, staring into space before she sees us. I wonder about what time must be like for her now that she's nearing the end of her life with only her daughters' visits to look forward to. To the young, time is an endless road. So much want, desire. Later, as we age, time is something to savor. "Life is desire, and desire is life," writes Thomas Mann in *The Magic Mountain*. Mann considers time to be circular and writes "we measure time by a circular motion closed in on itself, we could just as easily say that its motion and change are rest and stagnation—for the then is constantly repeated in the now, the *there* in the here." Death is the novel's central preoccupation and problem. Hans Castorp, the protagonist, is safe on the Magic Mountain, sheltered from the suffering and decay of society in Europe before the First World War. For the seven years in which he resides there he loses his sense of time. In essence the mountain "quarantines him," as my mother, too, is quarantined in an institution.

Like the characters in the Berghof sanitarium of *The Magic Mountain*, the residents in the Fairmount Unit live a hermetically sealed and ordered life. There is no stopping the progression of the body's demise. Though the residents in their wheelchairs, weakened by illness, numb from lack of stimulation, mostly sit staring directly in front of them, or with their heads bowed, they are still alive. Still part of the process of life. Even after a person expires, Mann writes, the dead partake of life processes in much the same way that a leaf slowly dies, expiring eventually into particles, and being absorbed back into the earth.

Hans Castorp falls deeper under the influence of the Magic Mountain the longer he stays at the Mountain's sanitarium. The days go by one after the other and soon he can't remember how long he's been away. His cousin Joachim tells Hans, "You wouldn't believe how fast and loose they play with time around here. Three weeks is a day to them." And Hans falls under this spell of timelessness, existing in an "eternal now." The residents live in a place where most have come to die. Iris, too, is living in an eternal now.

Like Alzheimer's, there was no cure for tuberculosis during Mann's era, though the mountain's residents live under the illusion of one. The two doctors on staff take their patients' temperatures daily as if they have some control over their fate. The residents are bound by their illness. They give up their past lives, past relationships, and enter a new life of ideas, a new society of people, they form bonds, even have love affairs, as people move in and out of the institution. Some, of course, die there. Residents take the horizontal cure wrapped up in their blankets and enjoy the vistas, mountain walks, company, decadent food, wine, and spirits, even cigars, away from historical events and the everyday responsibilities of living in the world below the mountain.

Up on the mountain, life is bountiful, a utopia. Hans Castorp, engaged by his walks through the mountains, by what he learns from his companions about himself, about life, love, literature, ideas, loses all sense of time, falls into the mountain's snowy trance, and eventually becomes part of the timeless spirit of the mountain, a metaphor for the meaning of existence and eternity. The sanitarium is a microcosm of life itself for those confined there.

Iris is in a trance of sorts, her own magic mountain, where consciousness is fluid. I think of it as a stream, a swirl of snow, no longer regulated by months and years, by the way in which we each form our own narratives of who we are. She's winding down, down, down. I'm not sure she can take in or follow the narratives and plots in literature, but nevertheless I sometimes read her a poem or passages from a book I'm enjoying when I visit. I know she can still take in the beauty of a flower, the face of a loved one, the sound of words.

Here each day is especially like the last. Time is organized into a strict schedule revolving around three meals. Residents

are woken up, dressed, wheeled into the main room for breakfast by seven or eight. After some napping in their wheelchairs
following a trip to the lavatory, lunch begins at eleven thirty
back in the main room, then another activity, an endless stream
of television to view, chair naps. Dinner begins at four thirty.
Before bedtime, the residents are offered a snack, some nights
a cup of pudding, a popsicle, ice cream bar, or cookie. After
dinner, residents are taken one by one from the main room
to be bathed, or if it isn't their shower day, face and hands
cleansed with a washcloth. The aides brush their teeth, change
them into their gowns, ready them for bed by seven thirty or
eight to sleep and the same day begins again the next morning.
Perhaps the same schedule every day is comforting. I hope so.

———

WE SLOWLY APPROACH Iris's table to surprise her and
tap her shoulder in greeting—*Hi, Mom*, we call out—and
she recognizes us. She's slightly hunched in her wheelchair,
wearing a royal blue blouse. She perks up, her head crowned
with shiny white hair cut close to her chin with her glasses
strung on a chain around her neck. It's as if the lights have
been turned on in a dark theater. We embrace her and give
her hugs. "Jilly, Dee Dee," she calls out, her pet names for us
since childhood. Tears sting my eyes. She remembers us. "I'm
so glad you're here," she says. Iris is sitting at a two-seater table
in the main room, a turquoise terry cloth bib pinned over her
blouse. All the residents wear them as they await their meal.
Sitting across from her is a woman who has lost her teeth and
wears a hairnet. Why must patients sit across from each other
at the table when they are unable to converse? It's awkward.

I make a note to ask the social worker if Iris can be moved to a different seat where she can face the television or a window. As we greet my mother, some of the other residents look on, wishing, I think, for the same attention. I look at them and share a sympathetic smile. I wish there was time to say hello individually but all our attention on these short visits must be given to our mother.

We kick open the lock on Iris's wheelchair and push her back to her room and we are free from the dreariness. She'll have her lunch with us, eating the goodies we've snuck in. When one of us is behind the wheelchair and she can't see us, she frantically waves her hand and asks where we are. She's afraid if we're out of her sight, we will be gone. In her room we are met by the sweet, sour smell of illness.

"Why am I here, what is happening?" my mother asks, confused once we're in her room. I tell her she's fine. Remind her that this is her new room, and she relaxes. I'm startled by the gray color of her skin and her cadaverous eyes; she has sunk into herself, grown inward. The recent move has caused more disorientation. My mother doesn't belong here. And yet, because she's immobile, she does. Grief, anger, denial spiral. Neither of us is ready to accept. Her room is full of her possessions: a small floral sofa, two antique chairs, her paintings and photographs on the wall, a nightstand that used to be by her bed at home, a television on the dresser, and once we are inside the room, away from the sadness of the others on the unit we can momentarily relax.

We unburden, taking our coats off, and settle her in. There is a screamer in one room on Iris's new floor, and a wailer in another. We slowly learn that this is something we must get used to. For some Alzheimer's patients, it is a way of life. It's steaming hot in her room, and we adjust the temperature. Cindy accidentally sits down on her bed and the alarm goes off. Perhaps because the staff knows we are with her no one shows up. But what if my mother had fallen? When my mother's eyes are closed, I slink away like a coyote into the large rocks for a breather. I pace the long corridor and get a cup of fresh water from the cooler. Return. Then it's Cindy's turn. Literature for those dealing with relatives with Alzheimer's suggests keeping visits short or taking frequent breaks. It can be exhausting spending time with a loved one in a diminished state, and the trapped air makes it worse. Observing my mother, and the lives of the others here who are also suffering, overwhelming sadness seeps in. It takes work to push through and keep our spirits up.

———

WE UNVEIL THE gifts we've brought her. Mom smiles, though I can see even a smile takes effort. Sometimes we bring new socks and brassieres. On this visit, we noticed the aide neglected to put on her bra, and her bosom had fallen to her belly. Dignity throughout the life process. My poor mother, she derived such pleasure in appearance. She wore bras to bed to keep her breasts from sagging and slept with satin pillowcases to keep her skin from wrinkling and to preserve her hair-style. Another thing I must tell the social worker. In my small Moleskine notebook, I write: *make sure she has her bra when she is dressed.* But I wonder, too, if the need for Iris to wear her bra, for her to be nicely dressed at this stage of her illness is more for me than for her. And then I admonish myself. Of course, my mother would want to look her best.

We've brought her a new pair of lounge pants and a few new tops. We have learned our lesson about buying anything that might shrink. Here at the home, the aides put whatever is dirty into the laundry. Iris's favorite sweaters, gifts for her birthday from her sisters-in-law, have shrunk to the size for a baby. A wool blanket I knit for my mother to keep on her lap since she's always cold, I discovered on another visit had shrunk to the size of a bathroom mat. Perhaps my mother had spilled something on the blanket or had an accident. The sad thing is that I don't think my mother noticed it was gone. Maybe we can use it for a doormat.

We make sure to cut off the labels of her new tops and pants because the labels irritate her skin. Fran, Iris's private aide, tells us we shouldn't spend money on buying her nice things, they'll only be ruined in the laundry, but Iris likes to dress attractively, and again we must preserve her dignity. I retrieve lotion from her bathroom and rub some into her arms and legs where skin is flaking off from the dryness of the institutional air. I've read how important touch is for providing comfort and security to dementia patients. Her muscles are deteriorating and she's weak but she still beams out her appreciation that we're here now, taking care of her.

I rustle through her closet to see which tops or pants are stain-covered and must be retired to the trash bin, so we know what needs to be replenished for the next visit. The color of her blouses washes out quickly. I hold a faded and thinning blouse out to Cindy to see what she thinks, and she says to trash it. The same for the next one. They must use harsh detergent that washes out the color. It makes my skin itch to think of it. Iris always insisted on soft detergent. I must remind myself that my mother lives in an institution with many sick people where germs and illness are everywhere, where the staff are responsible for trying not to let germs and illness spread, and don't have a choice about laundry detergent. It's the small things we focus on, to distract us from how sad we feel that this is now our mother's life.

Over her years in Menorah Park, many of her belongings have vanished. One day, it's a watch with a tortoiseshell band. My mother used to twirl it on her wrist and admire it. Another time it's a black velour zip-up sweater. We have long removed her more valuable jewelry. Cindy is storing her collection of pearls and bracelets and earrings in a drawer in her home. Her diamond chip necklace and antique platinum watch are in the safe in my apartment. How are they to be divided among her three remaining daughters when she's gone? This is something we don't speak about.

We tidy her room, rearranging some of the artwork, one a painting of a street in Italy, another a small painting by the pop artist Peter Max, a man of Jewish German origin, revered among the Jewish community in Cleveland, and straighten family photos that have shifted on the thin cardboard walls. We throw out the Mother's Day plant we sent, now nothing more than some crumbled leaves in a pile of dry dirt, another reminder that I am not there to make sure my mother's room is tidy.

Once we lock her wheelchair in place I take a moment alone in her bathroom to restore. It is tidy and clean.

How can Iris maintain her dignity amid such decay and sadness? My sisters and I quarrel because we're unable to fully take in what is happening to our mother. One of us thinks we could do more. Get the physical therapist to come in. "Maybe if they move her limbs, she can walk again and be moved back to Weinberg," she says. "We should have insisted that she had seen the physical therapist when she was confined to her wheelchair in the Weinberg Unit." We call the physical therapist, and she tells us that nothing can be done. It's magical thinking to believe we can turn back time. With Alzheimer's, calcification occurs in the areas of the brain that control movement. We can't stop the disease's progression; we can only make Mom comfortable. We quarrel because we don't want to accept that our mother is severely incapacitated.

While Cindy stays in Iris's room to finish going through her clothes, I go to investigate. There is a room with a curtained doorway; I peek in. It is where the residents shower. There is a construction-like lift next to the shower head. I learned that to shower, an aide must attach a belt to my mother's waist so that the lift helps her to stand. She's so frail that I worry that the apparatus will hurt her, but there is nothing to be done about it. I see bruises on her wrists, muscle melted away so there is only skeletal bone and wonder if it is caused by an aide's grip.

The aides on the Fairmount Unit are mostly floaters. The residents are at the end of life and incapacitated, and it may be hard to find staff who can regularly handle the difficult job of caring for these residents who not only requires patience and a strong constitution, but physical strength. Hence, the aides on this unit don't seem to have personal connections with any of the individual residents. Occasionally I will hear one in a loud, cheery, chirpy voice say, "Good morning, Iris," to my mother, as if speaking to a child. I understand the need to close one's eyes to pain and decay. To give out pleasantries. Sometimes a soothing tap on the shoulder. A word or two, "Iris, it's time to take your medication," maybe a pat or rub on her hand, before they give Iris a mini cup of a pill mashed into pudding. I appreciate any attention given to my mother.

Over the last several years, on my many visits from New York, I've witnessed her slow decline, loss of appetite, inability to form more than a few words in a sentence, and wheelchair-bound. I count on her smile when she first sees me enter the floor, where she sits in her wheelchair at her table near the window. The little tap of her hand. I pray that her life will end before my mother no longer remembers me.

There are days now when the burden of my mother's care has grown so great, and the quality of her life so minimal, that I question whether keeping her alive is the right thing. She has long lost her ability to walk, to go to the bathroom on her own, to shower and dress, to speak in more than a word or short phrase. She used to love reading the *Plain Dealer* every morning, doing crossword puzzles, and watching old movies of her favorite actors like Cary Grant or Gary Cooper. I wonder what she considers, or if she even knows, about her diminishment—why one day she could solve a crossword puzzle and the next the letters did not form words. She liked to watch *Jeopardy!*, and later, when her cognitive abilities failed her, she succumbed to the loud but addictive pleasure of *Family Feud*. But now even television game shows are of no interest.

When she was in assisted living at Stone Gardens, and then later Weinberg Unit, our first stop was the library so she could choose large print books to bring back to her room to read. But it is long past the time when she can read a novel or focus on a film. She's lost her appetite. The fresh bagels and lox we bring, or the donuts from her favorite bakery, the pizza from Geraci's, her pizzeria of choice, treats we must sneak into the kosher care home, no longer tempt her. Her body has dwindled to 98 pounds, her veiny wrists so thin I fear they'll break.

Atul Gawande, surgeon and writer, writes in *Being Mortal* about the eight activities of daily living required to be independent:

"If you cannot, without assistance, use the toilet, eat, dress, bathe, groom, get out of bed, get out of a chair, and walk—the eight 'Activities of Daily Living'—then you lack the capacity for basic physical independence. If you cannot shop for yourself, prepare your own food, maintain your housekeeping, do your laundry, manage your medications, make phone calls, travel on your own, and handle your finances— the eight 'Independent Activities of Daily Living'—then you lack the capacity to live safely on your own."

My mother has exhausted her ability to perform all sixteen.

Alzheimer's is a heartbreaking disease. It's impossible to predict how it will eventually alter one's entire being until the progression begins to happen. It slowly affects memory, behavior, and thinking. Life constricts rather than expands. Communication is limited to one or two words, sometimes a few phrases. Sufferers often lose the ability to communicate pain. The senses narrow. Walking, sitting, eating, and swallowing are challenges. Help is required for basic personal daily care such as getting dressed and bathing. Taste and smell also diminish as Alzheimer's penetrates the areas of the brain that enable the senses. Individuals experience greater memory loss and cognition as the disease progresses. The poet Yusef Komunyakaa, in his poem "Blue Dementia," describes the inner life of one who has dementia as if one "woke up dreaming one morning/& then walked out of himself/dreaming?" The body becomes a casement, the mind like a wilting tree. Sometimes I imagine Mom will wake up and be herself again.

Some patients develop personality changes. Some become mean and angry, say cruel things. Swear. Shout. Scream. Iris has become more subdued, sweet, softer, less needy. It's easier to feel connected to her in this state even though conversation is limited. I want to call her "Mommy" as if I've regressed to a child again and my life has come full circle. I'm told by the staff that my mother sometimes cries and calls out one of her daughters' names. When I hear this, my throat catches. She may be remembering sad events, and my mother has plenty of those to remember. Or she misses us. Or maybe also she's bored sitting in her wheelchair all day because there is so little she can do. Even lifting her hand seems to take strength. Does she recognize what she can no longer remember or do? In Alice Munro's story "The Bear Came Over the Mountain" (later made into a film called *Away from Her*), Fiona, the main character, is suffering from the early stages of Alzheimer's disease. In her kitchen, after she has recognized her condition and has made the decision to move to a nursing home, she wipes away with her finger a mark left on the floor from her shoe, an apt metaphor, since her own marks, traces of memory, of physical erasures, will soon be wiped away. Munro has Fiona comment: "'I thought they'd quit doing that,' she said in a tone of ordinary annoyance and perplexity, rubbing at the gray smear that looked as if it had been made by a greasy crayon. She remarked that she'd never have to do this again, since she wasn't taking those shoes with her."

It makes me feel panicky when I think about how it must have felt to Iris when she noticed her memory was disappearing.

———

ON THIS VISIT my mother notices my manicure and tells me she likes the color and then looks at her own hands. She has always been meticulous about her cleanliness and grooming; she looks forward to having her hair done, nails manicured. She often holds out her frail hands with visible veins running from her knuckles to her wrists to examine her manicure. Since she no longer can go to the beauty parlor due to her diminishment, the staff gives her quick manicures, the polish caked on layer after layer and some of her nails are chipped. I take out the nail polish from my purse. "It's called Russian Roulette," I say, "fancy," and we laugh. I go into the bathroom and get the nail polish remover, then file her nails and polish them. I always bring my nail polish when I come to visit because Iris always wants the color I'm wearing. "Thank you, darling," she says, and holds out her hands to admire the not-so-great but doable manicure I've given her.

Afterward, Mom points to her abdomen which means she needs to use the bathroom. One of us must go find the aide. I go out to the hallway and ask an aide who is emptying garbage pails from residents' rooms into a bin if she can help. I am given a face that is not quite a scowl but more an irritation. The aides sometimes move slowly. Lackadaisical, tired. Granted, it is a difficult job, and unpleasant. Still, *do your job*, I want to scream, *my* mom *has to move her bowels*, as my impatience and anxiety mount, but I must be nice and understanding to the aides so that they will not take it out on my mother later.

Thank God for Iris's private aide. Fran's been attending to my mother since she was admitted into the Weinberg Unit. Fran is retired but she remembers Iris from when she cared for another resident at Stone Gardens. She's religious, goes to church on Sundays, has two grown sons, is perhaps close to my mother's age, but her cognition is perfect. She wears a blue smock over her neatly ironed slacks and blouse and has soft eyes. She'll hold my mother's hand, give her a kiss on the cheek, fold a blanket in her lap, tell her she loves her.

Fran brings Iris new soft socks and juicy clementines, takes her for a kosher ice cream at the ice cream parlor, somehow discovers Iris loves to watch sports. So now, most afternoons, Fran takes my mother to her own room rather than the main room to watch whatever sporting event, no matter if soccer, baseball, or football, is available on cable. She's content watching the strong and able bodies perform their visual magic. Iris's favorite sport is baseball. Laura thinks it's because watching the players is eye candy. My mother has always loved a good-looking man. That, too, and because with sports my mother doesn't have to follow a plot. She can watch the action in real time. The games seem to soothe her. She watches intently, but I can't tell if she is focusing, or drifting.

It's a relief not to have to call the busy aide stationed on the floor, or the hard-to-reach social worker to find out how my mother is doing when I'm back in New York. Even getting an answer from the social worker about whether they can find a certain wheelchair for my mother, or an update on her health and weight can take days, even weeks of back-and-forth emails. Fran is always available to take our calls. She tells us that we are good daughters. That we are doing the best we can. Some families I've worked with, she says, never come and that assuages, for a time, some of my guilt. Fran feeds my mother her meals, or whatever she will eat of them. Fran reports that Iris likes to have ketchup on a hamburger or hot dog to disguise the taste, she won't touch the overcooked vegetables, the canned fruit. If only we had known about the ketchup before Mom reached this stage in her illness. Now she subsists mostly on cartons of Ensure and peppermint patties. I'm told by one of the nurses that she likes sweets because she can still taste them. Knowing Fran is with my mother for at least part of the day helps me to feel less anxious.

———

WE MOVE OUR antique chairs whose embroidered cushions are sinking into coils that once belonged to my great aunt Florence next to my mother's wheelchair and catch up, telling her about our work, our families, showing her photos on our phones. Cindy likes to show her pictures of her two cats—my mother loves cats—and tells her the story about the time she found Einstein in the dishwasher! Mira in her shower! Mom laughs. I show Mom pictures of my garden and photos of my son, and this time a copy of a poem I've published in a journal and read it to her. "You wrote that," she says with a sparkle. She has a collection of my books on one shelf in her room, and before she became ill, created a scrapbook for me of clippings of reviews and photos from my book signings and publications. One Christmas she stayed up all night making each of her daughters a photo album filled with baby pictures, school classroom photos, wedding photos, all the way to the present. Mine has a forest green floral embossed cover and is one of my most treasured possessions.

Next, we flip through the voluminous photo albums Iris has carefully curated throughout the years. The albums tell the story of her life from before she was even born. Inside are photos of her parents and grandparents, photos of her as a newborn, toddlerhood, girlhood, through her teens and early twenties, her marriage, the early years of our childhoods, our coming of age, of her two grandsons. My mother points to a photo of me as a toddler and smiles. When she was more verbal, she used to tell the story about what she called "my dancing eyes," and about how shy I was as a toddler. When company came over, she said I walked into the living room with my eyes closed; I thought if they were closed no one could see me. She points to a photo of Cindy and laughs. We remember the story of how Cindy was such an active baby that to diaper her, my mother had to sit on her. Now we tell the stories and Mom laughs as if she's hearing them for the first time. Occasionally she makes a gesture, for us to hide the cord of the standing lamp. Fix the still tilted painting. OCD is common among demented patients. The obsessive attention to details is a way for them to control their inner anxiety.

After the photo albums we turn to her scrapbooks from junior high school and high school when Iris was popular and had a ton of dates (more of this to come). "Mom, you were hot," I say to her turning the pages when we come across a photo of her in a swimsuit and others from clippings from the school paper. "How many dates did you have?" Cindy says as we flip and flip the pages filled with matchbooks, napkins, and corsages from one date after another. "That's a lot of guys," Cin says, and Iris covers her hand with her mouth and laughs again delighted—I've always loved my mother's exuberant laugh—and for a moment she seems to sink into memory.

———

WE WHEEL MY mother out of her room to take her for a stroll and are interrupted by a volunteer who roams through the unit visiting residents. This man seems to have a crush on my mother. Every time I'm there, I see him. Short, bald, mustache, dressed in the same brown suit, shirt, and tie, Eastern European accent, maybe in his seventies. He comes close to my mother, taps her shoulder, takes her hand. "Iris, give me that beautiful smile," he says, and of course, Iris raised to be polite, complies. Then he kisses her on her hand. He reminds me of the emcee in the movie *Cabaret*, always arriving out of nowhere waving his hands back and forth, taunting, and sinister. I imagine him whispering the show's title song:

> What good is sitting alone in your room? Come hear the music play. Life is a cabaret, old chum, come to the cabaret.

After he leaves to move on to the next resident, my mother gives me a look that is not quite an eye roll but one of exasperation. I get it. She's now in a stage in life where she must accept certain conditions. And one of them is making a volunteer happy.

We hear music in the unit and wheel Mom to the main room. The goodhearted and sprightly activity coordinator in her green uniform stands in front of the residents sitting in their wheelchairs and begins to sing familiar songs, "Singin' in the Rain," "You Are My Sunshine," "Moon River," and instructs the residents to tap their hands on their laps or clap to the music. A few residents perk up and join in, others stare in bewilderment.

Call Iris a snob, but she refuses to participate. She sees this kind of sing-along as a form of infantilizing. She is a woman who has led a long and complex life. I can tell by the look on her face and an eye roll that it makes her feel embarrassed. Or maybe she feels ashamed of her condition in front of her daughters. I'm not sure what kind of music would connect her back to her identity, as certain songs are said to do with dementia patients, but this sing-along isn't working. My mother instructs us with a wave of her hand to take her back to her room.

———

SITTING IN HER wheelchair, Iris has a blank, expressionless stare on her face, her eyes barely blinking, facing the TV where we've put on a soccer game. It's as if she's looking into a no man's zone. Perhaps she's tired. Reduced gaze is the clinical term for this, a dementia symptom that changes a person's ability to move their eyes normally and makes them look like they are staring. Maybe she's adrift in a wheel of memory. Or maybe she can't recall her thoughts, maybe she's dreaming.

There's a distracting buzzing against the window, strange in January, but flies can survive the cold. I open the curtain. The fly is caught between the screen and window glass, trapped, soon to die, it buzzes as if wanting out. I'm reminded again of Emily Dickinson's poem, "I heard a Fly buzz—when I died," in which Dickinson imagines her own death, and I wonder if my mother considers her own dying and is slowly preparing. Outside, snow has fallen over the withered plants in troughs in the little garden. Rests on the branches of the trees further afield. The world outside is wrapped in a snowy blanket.

Maybe this is okay, I think. Maybe it's time for Iris to simply reside in solitude. To rest. I wonder how much at this stage she knows of her disease. Sometimes she will ask why she is here, and I tell her that it is because it is safe, and she is getting the care that she needs. What use would it be to remind her?

I hold her hand. I have always admired my mother's hands. Those hands embraced me when I was a child. They wiped away my tears, rested on my forehead when I had a fever. Those hands made my dinners, washed my clothes, were raised in ecstasy or clapped when she was proud, urged me forward when I was shy. Held my hand when I lost my first child. I admired those hands with their long, elegant fingers and now when I look at them, aged like the bark of a tree, veiny, freckled with arthritic knuckles, I think of all they have been through.

Since she can't communicate verbally, our conversations are one sided. Her responses: a nod, or a smile, or a grimace if she's unhappy or in pain. I have learned only to ask questions that require a nod of the head, a short answer, or a question that will allow her to point or gesture. I look into her sunken brown eyes when I speak to her. I softly rub her arm. I give her a glass of water, a sip of her Ensure. I hug her though she can't hug me back.

———

IT'S FIVE O'CLOCK. Dinner. We wheel Iris into a small
private dining room available for guests to dine with a resident
with her tray. She barely touches her meal. Today it's turkey and
gravy and mashed potatoes. She allows a spoonful of mashed
potatoes and picks at a slice of chocolate cake. There is no way
to persuade her. My mother's weight is dropping. Soon she
will be the weight of a child. I fantasize about how I might
get my mother out of here. A friend told me that she and her
two sisters alternated care of their mother, bringing her into
their homes, each for a year. But I'm not sure their mother
needed the round-the-clock care my mother requires. I try to
add up the cost for even a day. Where would she live in our
1,200-square-foot Manhattan apartment? In our living room?
We consider moving her to a nursing home closer to where
we live but become daunted by long waiting lists and by the
fear that the move would unsettle her further. That the care
homes we've looked at seem no better, some worse, than where
my mother resides.

While the other residents are still eating in the main room,
we take Iris to the little private sitting room with mismatched
chairs, mostly empty bookcases except for an antiquated set of
encyclopedias, a Bible, a Jewish prayer book a family member
must have donated, fake plants gathering dust, and a TV with a
DVD player. We discover an old DVD of *The Sound of Music*
near the television. As kids we used to watch this movie every
year with Mom when it was shown on television. One of the
songs from the musical suddenly forces itself into my mind:

There's a sad sort of clanging from the clock in the hall
And the bells in the steeple too

And up in the nursery an absurd little bird
Is popping out to say "cuckoo."

We pop in the DVD, I can tell even my mother is a little pumped, smiling as we eagerly await Maria and the children, the nuns, and the captain. There is something comforting about rewatching favorite movies, remembering the times we watched it as kids sprawled on Mom's king-sized bed, but unfortunately the player jams.

So long, farewell, auf Wiedersehen, goodbye
Goodbye, goodbye, goodbye
Goodbye!

The day is dwindling. We take our mother back to her room. I tell her that I'm proud of her, that she's doing well, that she's in my thoughts every day even when I am not with her. She seems to understand and looks deeply into my eyes, fixated on my words. "Love you, Mom," Cin says. We're exhausted. Spending most of the day and early evening tending to my mother is bittersweet and wearying. It comes with the scourge of guilt on top of the pain of seeing her decline. Who will offer her a sip of water in the night if she wakes up and her lips are parched? Who will soothe her if she cries out in pain? How can we leave her? But we do. By the time the sun fades into darkness, we wheel Iris back to the main dining hall—the only time she is allowed to be alone in her room is at bedtime—and say our goodbyes. We promise we'll be back soon. To soften the blow, we give her two peppermint patties, a gesture that saddens me, as if we are giving them to soothe a child. But Iris isn't a child. I come back and give her another kiss. My spirit sinks as we slink away.

———

DEATH IS ALWAYS at the forefront on these visits, but I don't know what it will mean to see my mother go. Sometimes I wish it would come, as I wonder if death is better than her current living. Would it be better to die before losing one's faculties? I think so, but I can't know for sure the inner world my mother or others with Alzheimer's inhabit. There are times when I've contemplated whether we could or should help her to die. In a personal piece in the *New York Times* called "The Last Thing Mom Asked," Sarah Lyall writes about her mother who, in the endgame of stage four lung cancer, was ready to go. She asked her daughter to help her die by giving her enough morphine to kill her, knowing that the end of her illness would be extremely painful. But after contemplating this, and storing away medication, Lyall discovered that she didn't know the exact dosage that would work, and even amid her mother's pressing demands, got cold feet. Her mother's pain was getting worse. Lyall writes that the one thing she could do would be to withhold food and water, she tells her mother and this is what they eventually did.

Does my mother want to die? I'm afraid to ask her directly. Not too long ago, I saw her wincing. She seemed in pain. I held her hand and told her that if she was ready to go, she didn't need to hold on for us. She squeezed my hand and tears formed in her eyes but I'm not sure she fully understood. I know that when her time does come, she will stop eating and drinking. That is what is usual for an Alzheimer's patient, and we decided long ago that she would not be kept alive on a feeding tube. In her living will she requested not to have any life saving measures. She is not in a dire state of pain, as far as I can tell, though from time to time she complains that her bum is sore. Now it's all bone with no padding and sometimes she says her body hurts.

When I tell this later in a phone call to the doctor on the unit, he insists that her vitals are fine and offers more anxiety meds to keep her comfortable. Atul Gawande recalls that when he was in training, a geriatric doctor told him, "'The job of any doctor . . . is to support quality of life,' by which he meant two things: as much freedom from the ravages of disease as possible and the retention of enough function for active engagement in the world." I suppose that in this stage of my mother's life, both these objectives no longer apply, and yet it is her state of being that troubles me. "When one day is like every other then all days are one," says a character in *The Magic Mountain*. "Habit arises when our sense of time falls asleep, or at least, grows dull; and if the years of youth are experienced slowly, while the later years of life hurtle past at an ever-increasing speed, it must be habit that causes it. We know full well that the insertion of new habits or the changing of old ones is the only way to preserve life, to renew our sense of time, to rejuvenate, intensify, and retard our experience of time—and thereby renew our sense of life itself." But there are no new habits available to my mother at the end stage of Alzheimer's. She is in a state of stasis, able to receive, but not able to give more than a smile, a fragment of a sentence. Accept a kiss. A nod. Her body is no longer her friend. Her mind, without enough words to express itself, is largely unavailable to us. And yet, her mind and the soul, if the soul is the essence of an individual, are both for the time being, forging on.

She tunnels further inward. I'm afraid soon I won't be able to reach her. I wonder where her mind goes when she drifts. What she thinks about day after day when she's alone and the days blur. Thomas Mann writes, "The days began to fly now, and yet each one of them was stretched by renewed expectations and swollen with silent, private experiences. Yes, time is a puzzling thing, there is something about it that is hard to explain." But what is time for the Alzheimer's patient when she loses track of the days, months, seasons, years? When for hours she sits in silence with little to break up the time except for a tap on the shoulder to take her meds or to bring her to the toilet. Time exists in the present and the deeply meaningful events of the past, including the memories of relationships ensconced in long-term memory that can last a lifetime.

———

WE WALK THROUGH the halls, back through the purple vestibule, give a nod to the maestro slumped over the piano, he looks tired, too, and walk out the door into the fresh air. There's a woman on the sidewalk walking her dachshund. Birds call out to each other, *trulee, trulee, trulee,* as if on repeat. Cars rush past on the street we see beyond the care home. It's as if the gates have opened back to the world we inhabit and like horses being let out of their stalls we are achingly set free.

4.

Iris is eighty-three and has been living in an assisted living facility called Stone Gardens on the Menorah Campus in her own apartment for the past five years. She's become incontinent, gets lost finding her room from the dining hall or the movie theater, or one of the activity rooms. She's more confused. She's been having falls in her room getting out of bed. It's no longer safe for her to be alone. Without long term health insurance, we can't afford twenty-four-hour private nursing care along with her monthly costs at Stone Gardens. My mother's physician recommends that we move her to the Weinberg Unit in the skilled nursing home residence on the Menorah Park campus for residents with memory loss related to dementia, aging, or strokes, and luckily there is a room available.

Laura, who is then living in New Jersey, makes the trip to Cleveland to help move our mother into Weinberg from Stone Gardens. It isn't easy. Iris doesn't understand where she is or why she must move. She misses her friends, particularly John, a man she grew attached to, holding hands with him every afternoon while watching a movie in the assisted living's small theater. She misses the freedom of traversing from meals to her room, to the art room, and back on her own. Laura tells us Mom has it in her mind that a resident at Stone Gardens who scolded her during a program for walking in late and sitting in front of her somehow kicked her out and that is why she is moving to Weinberg. We tell her it isn't true, that it's because she needs more help, and it isn't safe for her to live on her own. We remind her of her falls, of her getting lost, of her wetting the bed when she lived in Stone Gardens, but my mother doesn't believe us. She keeps agonizing over why she has been asked to leave. *Who are these people? Why am I here? I don't like it,* she says when I call her to check in. This pains me. I don't like the idea of my mother feeling dislocated from the apartment she considered home. I call a florist in Cleveland to send my mother a flower arrangement, to give her pleasure and to ease my guilt that I'm not with her. A plant won't work because it would require someone to water it.

The move has caught me off guard, too; suddenly my mother's mortality is closer. I am uncertain and adrift. I wake in the middle of the night in fear, or worse, in a cold clammy sweat. I don't like to think of my mother alone in this new unit, with a new room and a new schedule and not having anyone familiar around her.

I download a French film called *Amour*, knowing from reviews that it will be upsetting, but I want to know all I can about what awaits me. It's about a married couple, retired music teachers who share a deep bond, and after decades together are still in love. Georges and Anne sit at the breakfast table. Suddenly Anne is confused and disoriented. In the hospital, we discover she's undergone a stroke that is further complicated by vascular dementia. The director Michael Haneke doesn't spare the audience the indignities of Anne's slow decline. In one scene Georges has come home from a funeral of a friend. He describes the funeral to Anne, and she says, "I don't want to go on. It's touching how you try and make it bearable." As Anne becomes more infirm, Georges makes himself her caretaker. He washes her hair, exercises her legs, feeds her. Near the end of the film, Anne loses her ability to walk, speak, and swallow; in bed, she moans in pain and, unable to bear her suffering, Georges smothers her. The film is incredibly convincing, and one feels intensely for both Anne and Georges as we view the horror of seeing Anne slowly succumb and the emotional pain Georges endures before he takes his beloved out of her misery. How much suffering should people have to endure? I suppose this is the paradox of living. The slow disintegration and disgraces of bodily functions will soon come to pass for my mother, too, but I am not ready.

————

IT'S NOT ALL bad at Weinberg. The unit is abuzz with activity and Iris is an avid participant. Many of the residents can still walk and communicate. Family members and staff come in and out of the unit. There's lots of chatting, beepers going off, bingo games, and a slate of planned events. There are long tables where residents might read the paper, work on a puzzle, or do an art project.

Iris is initially anxious and confused about the move from her apartment and it signals for me the reality of her slow decline. Her mind can no longer control her body. She has lost her short-term memory. I call her on the phone, and she says that she needs new shoes. I tell her that I will take her to get some the next time I visit. A few minutes later she says she needs new shoes. And again, I will remind her. And it goes on like this. While her short-term memory has failed her, she can still concentrate on the art projects offered, such as making bookmarks and stringing together a necklace of beads, and can still read the paper and play bingo. She can no longer control the narrative of her life, but she is still experiencing and participating, still a person with inner depth and a life history. Hence, what does forgetting really mean to someone who is in a diminished state?

After reading about it, I purchased a copy of *This Little Art* by Kate Briggs, translator of Roland Barthes's *How to Live Together*. I discovered that Briggs begins her book coincidentally with a telling of a lecture Barthes gave where he spoke of the "strange age of his body" in relationship to rereading Thomas Mann's *The Magic Mountain*. He realized, rereading the novel set in 1907, that his own tuberculosis was the same version "down virtually to the last detail" as that of Hans Castorp. Briggs writes that "this made his body historical. In a sense, the contemporary of Hans Castorp." This realization prompted Barthes to say, "I must fling myself into the illusion that I am contemporary with the young bodies present before me . . . and start a 'new life' with new concerns, new urgencies, new desires." Briggs continues: "The question that the lecture comes around to ask, is— 'What to do in this old and untimely body.' What does aging mean? And 'forget' is the answer he'll offer . . . Forget and be carried forward by the force of forgetting, which is the forward-tilting force of all living life: forget the past, forget aging, and press forward. Which is to say: begin again."

Might we be comforted by the idea that forgetting isn't tragic? That one can begin again in a new state of mind? The Alzheimer's sufferer eventually regresses to a state of infant-hood, unable to survive without assistance by another individual. Unable to speak, walk, bathe herself, or brush her teeth, in essence, she is moving backward. Even though the physical body and mind regress, the disease does not strip the individual of her personhood. Memories and dreams are alive, a form of time within time. The loss of short-term memory is confusing and frustrating for others who are engaging with the person with dementia; but for the afflicted they are existing in another reality and hence perhaps forgetting is not as important a loss.

———

LAURA HAS BEAUTIFULLY and carefully arranged Iris's new room, hanging photos and artwork on the walls, placing Iris's clothes into drawers, her books and photo albums on the bookshelf. Her belongings from one house have dwindled to this one room, but the ambience still feels like it belongs only to Iris. I arrive a few weeks later with my husband and son to visit. While they're seeing other family and friends in Cleveland after spending a few hours with us, I share the rest of the day with my mother. In her room we sort loose photographs into a photo album. We look at the photographs of the house where I grew up and where Iris lived for more than fifty years. She gazes at a photo of the kitchen with her collection of Fiestaware orderly arranged on open shelves. She turns to a photo of my youngest sister when she was a teenager wearing a Cleveland Browns sweatshirt. "I can't believe she's gone," she says. "My baby." And then to another photo of Iris at my wedding. Her auburn hair is shoulder length, and she's elegantly outfitted in a gold and black evening dress. "Who is that?" Mom says. A few years ago, she let her hair go gray and she doesn't recognize herself in the photograph. "That's beautiful you," I say, and Mom laughs in embarrassment and amusement.

———

AT WEINBERG, THE more ambulatory residents are allowed to roam the unit, their beepers strapped to their ankles, but invariably, someone forgets to type the code onto the pad next to the door. Throughout the day, beepers and alarms go off. Once a month, the activity coordinator takes the residents on outings in a van, whether to the baseball stadium to see the Cleveland Indians play (my mother has become a die-hard Indians fan), the art museum, or to a dinner at the Italian Rose Garden and my mother enjoys these excursions. They're the highlights of her month. She especially loves going to Olive Garden, one of the restaurants she took Aunt Harriet to before she moved to assisted living. She still reads the Cleveland *Plain Dealer* every morning.

In Iris's first weeks at Weinberg, she's ambulatory with her walker, though she must wear an alarm bracelet on her ankle in case she wanders off the unit. Iris is not a wanderer; she abides by the rules of institutional life. But gradually it is harder for her to walk and maneuver her walker and out of fear of falling, she is relegated to a wheelchair. With assistance she can be lifted from her wheelchair, to use the toilet and get into bed, but she dislikes the wheelchair intensely. Gloria, her favorite aide on the floor, gives her a plastic weighted pillow (in case she leaks) to sit on. Being wedded to her wheelchair marks another stage in her diminishment of freedom from the most elementary of acts. We rarely think of freedom until it is taken away from us. The small undertaking of being able to go into the privacy of a bathroom, sit on the toilet for as long as is needed or desired, sometimes to read a magazine or a book, to escape the bustle of others, to stare at the color of the tiles while contemplating a conversation with someone, or to cry in privacy, is a form of liberation that Iris is now deprived of.

———

ON THIS VISIT, she's dressed in black velvet lounge pants from Talbots and one of the soft sweaters that she likes. She looks pretty with her lipstick on and her white hair freshly washed and cut in a bob. I take one of her beaded necklaces and put it around her neck and tell her she looks beautiful. Talbots is where we buy her clothes because my mother insists that she needs to wear "petite" sizes, not just medium, medium petite, she says, I can only wear medium petite. This is another new obsession she's developed.

When we're coming to visit, we call ahead so the aides are aware, and Gloria helps her to apply lipstick. Gloria is from Cuba and loves my mother. When she sees me, she says to my mother, "See Iris, I told you the girls would be back soon." She tells me I look just like my mother, and Iris smiles. "You have such beautiful daughters," Gloria says. "And look how young she looks," Gloria says. My mother looks at Gloria, nods, and says "and she's not even wearing makeup." I'm astonished by what my mother observes and doesn't observe.

In the Weinberg Unit, you might occasionally see two table mates conversing with one another at dinner. Many of the residents read the paper and play bingo (Iris is an avid bingo player and keeps a little change purse in the basket of her walker for her winnings) or participate in Exercise with Mike (exercising in a chair). A typical day on the Weinberg Unit might include a half-hour session of chair yoga, Hot Topic with Rabbi Saul, Inky Pinky and Other Word Games with Noah, or adult coloring with hot cocoa in the Piazza.

Iris's stay at Weinberg coincides with the presidential campaign between Hillary Clinton and Donald Trump. Iris is an ardent fan of Hillary Clinton. She watches the news and the debates on CNN and MSNBC on the TV in the unit and becomes obsessed with the upcoming election. The care home has given her a Hillary Clinton T-shirt and she is glad that she can still use her privileges as a citizen to vote. It's the first time in American history that a female is a candidate in a presidential election. It is monumental, especially for my mother's generation. Slowly, Iris has adjusted to living in Weinberg, and on this visit, she seems happy.

———

IN THE MAIN room of the Weinberg Unit, a door opens to a little garden with an iron table, umbrella, and chairs. I take Iris out to the garden to soak up some sun. She wears her straw hat and a scarf around her neck, reminding me of the actress Catherine Deneuve. Once she discovered how bad tanning was for skin—maybe it was in the '80s when the pendulum turned, and suddenly the dangers of sun exposure were in the news—she religiously applied sunscreen on her face and wore a hat outdoors and doesn't have a single wrinkle on her face.

In the garden, I ask her to tell me about my father, one of her favorite things to discuss. Her face still lights up when she remembers him. Years after she divorced her second husband, she took to wearing her diamond wedding ring from my father and had her name legally changed from her second husband's name back to my father's. My father is her true love, like the lovers in the novels she reads. She has always imagined that she will be reunited with him after she dies. I'm not sure exactly how she envisions this happening but I'm glad for her belief.

Iris is not one for religious doctrine. Her religion is love, nature, and beauty. When she sees a garden of blooming flowers, she will say that there must be something more in the afterlife because how else can we explain the miracle of flowers and nature? She doesn't see the point in cemeteries—the soul is gone from the body, she says. She never returns to visit the graves of my father, her daughter, or her parents. She never took us girls to see my father's grave, and it was only when my paternal grandmother died that I saw his grave for the first time, the headstone battled and worn from weather, next to the plot where my grandmother was to be interred. Iris prefers to embrace the idea of a reunion in the afterlife.

———

"HE CHOSE ME," my mother says, about my father. Iris is still verbal but mostly uses short sentences. It is a refrain she has repeated maybe a hundred times or more about my father, and then she looks down at her diamond wedding ring and twists it again around her finger, and for a moment, she's lost in a misty remembrance. "If only you'd known him. Everyone loved him," she says with teary eyes. "He was the kindest, most loving person I've ever known." I used to wonder if my mother romanticized my father. But over the years, anyone I've encountered who knew him, friends of his, relatives, always said how special he was and became so moved upon seeing me—his daughter—they could barely speak. "I wish I had, too," I say. I think for a moment. "And Mom, you chose him, too," I say. "From your scrapbooks, it seems as if you had plenty of suitors." Mom's lips break into a smile.

———

THE UNIT IS getting ready for lunch. I wheel Iris back in and take her to her seat at one of the long tables. There's soup in a plastic bowl on her plastic tray and a grilled cheese sandwich on white bread, a handful of potato chips, a twig of red grapes, a cup of pudding and the kind of tinny cutlery you might take on a camping trip. Mom eats half her sandwich, picks off a few grapes and pops them in her mouth, and that's it.

For the patients sick with tuberculosis in *The Magic Mountain*, food is a source of plentitude, a comfort. A privilege. There are frequent rich meals and libations. Rest and food are thought to offer the best outcome for the disease. Here is a description of breakfast on the mountain:

> There were pots of marmalade and honey, bowls of oatmeal and creamed rice, plates of scrambled eggs and cold meats; they had been generous with the butter. Someone lifted the glass bell from a soft Swiss cheese and cut off a piece; what was more, a bowl of fruit, both fresh and dried stood in the middle of the table.

Such luxuries. But indeed, comfort is the best that can be offered to the dying. Of course, there are budgets in institutions, and the unit where my mother resides is hardly like the Swiss sanitariums before World War I, save for its hermetic nature, a place where time stands still and where the residents have come to die. A world under a glass bell. Still, at this Five Star institution (nursing homes, like Michelin restaurants, are rated), known according to their website as "Northeast Ohio's Trusted Premier provider of health and wellness services," one might expect something better on Iris's plastic tray.

I wheel Mom back to her room and do what I can to dress up the institutional strangeness. I fluff pillows for her bed and unfurl a new duvet I've bought her with a cabbage rose print—one of her favorites (only to find out on another visit that the staff has stuffed it in her closet, preferring the institutional flannel blankets for her bedding). She's only allowed in her room alone when she is put to bed. Otherwise, she's parked in the dining room. The administration will not let residents stay in their own rooms unattended out of concern for their safety unless the family signs a waiver to protect the institution from any liability.

In her new room, she has a window that looks out to a garden, and even though the garden is neglected, and some dead bushes and plants are still in their pots, I am glad my mother has a window with a view. Across from her bed is a horizontal frame containing separate portraits of her four daughters. Years ago, when all of us were home, Iris hired a photographer to take professional black-and-white portraits of each of us and they are now, all four, in one horizontal frame on the wall so that she can see the photos of her daughters when she lies in bed. We are the crown jewels of her life.

A man is screaming (another symptom of dementia for some) in one of the rooms a few doors down from my mother. It's an insistent sound, like one of an animal in pain. I look at Iris to see if she notices, but she is staring straight ahead at the TV with a thin flannel blanket I've draped across her legs. This patient on my mother's floor seems to be on autopilot. Why? And worse, why is he being ignored? Though many here can't communicate and are confused and frightened, they still feel their emotions. I wonder if my mother has days like this where she loses it and if an aide or a nurse will try to soothe her. It's so hard to know.

The caregivers have given up or tuned out on our screamer, but I've had enough. It's painful to listen to someone in agony and it seems incomprehensible to me how the screamer can be ignored. I suggest we go to the Piazza, which is a common space available to all the residents in the separate units and buildings on the campus, and Mom agrees.

I wheel Iris into the Piazza, an open high-ceiling room as big as an auditorium made to look, as the brochure says, as if residents have "just sat down in an intimate café in an Italian square." On one side are three other smaller rooms that house a small reptile and bird room, a library, and a beauty parlor. The beauty salon dons a black and white striped awning at its entrance as if to look like a barber shop in a small town. Inside live one empty manicurist table, three sinks, and corresponding chairs for shampoos, cuts, and hair color. It is closed on the weekends.

The Piazza is a nice and airy space, but there is nevertheless a feeling of trying too hard about it. Plastic trees in pots, fake iron café tables with umbrellas, even though we are indoors and there is no skylight or sun. Fixed to the floor on one side of the large room is a statue of a yellow motorcycle which I suppose is to give the illusion that we are in Monte Carlo and some handsome Italian gigolo is waiting in the wings. Italian posters advertising operas adorn the walls, and there's a wine bar that looks like something on a Hollywood set where you might take your resident for a drink. Mom watches as I peer in the bar, and notice the refrigerators are locked. And so are the cabinets. Where's the booze. Is this, too, a façade? I google the care home and find out that the "Piazza has a free wine bar and serves cheese, crackers, and gelato every afternoon." The happy hour must take place on weekdays when we are not there. Still, I'm again reminded of a Fellini movie where nothing is quite what it seems. I ask my mother if we should sneak in some wine next time we come to visit, and she laughs.

To our left is the doorway into the reptile and bird room. We shuffle in. It smells like the zoo. There's a reptile cage housing snakes, slow-moving turtles, and crusty iguanas. Also, an overcrowded fish tank. In a large open cage resides an old blue and yellow parrot who repeats, *Hello, Polly Want a Cracker, Pretty bird. Pretty bird.* Iris likes the parrot, and she calls out, "hello." She is amused when the parrot says *hello* back. In another cage are colorful and tropical birds perched on wooden platforms. I'm sure it wasn't intentional but keeping these birds institutionalized in a room only serves as a reminder that the residents are similarly confined. Maybe it's all here to please the grandchildren and the relatives. Or to further furnish the illusion of Fellini's theater of the absurd. I see in the brochure they offer tours.

After visiting the birds and reptiles, I wheel Iris into the library. The doorway barely fits her wheelchair, which is strange since so many residents are in wheelchairs. It's small and cozy, like a cubbyhole, stocked with new books, one shelf of fiction, another shelf of nonfiction, and a shelf of large-type books. In the center is a small table with current magazines on top and a few chairs scattered around the room. Iris likes to take a few books back to her room to read. Her favorite is *The Notebook* by Nicholas Sparks, though I am not sure that she connects the protagonist, who is slowly losing her memory, to herself. My mother has always been a die-hard romantic and is a sucker for love stories. She likes books by Nora Roberts and she is a fan of Rosamunde Pilcher's *The Shell Seekers*. Before Alzheimer's, she was a more sophisticated reader, enjoying classic novels or literary novels that I edited and would send to her, but now, she reads more for plot and entertainment. I'm not sure how much my mother remembers of what she reads, but it is important to her always to have a book with her that she keeps in a tote bag along with her Kleenex, the *Plain Dealer*, throat lozenges, and change purse. I go through the shelves, calling out titles. "I need large print," Mom says. I find a copy of *The Notebook* and hand it to her. "I love this book," she says and smiles. "I know you do," I say, sliding it next to her in her wheelchair.

Leaving the library, we encounter a train of wheelchairs pushed by family members or an aide going into the Piazza for the daily 2 p.m. musical performance. The room begins to fill, and we take our place toward the back. In the front are the more attentive residents. A few are on stretchers propped up with oxygen tubes coming out of their noses, dragging oxygen carts. So much sickness and sadness to observe. Some are huddled over in wheelchairs, withdrawn, unaware of others; it's as if they are horses with blinders on. It's the family members who seem to appreciate being able to bring their loved ones out for a show. And why not? We, too, must endure.

———

DO THE RESIDENTS believe they are in an Italian square when they visit the Piazza? Or is it the illusion that the Piazza offers? In *On Being Mortal*, physician and author Atul Gawande writes that when he was in medical school, in a weekly seminar, he and his classmates discussed Tolstoy's *The Death of Ivan Ilyich*, a novella about a judge with a terminal illness, as a way of contemplating how doctors should confront the "basic responsibilities of a modern doctor" to act compassionately. Quoting Tolstoy, Gawande points out that Ivan Ilyich's greatest torment "was the deception, the lie, which for some reason they all accepted, that he was not dying but was simply ill, and he only need keep quiet and undergo a treatment and then something very good would result." Ultimately, Ilyich only wanted simple comfort and companionship, which only his servant could give him. I suppose this is what I want for my mother, but that I can't always give her.

Does a fake Italian garden please some of the residents— an attractive space that provides a reprieve from the more utilitarian furnishings of the units? I'm sure it must. But I'm not convinced that they all associate the space with the feeling that life is still ongoing in the same way it had been before they'd gotten sick. I don't know why I'm so down on the place. I suppose I want more for my mother, and I should be grateful that she is in a residence where she is taken care of.

Some of the generous performers are guitar players, one

with thin graying hair tied in a ponytail strumming tunes of Simon and Garfunkel and James Taylor. Others sing numbers from Broadway musicals that the more agile residents clap along to. Occasionally there is a solo pianist or a violinist, which I know my mother prefers. Once a men's choral ensemble. Another time, National Council of Jewish Women sing-along. It's clear that many of the patients, especially those who secure spots in the front row, hear and enjoy the music. No one knows how the residents who seem more out of it may respond internally. Nevertheless, I'm glad the Piazza offers these daily performances.

I can see by the look on Iris's face that today she doesn't fancy the men's choir rendition of "Seventy-Six Trombones" from *The Music Man*. Her hand swats back and forth, and she grimaces. "Let's go, Jill," she says. I wonder, too, as she looks around at the other residents in wheelchairs, many severely ill and compromised, if she simply does not want to be included in this club. She doesn't want to see herself as she sees the other sufferers.

While bird zoos and piazzas, mannequins, performers, and activities are necessary distractions and are meant to reassure residents that life still goes on, the end of life is not just something to be appeased only by illusions and fantasies.

Larissa MacFarquhar, in a piece in *The New Yorker* called "The Comforting Fictions of Dementia Care," cites the philosopher Ronald Dworkin, who argued that "people don't just live for pleasure . . . they also want to preserve their dignity, and to feel that their life has integrity and coherence." For those who are aware of their condition, Dworkin believed that they would "dread the total dependency of late-stage dementia, they don't just dread its effect on others; they dread the way it warps the shape and story of their life. For some the prospect that they might live their last years content with childlike pleasures, kept happy with benevolent lies, would not be a relief but a horror."

Atul Gawande, continuing his discussion of Ivan Ilyich, writes, "As we medical students saw it, the failure of those around Ivan Ilyich to offer comfort or to acknowledge what is happening to him was a failure of character and culture." What did he want? What do the residents need and want? To be viewed as they are, as human beings who have led full lives. Like Ivan, I wish for my mother only comfort, love, and support as she must transition toward end of life.

How do you maintain the elderly's dignity and not reduce them to children? This is a difficult and perhaps impossible question to answer. Can one expect this in an institution? In many cultures, the elderly live with their families, even when they are incapacitated. Perhaps, too, in these cultures, the matriarch in the family may not work outside the home while raising her children and can offer full-time care for their parents. I can't imagine what that would be like for me, given my mother's condition and the commitment that would entail. Still, the remorse of not being able to provide this for my mother and the flood of guilt is always with me, especially during and after these visits.

———

I UNLOCK IRIS'S wheelchair, and we are on our way. One of the perks of the Menorah Campus is that residents can use all the facilities of the other buildings, that is if a family member or an aide is available to serve as an escort. I take Iris to Stone Gardens (where she used to live) so we can go to the movie theater. On the way we pass an aquarium where giant fish swim in a tank. Then pass by the main auditorium where another performance is taking place. Wait, is that a clown? Or is it someone in drag?

I wheel my mother down the long corridors and then hit a button to open the double doors to Stone Gardens. In the theater, they show films twice a day, one screening at 2:30 p.m. and the other at 7:30 p.m. Some of Iris's favorites are older films with Katharine Hepburn and Audrey Hepburn and some more contemporary ones like *A Fish Called Wanda*. The movie theater is the one place at Menorah Park that feels immune to disease, smell, weariness, and melancholy, and when Iris lived in Stone Gardens, she went daily, transported by the films to another world. Once I situate Iris's wheelchair next to the row of velvet theater seats, where I can sit next to her, I take out a bag of pistachio nuts, open the shells for her, and we eat the nuts and sip water from tiny Dixie cups I fill from the water dispenser. Sometimes, I hold her hand, and it seems in the theater's darkness that, at least for a time, we are mother and daughter in our own wonderland. Iris rarely stays awake for the entire movie.

When the credits roll, I wheel her back to her new room at Weinberg to say my goodbyes. As the day has dwindled, she's gotten more and more tired. The move has caused confusion, paranoia, and agitation. She obsesses again over a lamp's electrical cord and tells me to hide it behind the little sofa. She wrings her hands. She gets more distressed at the end of the day. "Why am I here," she says to me. "I don't live here. I want to go back." What she means is that she wants to go back to her apartment in Stone Gardens, where she had lived before the move. "Fix it, Jill," she says to me. "I don't belong here."

I tell her this is her new room, as I've done repeatedly, and that she'll be safe here. She's been here for over a month and likes the activities and outings. "I know it's hard, Mom," I say. "I wish it could be different." I tell her it's hard for me, too, and that I wish I didn't have to leave her. For a minute, I look into her eyes and see she understands. I squeeze her hand and tell her I love her. "My Jilly," she says. And then, when I look at her again a moment later, I can't seem to find her.

―――――

BACK IN MY own home, exhausted from the trip to Cleveland, recollections churn. I can't settle down. My mind swirls. I think of Eliot's lines in "Four Quartets": "Time past and time future/ What might have been and what has been/ Point to one end, which is always present." I know I can't change the past or the present, what has been and what might have been; nevertheless, I'm filled with panic and sorrow for what's to come.

I roam the house, then outside, pick the dead leaves off the geranium plants. I weed one of the garden beds. The irises, the matriarchs of the garden, stand erect, exerting their authority. Her namesake, I planted them years ago in her honor. How to define an iris: dark purple glory, tall, erect spine, crown of petals, yellow stamen, long green stalks like palms cupped, fingers outward, protecting its flower. I take the flowering as a good sign, but nevertheless, my mood is bleak. I go back inside. Suddenly I want to fill the room with plants, with life.

The next morning, foggy from waking up and still half in a dream state, I stand on our old, small deck and look out to the expanse of trees beyond. There are knots on the trunks where dead branches have been removed. I wander to the garden where the hostas begin showing their early leaves. I pick weeds to make room for the perennial plants. For years, my lavender has shared its sweet scent, but it is suddenly withering. No matter how much you attend to them, some will not survive the frost or thrive.

A tiny frog swims in a deep puddle, legs splayed out in swift breaststroke kicks. I'm squeamish regarding the rodents, bugs, and bats that have their home here. Once, I opened our sun umbrella, and at least ten or fifteen bats flew out. Last summer, a fawn with a broken leg lay crying in the woods behind our garden. I called the animal rescue service and waited until a heroic woman with her young daughter drove up in an SUV. She gave the fawn an injection to sedate her, scooped her up in a blanket, and put her in the back of the car to take her to the animal refuge, where they would set her leg in a cast. Another time, a small bird got trapped between the screen and the glass door on our deck. Nature's fragility. I sit on the chaise for a moment, and slowly, my heart rate returns to normal. Some things can be fixed and saved, at least temporarily.

Deeper in the woods, some trees are more desolated, others dwarfed. Thick vines tangle branches and threaten to choke. The deer have eaten the bottom limbs of the evergreens, leaving only dead brown branches. Moles make underground tunnels in the ground. Everywhere I look, I see the passage of time and its sometimes-cruel ripples of ravage.

I notice the color of my blue spruce becomes bluer as it forms new leaves. They are constantly being replaced as cells age and die. Every year, perennials return, having survived the winter. A bee lands in the center of a flower and curls into it. The hair on her body will collect the pollen and stick to it. When she moves to another flower, some of the pollen is rubbed off onto the tip of the pistil or the stamen, the flower's female reproductive organ, which allows the flowers to reproduce. Perhaps there is, as Roland Barthes suggests, some rebirth that comes along for the aging.

5.

Iris is in the hospital recovering from a breakdown when she is diagnosed with the disease. She's seventy-eight years old. Her geriatric psychiatrist is emphatic. She can no longer live on her own. He recommends Stone Gardens, an assisted living facility on the Menorah Park Campus. In assisted living at Stone Gardens, residents are expected to live on their own, and if they can't, they must hire a private aide. The online brochure advertises, "It is designed with profound respect for the fact that people who may need assistance with daily activities as they age, still have high standards of residential living, still value their independence, still relish their privacy, and still retain their individuality."

Iris's physician believes she will do well at Stone Gardens. They have an opening for a one bedroom, and we decide this is the best option. She knows it well. It is the place where my mother's aunt Harriet, who was like a second mother to her, lived during the last decade of her life. My mother took care of her there. She set up her apartment for her when she initially moved in, visited her weekly, accompanied her to programs on the schedule, films in the movie theater, and always to the famous monthly bagel brunch. I've been fearing my mother's impending move, worrying about her loss of independence. But having her personal needs met in the assisted living community, without the worries of going grocery shopping, cooking meals, or keeping up with yard work, will be a boon. Over tea in the hospital, I take out the packets of literature about Stone Gardens and show my mother the schedule of activities. The facility offers yoga, current-events discussions, book clubs, and twice-a-day film screenings. She'll be moving to an apartment at Stone Gardens directly from the hospital.

"What about my furniture and all my belongings at the house?" Mom asks. My son is with me. He comes up with the idea: he'll take photos of her paintings, furniture, and objects from her house on his iPad and she can select from the photos which items she wants to move to her apartment and which we can sell or donate. Amazingly, Iris is calm about it all. It's as if the weight of her worries is sliding off her shoulders. She seems to embrace the move.

Stone Gardens comes with housekeeping, once-a-week sheet changing, medicine dispersion, and three meals daily in the dining room with many different meal options. It's pleasant, sparkling clean, and sunny in the living areas. The residents seem to be mostly lucid, are dressed nicely, and appear to be well cared for. Many have led interesting lives—artists, former doctors, lawyers, teachers, clerks, mothers, fathers—and are the generation in which my mother came of age. Upstairs is a sunny art room and a well-stocked library. In the bright hallway is a bird cage with pastel-colored parakeets, which we discovered later that my mother likes to visit. One of the living rooms is decorated with comfy armchairs and coffee tables, a fireplace.

There's a tea room and a small game room where the residents can play mahjong, bridge, and board games, replete with a hot chocolate machine and a popcorn dispenser. Lovely gardens are outside with benches to sit on and pathways to walk. Activities happen throughout the day in two large community rooms on the first floor.

On March 3, 2011, we move Iris into her apartment on the second floor, with its snug galley kitchen and open shelves for her Fiestaware and a mini-refrigerator. There's room for her small dining room table and four chairs. The living room fits her small sofa and antique walnut chairs with their floral embroidered cushions that once belonged to our aunt Florence and aunt Harriet, and a beautiful bell-shaped rose glass lamp, one of Iris's antique shop finds.

She instructs us where to put her furniture and hang her paintings and art, and as usual, this process is endless because my mother is a perfectionist. She can't bear a cord from a lamp showing, nor a picture that is not hung perfectly straight. She winces if we place a Starbucks plastic cup on her dark chestnut table without a coaster under it. Her OCD condition has gotten worse with the onset of dementia. The day is bright and sunny without a cloud in the royal blue sky. Mom's little apartment is cozy and warm; most of all, she is safe. My heart dances with relief.

To afford for her to live at Stone Gardens, we will sell Iris's house. She has her AARP insurance and is also on Medicare, still receives monthly social security and has some money left from a trust Aunt Harriet left for her that will cover the monthly all-inclusive fee until we sell the house. Once her funds are exhausted, my sisters and I will split the fee. We fund her daily expenses, clothes, and necessities like shampoo, soap, and tooth-paste to preserve her funds as long as we can and handle her bills.

The first day after she is settled into her apartment, we escort her downstairs to the dining room for dinner before we say goodbye. Ironically, I'm the one who succumbs to emotion and becomes tearful, not my mother. Years ago, when she was well, she asked me to promise never to put her in a home, and I failed her. I would never have imagined this debilitating disease would plague her. One of the staff members is with us, waiting to take Iris to her table to meet her table mates. We hug goodbye, and I look at my mother, anxious about how she will adjust to this new life. She notices I'm upset, tells me she's fine, gives me a reassuring smile, and hugs me again. I watch her walk stoically into the dining hall dressed in slacks and a blazer and linger as she's introduced to her new table mates. She sits at the table without turning back, and I swell with pride. It's as if she's just sat down to dinner at a country club. And for a time, she is fine. Surprisingly, she doesn't ask about her home on Lytle Road where she's lived for fifty years; it's as if she's shelved it in a private place.

———

IRIS IS CONTENT not having to shop, prepare food, remember to take her medications, and manage finances. Now, she doesn't have to worry about the endless repairs on her house, the persistent and agitating notices of violations telling her to repave her driveway or fix the roof she receives from the Shaker Heights Housing Inspections that require more money than she has. We have taken over these responsibilities so we can sell her house. She likes her life being reduced and managed.

The activities and schedule give her a sense of purpose and fight the melancholy and anxiety associated with her disease. We've gotten her a special phone in her room where we have each programmed our phone numbers, so she only needs to push one button to call us.

I don't know if my mother fully understands that her cognitive abilities have been compromised enough to impair daily function, if she can fully understand how much her life has changed or if these changes have become part of her reality. I'm reminded of the novel *Dogs at the Perimeter* by the Canadian novelist Madeleine Thien. It is about a young Cambodian researcher, Janie, and her scientist friend, Hiroji Matsui, who both work at a Brain Research Center. Hiroji has been studying a patient with Alzheimer's.

"Elie was fifty-eight years old when she began to lose language. She told Hiroji that the first occurrence was in St. Michael's Church in Montreal, when the words of the Lord's Prayer, words she had known almost from the time she had learned to speak, failed to materialize on her lips. For a brief moment, while the congregation around her prayed, the whole notion of language diminished inside her mind. Instead, the priest's green robes struck her as infinitely complicated, the winter coats of the faithful shifted like a collage, a pointillistic work, a Seurat: precision, definition, and a rending beauty. The Lord's Prayer touched her in the same bodily way that the wind might, it was the sensation of sound but not meaning. She felt elevated and alone, near to God and yet cast out. And then the moment passed. She came back and so did the words. A mild hallucination, Elie thought. *Champagne in the brain.*"

Champagne in the brain. It doesn't sound so bad now that she's in a safe place with staff to care for her. Maybe I'm suffering over the loss of my mother's cognition more than she is.

When Iris lived alone in her home on Lytle Road, she grew isolated and lonely. Now, she's part of a community. She likes the yoga, tai chi, and Zumba classes, the art room projects, the films and lectures, and the daily reports on news events, and she has made new friends. She sits at a table for dinner with two men, one a former dentist and the other a ninety-three-year-old artist who has a crush on her. When I ask about them, she says she likes their conversations and they make her laugh. She breakfasts with two ladies, one a former dancer. A mock ball to celebrate Prince William and Kate's wedding is on the calendar. Iris adorns herself with the colorful Bakelite bracelets she collected from her flea market days and a strand of beads and dances with the artist under colored lights. Even in her late seventies, she can still draw a man's attention. The warmhearted, loving, sensitive, slightly bohemian woman with a love of life, even though at times a little eccentric—Iris would never be common—has returned to us and, out the door, slips her melancholy ghost.

But the hours after dinner are difficult for her. They call it "sundowning." It can bring agitation, confusion, and anxiety. Her mind is tired, having spent all day keeping up. I call her sometimes from New York before I leave work, and she says she can't wait to get into her pajamas. She's usually in bed by eight. Though I know she's content and safe, I worry that even among the company of others, she's lonely, but perhaps I'm projecting my own sense of what life must be like for her now.

One month, my mother's paintings (of flowers, of course!) she created in the art studio are on display at the entrance hall in Stone Gardens. She is voted Artist of the Month. She calls me to read the citation. Hearing the delight in her voice is a boon. For so long, she's been depressed, and seeing her busy with activities, her spirits bright, I recognize what depression and anxiety have stolen from her.

With her day-to-day needs managed, her anxiety has decreased, lessening my own, and as a result, our relationship has deepened. But the realization that she is now my sisters' and my responsibility is daunting. She'll eventually outrun her money from selling her home. Since Stone Gardens is a private facility, they don't take Medicaid. The future is unknown—we can't know what the disease will bring—but for now, she's safe and comfortable.

———

IN JUNE MY mother attends the senior prom (the irony of the name does not escape me). She dances with a man she met for the first time that night. His name is Paul. She's crowned the Stone Gardens Prom Queen and Paul is the Prom King. I imagine the two of them dancing together under twinkling lights like young lovers. Perhaps dancing in each other's arms reminds them of their early years. Paul is a former doctor. He is eighty-three, fit and handsome. Paul has aides around the clock with him. He, too, suffers from dementia, but his dementia is worse. "He's often lost," my mother tells me. "It breaks my heart. But he looks to me. I can feel his soul," she says. Sometimes, he comes by her apartment after dinner, and his aide will leave Paul with Iris for an hour or two. They watch the Indians game on TV. My mother occasionally mentions her concerns about Paul's dementia and whether she can have a relationship with him. I think she means sexual, but I don't go there. I tell her I don't know. I want to say to her that she has dementia, too. I'm not sure she knows that she does anymore. "It can't be reversed, can it?" she asks me. I shake my head and tell her no.

John Bayley, in his memoir *Elegy for Iris* about his wife, the novelist Iris Murdoch, and her dementia, writes that even with the disease, so much of her remained the same. "Only memory holds reality." And it's true; we are all made of our experiences and our memories that chart the narrative of who we are. Paul and Iris remind me of Fiona and Aubrey, who form a strong attachment at the care home where they meet in Alice Munro's story, "The Bear Came Over the Mountain." Like those two, they have immediately found a connection, that spark of life that new love can bring. It's as if their past lives no longer matter. Their essence and spirit bond them.

———

IRIS IS MORE buoyant—it is a joy to hear her burst into laughter when she repeats a joke that one of her dinner mates tells, or shares gossip about one of the residents, one who is cranky and gets mad if anyone takes what she thinks is her reserved seat at the movie theater or another who sits in the same chair by the doorway as if she is waiting for someone to arrive. Still, I can see the disease taking its toll. Iris soon becomes incontinent. We discovered that there is a bladder therapist (the things one learns!) that my mother's insurance covers, so this is the first step. Whatever she is told to do, it doesn't last long. She has accidents frequently, and now she is dependent on Depends (yes, the irony there, too). One of us arranges for the Depends to be shipped weekly by Amazon. Before then, we bought them at the Stone Gardens shop, but the expense became too much. If she has an accident during the night, housecleaning will help, but she is having accidents throughout the day, and without an aide, she is having difficulty. She still knows how to push my number on her phone. She'll call me in the office and tell me she had an accident again. I shut my door lest any of my colleagues hear to try to walk her through what she needs to do to change out of her clothes, wash herself, adhere the Depends to her panties, and put on new clothes. She also suffers from frequent urinary tract infections, which can be a common feature among dementia patients faced with incontinence. But still, Iris is mobile, content with the daily bingo games on the schedule, the lectures that are offered, and the occasional outings. If, on a visit, I bring her a new fashionable lipstick or nail polish, her face brightens with gratitude and delight.

Then, devoted Paul is suddenly gone from Stone Gardens. My mother doesn't know what has happened to him. I inquired with the receptionist and learned he had passed away. I don't know why the staff doesn't share this news with the other residents. Or maybe they did, and my mother wasn't aware or had forgotten. She is sad for a day or two but stops talking about him. She's made a new friend. Her name is Elizabeth, and she is from the suburb next to where my mother used to live. She's an elegant and intelligent woman who dresses in plaid skirts and cashmere sweaters or blazers. Her daughter lives in town and often comes to visit, and she will, on occasion, take my mother with Elizabeth to her house for dinner. I'm glad my mother has a new friend to sit beside at the movie theater, programs, and dinner.

And now there's a new man she likes. He's called John. A strong jaw defines his face; even with a slump to his shoulders, he towers over Iris. His family doesn't visit, but he has around-the-clock aides. My mother and John meet at the movie theater. They sit next to each other and hold hands. Sometimes, John kisses her. When I visit, they're always together, whether sitting on the couch in the main living room or on a bench looking at the parakeets. I meet John and see that he has a soft heart and is kind with no airs. It's becoming more difficult for my mother and John to converse. Holding hands is what they do. I don't know how long this period will last, but I try to keep it close. I don't like to think of my mother as afraid or alone at the end of the day, and even when I am tired or overwhelmed with work or other responsibilities, I call her. Sometimes I ask her what they served for dinner or what movie they are showing that night. She likes to read me the blurb on the program about the movie. I ask her how she likes the residents at Stone Gardens. "There are some nice people here," she says. "But there are people here with a lot of problems. There's one older woman who calls for her mama all the time. It makes me feel grateful." "So, you like Stone Gardens?" I tentatively ask. "I feel taken care of," she says. It's what my mother has wanted all her life. I put down the phone, close my eyes and exhale. All worries for another day.

———

IRIS HAS A long shopping list of what she needs when we visit. Shampoo and Charmin toilet paper because it is extra soft, with special toothpaste for her gums, Colgate or another common brand won't do. Post-its, pens, bottled water, sometimes the lists get too long, and we're exhausted, but who else will shop for her? Her OCD is getting worse. If we leave any papers or brochures on her table, she picks them up and hands them back. Everything must be immaculate and organized. If we buy her new clothes, we must cut out the labels immediately. We must open each plastic bottle of Dasani water, leaving the lid on slightly because her hands are too weak to open the bottles. And Dasani is the only bottled water she will drink because she says it doesn't taste like chlorine. Sometimes, she has more needs than we've budgeted time to handle, or we bring home her toothpaste, which is the wrong kind, and no other kind will do. I can't control my frustration and anger, and we quarrel. There are responsibilities at work, at home, anxieties that arise from being the mother of an adolescent, my own hurts, and memories from the past that surface when I'm with my mother. In one way or another, it feels as if we sisters have tried to hold our mother together for most of our lives, and now it will only get worse. I regret snapping at her and ask her if she'd like to watch a movie. We turn on TNT, the classic channel, and settle on something with Gregory Peck, another of Iris's favorite actors. Then I notice that she isn't really watching. There's a blank stare on her face that scares me. John Bayley, in *Elegy for Iris*, describes it as what he calls a "lion's face":

"The features settle into a leonine impassivity that does remind one of the king of beasts and the way his broad, expressionless mask is represented in painting and sculpture. The Alzheimer's face is neither tragic nor comic, as a face can appear in other forms of dementia, suggesting human emotion in its most distorted guises. The Alzheimer's face indicates only an absence. It is, in the most literal sense, a mask."

As I watch my mother, her stare unmoving, I'm aware that more distressing changes are to come. *Where are you, Mom,* I want to say. *What's happening?* It's painful watching my mother trying to hold on to her identity. I move my chair closer to her and rub her arm. I notice, too, that her walk has changed. She shuffles, barely lifting her feet, and is unsteady. It's the dementia shuffle where parts of the brain that control the ability for the brain to signal the body are impaired; I'm later told when I ask the nurse about it. I want to close my eyes and pretend that the disease won't progress, but I know that I'm fooling myself.

———

WHEN IT IS time to return to New York on Sunday after a weekend spent taking care of my mother, my sisters and I are comatose and exhausted. We catch the 7 p.m. flight back to LaGuardia and can barely speak in the car on the way to the airport. Before our flight, we stop at the airport wine bar for a glass, split a cheese plate, and worry together about what the next steps will be and decide when we should plan the next trip.

6.

I call my mother in her home on Lytle Road from New York and am slayed by how depressed she sounds. It's as if she's been lured away. She's so fatigued she can barely speak. I imagine her curled up in bed with the blinds drawn in her room, black as a bottle of spilled ink. She's in her early seventies but still looks like she's in her sixties. Depression has haunted her life for as long as I can remember, and when it strikes, its dark tentacles infiltrate every part of her. I ask her if she's been taking her medications—she switches so often that it is hard to keep track. One makes her dizzy; on another, she can't consume eggs; on another, it's white wine; another leaves a metallic taste in her mouth. Sometimes I call, and her voice is hoarse as if she hasn't talked to anyone in days. For the rest of the afternoon, her mood weighs on me. I know what the crushing heaviness does to her. Days she can't get out of bed, filled with helplessness and loss of hope, lack of motivation, and persistent despair. Whatever I say or do to try to assuage makes her more agitated. Though I dread it, I must force myself to call. I miss her warm and upbeat voice—*Hi, darling*—when she's eager to hear from me and not the tired voice of someone who wants only to sleep to pardon the pain. When she's depressed, her tone is flat and needy and I feel helpless to know what to do to help her. My mother's two sisters-in-law live in Cleveland and have become increasingly worried about her. One is six months older than my mother, and the other nine years younger. One is an artist. The other is a homemaker with four children and nine grandchildren who comprise her world. Both are sharp, present, and aware.

Concerned, I return home to Cleveland, always that pit in my stomach, to see how she's managing. Iris greets me at the front door, looking frail and thin wearing navy sweatpants and sweatshirt. Gray hair has grown in near her roots, a sign she's not taking care of herself. She's wearing no makeup and walks in slow motion with her shoulders slumped and a distracted, blank, and hollow expression on her face. I can't discern whether the lethargy is a symptom of her medications, her depression, or something else. My mother has always looked a decade younger, staying out of the sun in her later years, careful of her weight, mindful to get her hair colored, with a youthful, easy laugh and spirit. Now she looks smaller, feeble, uncertain.

It's January, and Cleveland is as cold as I can remember. Branches sheathed in ice. The landscaper who also plows the snow from her driveway comes by. He tells me that my mother asked him if he would come inside and help her figure out what was causing the draft in the house. He discovered that she'd kept a back window open in the den, possibly since the summer. The house was so cold that he could see his breath downstairs. "Your mother is a very sweet lady," he says. "But I think she's become reclusive." I dig my foot into the soft snow and underneath reach a patch of mud. I don't want to face what's coming. Inside her freezer, I notice stacks of frozen blintzes and Stouffer's spinach soufflés and pizzas. Now, she no longer cooks for herself. Recently, she couldn't find her way home from the grocery store, a route she's traveled thousands and thousands of times. It is no longer safe for her to drive. I worry about how she will get around. Cleveland is not a walking town.

Iris is convinced she has a terrible disease. And she does, only we don't know it yet or what it is. She's lost twenty pounds, is not eating, and suffers debilitating migraines. She sees a battery of doctors, has blood drawn, X-rays taken, a colonoscopy, MRIs, stress tests, and sonograms. Her physical health all checks out. On another earlier visit, my sisters and I took her, along with a close friend who was also concerned about her, to the Cleveland Clinic for cognitive and neurological testing by a team of social workers and a neurologist. The results from the evaluation concluded that her symptoms were a result of "pseudo dementia." It is defined by characteristics of dementia such as loss of memory, distraction, and confusion, but these are, in fact, symptoms of depression.

While I should have been happy that my mother was not suffering from actual dementia or Alzheimer's, or another serious disease, I was hoping for a remedy, something more concrete to return my mother to me. Instead, we are advised she should seek out treatment with her psychiatrist. That her current state could be reversed if her depression lifts.

However, my mother's depression seems resistant to medication. According to the Cleveland Clinic, "Treatment-resistant depression (TRD) is a type of major depressive disorder (MDD). It happens when at least two different first-line antidepressants aren't enough to manage the condition during a depressive episode. ECT, or electric shock treatments, are sometimes recommended but come with potential risks." One of my sisters wants my mother to try ECT. She is a psychotherapist and has seen good results with some patients, but my mother is not interested in pursuing it. ECT still carries a stigma, as if it is only used for severe mental patients locked in wards or asylums. It is reported that seven out of ten adults with major depression find a treatment that eventually works, but finding the right meds can take months, perhaps years of trial and error. And my mother has had many trials with medication. What about those who remain resistant? A sense of hopelessness sets in. Jane Kenyon in her poem "Having it Out with Melancholy" calls depression "the mutilator of souls."

"There is nothing I can do against your coming," she writes of a depression that began in childhood. At the end of "Having it Out with Melancholy," "High on Nardil," the speaker is "overcome by ordinary contentment" and wonders, "What hurt me so terribly/all my life until this moment?"

I, too, wish more than anything for my mother to be high on ordinary contentment, but her anxiety persists. I see that her plants by the windowsill are shimmering in their greenery, well cared for as they were through all my childhood years. My mother played classical music in the mornings for them, having read that music helps plants to thrive. I take this as a small sign that the compass may turn itself around.

Our focus turns to encouraging Iris to sell our house and move into assisted living, or an apartment. The house is too much to care for and she is too isolated, but the house is her only port of safety—she's lived in this house on Lytle Road in Shaker

Heights for fifty years—and she is understandably frightened
of what the change will entail, and her anxiety increases. She
refuses to consider independent or assisted living. She agrees
to live in a regular apartment complex we find nearby with a
gym, a card room for residents to play bridge or mahjong, a
beauty shop, and a connecting restaurant. But when offered
an apartment, Iris refuses because the apartment doesn't have
a separate shower, only a tub she would need to step into to
shower, and she is afraid of falling. Another year passes, the real
estate market tumbles, and her house does not sell. Because
she is unable to tolerate the other SRIs, her psychiatrist puts
her on Nardil, an inhibitor that breaks down proteins in the
brain that block norepinephrine, dopamine, and serotonin,
one of the earliest antidepressants, the same medication that
Jane Kenyon writes about in "Having it Out with Melancholy."
I hope that it will help, but I don't sense a change in Iris's mood
or the way in which she is functioning, half in a fog. She takes
Xanax during the day, a higher dosage before bed to help her
sleep, and Fioricet for migraines. She complains about needing
to restrict her diet due to the new medication and wants to try
something else. Her psychiatrist, by then no doubt weary, too,
tells her that he will no longer treat her unless she continues
the medication.

   We put her on the list for Myers, one of the independent
tiers of Menorah Park, an assisted and independent living
community in Beachwood, twenty minutes from my mother's
house. There is a two-year wait list. We regret that we didn't
apply sooner. Iris complains that the residents at Myers are too
old (and it's true, the average age is early to mid-eighties) and
infirm, many of them in wheelchairs and pushing walkers. She

refuses to go there. In the interim, we contact Jewish Family Services to help us employ an aide to care for her at home. The social worker sent to evaluate her reports back, after his meeting with my mother, that she presents as a woman unaware of her age. I ask what he means. He comments on the clothes she is wearing, tight-fitting leggings, a sweatshirt and running shoes, and her defensive demeanor when he begins to question her about how she is living. My heart catches, hearing any criticism of her. My mother told the social worker not to come back.

The combination of antidepressants, stimulants, and anti-anxiety medications Iris has taken for years is now proving ineffective. The painful absence and loneliness at the core of her life frightens me. Without purpose, what makes a life? I don't know how to improve it and berate myself for not always feeling compassionate. Why are the meds not helping? I wonder if she still regularly sees her friends or if she's been isolated. If she stayed active with the outside community, a job, volunteering, or taking a class, I keep thinking she'd feel better, but to wish this is like putting the cart before the horse. I want to take my mother's depression away, but I can't. Despair finds me in the mornings upon first awakening, a sense of dread, anxiety, and fear that momentarily makes me forget myself. But unlike my mother, I am not clinically depressed.

Back in New York, a call comes in from the ER in Cleveland. Iris is in an emergency room. She summoned an ambulance, convinced she was having cardiac arrest or that something else was terribly wrong. She called 911 and was taken again to the emergency room two more times within the same month. Once it was indigestion, another a panic attack. Later, I realized these visits were a cry for help, both figuratively and literally.

———

AFTER THE LATEST emergency room visit, I pull into her driveway from the airport. A real estate sign is planted on the snowy lawn. Even though the house has been on the market for a year and I have been working with the real estate agent from my home in New York City, the sign makes the impending loss more tangible. I want to run my fingers along the bushes snuggled close to the house, cut in between them, and then across the lawn as I used to do on the way to school, and hug the tree in the backyard. I'm possessive of this burnt-red house with the brown trim and door. My father bought the newly constructed house over fifty years ago in anticipation of having a family. It is where my three sisters and I grew up. Soon it will belong to a stranger.

From the windows hang thick icicles of different lengths and widths, all shaped like daggers. I remember ducking when I was little so one wouldn't spike me in the head. I don't duck this time. I let myself in the front door. I find myself study-ing each object—the dictionary propped up on the wooden stand in the living room; the grandfather clock in the hallway that once commanded my attention every hour, its chime long since silenced; the art deco dining room chandelier, another flea market find. The painting of Iris, maybe in her thirties, with shoulder-length hair parted in the middle and falling to just above her breasts, wearing a white silk blouse revealing her long neck, hung in the dining room. An artist friend she'd known since high school painted the portrait and it captures my mother's beauty, her empathy, depth, and strength.

I walk into the kitchen and see her copper pots and pans

hanging in a rack above the sink, her spices neatly arranged in small clear bottles on open shelves, the butcher block counter tops and the sleeve where she keeps her knives tucked into a cabinet so all you see are the handles, the long black walnut table where my sisters and I, as adults, made brunches of scrambled eggs, bagels, and cream cheese when we came to visit. We served birthday cakes to our little sister, Kimmy, who was ten years younger than me and who commanded the head of the table at her birthday parties. Iris's collection of yellow, blue, red, gold, and green Fiestaware is displayed on the open shelves, collected during her flea market days. When the house was remodeled years ago after she married her second husband, she planned the kitchen meticulously, from its ceramic tiles to the open windows overlooking the backyard. She is a fabulous cook, but now she only boils water for her tea and uses the microwave for her meals. I notice the dishwasher is broken and when I open it, I see it is the place where she now stores paper and plastic bags. Why does she need a dishwasher when she only uses a single plate, a fork, and a cup for her tea?

I peer at the old milk chute in the downstairs bathroom. It's now bolted closed, but it was a point of intense fascination when I was younger. I'd come down the stairs in the morning, open the chute and find that two bottles of milk—one white and one chocolate—had miraculously appeared inside. Later, when my sisters and I were teenagers, we'd crawl through the milk chute to sneak out to meet our friends late at night and then use it to crawl back in. When I observe how small it is, I'm amazed we could fit through, though I remember having to tip my hips to the side, nearly scraping the skin to make it happen.

I am transported to a time when the house was bursting with life. I hear doors slamming and my mother shouting from downstairs, *Would someone please turn up the air conditioner* during her menopause phase. We sisters screaming and bickering at each other, our angry tantrums. I smell something cooking on the stove. In my old bedroom, I see myself lying on my bed and looking at the wooden beams of the ceiling, daydreaming. As a teenager, I stared at the ceiling for hours. The house is on the corner of Norwood and Lytle Roads and stands like a matriarch with its upstairs shuttered windows that remind me of eyes looking outward, three trees on the lawn by the sidewalk, and the shrubs that line the walkway to the front door. It hugged us when we were cold; it was steadfast, unconditional, and never let us down even when the driveway began to chip, the paint on the outside walls bubbled, and we were embarrassed by the sagging roof when we walked home from school. It stood stalwart, a monument. The brightness of the walnut floors when the morning sun poured in and the shadow that fell over the house just before dusk. The street-lights going on and flickering through the lace curtains like the beam from a lighthouse. It kept us safe even if our mother was still in bed, even when we were bored and listless and had no place else to go, even when the furnace went kaput, and we slept in our winter coats. The house we wanted to escape, and then came running home to. The sinks that clogged and the toilet that one of us stopped up with a maxi-pad or vomited in. The windows that creaked when the wind slipped through. Now, the house is very quiet—so quiet that I can hear snow falling off the roof when a gust blows in a whiteout.

The house was a place to come home to when we were

directionless, a pit stop between college and being a grown-up. Its creaky floors bore the wear of our shoes and the print of our footsteps, it held our dreams and nightmares and then let them fly out the screened windows. It reverberated with the sounds of the music we played on the stereo in the living room—Neil Young, Buffalo Springfield, Cat Stevens, the Rolling Stones. It breathed in the winter chill and puckered in the humidity of a hot summer; it cocooned us and took in the chemistry of our personalities. And when we lost one of us, it continued to harbor us; the spirit of the one we had lost was held there, too, and would never be forgotten.

———

MY MOTHER IS upstairs in bed. She has been suffering from intense migraines—a slant of light will undo her. When she has a spate of these headaches, it is hard for her to function. There have been signs for the last year that things aren't right. First, it's the driving incident when Iris got lost; next, all the Post-its I notice around the house. Notes to herself in her perfect cursive handwriting. Notes with reminders of doctors' appointments, grocery lists, and when to take her pills. Then the constant phone calls when I'm at work. She's anxious because she wants to sell the house. She realizes she can't afford the upkeep and manage all the constant repairs, the roof on the garage that needs to be replaced and the driveway that needs to be repaved. She's been obsessing because there are strict rules and codes in the suburb where she lives, and she is being fined for the state of her driveway and other violations (owner-occupied homes receive an exterior inspection every five years). I learned that Maureen, the real estate broker, told her that the house won't sell with a one-car garage and was urging my mother to build a new garage. It would cost $20,000 that my mother doesn't have. I tell her that's ridiculous. I don't trust this woman. She pretends to be my mother's friend. She takes her to lunch. Sometimes to dinner. Flea market hunting. Maureen tells my mother that they can have a garage sale in the spring; she'll set it up and take a small percentage of the profits. When my mother tells me these things, she's confused. If I disagree with her, she gets angry. "What am I going to do?" she says. "Where am I going to live?" I tell her that we'll figure it out. There isn't a rush.

On the counter is a bottle of a miracle antiaging juice someone has sold to her. I tell her she's wasting her money. She gets mad at me. I need it, she says; it makes me feel better. I see jars of expensive creams in her bathroom and wonder how she can afford them. She's bought a Peter Max painting that costs $5,000. Anxiety builds. She's not acting herself. Who is going to do her shopping? Take her to doctor's appointments now that she's not driving? The psychiatrist she is seeing doesn't seem to be helping her.

When I come home after the rash of emergency room visits, Mary, who we hired to help my mother after she sank into depression, is upstairs with my mother. She's pleasant enough and my mother seems to like her. There have been a few of them, but they don't last long, and I worry they take advantage of her. Through the living room ceiling, I hear my mother's footsteps on the carpeted bedroom floor above, the same creaks I used to hear when I was making out with my high school boyfriend on the couch downstairs.

I go upstairs. From the hallway, I watch Mary help my

mother, who has just risen out of bed. She brushes Iris's hair
and clips back her bangs with a bobby pin. Mom used to spend
hours in front of the very same mirror with curlers in her hair,
doing her meticulous makeup regime. How young and pretty
she was then, with her brunette hair she colored auburn once
she began to gray, clear porcelain skin, long and slender legs,
and slim figure. She is no longer young, but when she smiles,
her wide-open smile, she is just as radiant. Only now, she barely
smiles. "I don't know what I would do without you," Mom says
to Mary, and I feel a whip of envy or maybe it's guilt that I'm
not living in Cleveland to help.

"You're going to be okay, Iris," Mary says. She has gray
hair pulled back in a short ponytail, rosy cheeks, and a stout
shape clad in a white uniform, which makes me feel better. It
is as if the uniform alone means she knows what she is doing.

Mom hugs Mary. Mom has never looked so tired and out
of it. Her robe is wrapped tightly around her, and she smells
like sleep, as I remember from childhood. Her eyes barely open,
though they look terrified, darting left and right as if she's
looking for something she can't find. I'm seized with a complex emotion: I have no name for it, but it has to do with the
passage of time and my fears of the future, of how my mother
will fare as she ages—of eventually having to live in a world
without her. "Hi, Mom," I say. "Oh, Jilly," Mom sighs. "I'm glad
you're here." I smile apologetically. She'd forgotten that I was
coming, even though I spoke with her the night before. Her
voice is soft, weak, and a little resentful that I haven't been to
visit sooner.

Thinking about moving, even hiring a real estate broker, has been overwhelming for both of us. She sends me the

documents, mail from the city citing the violations on the house, and agreements with real estate brokers. The folders in my desk drawers are stuffed to the brim. "Will you call the doctor and ask him about my prescription?" she asks me. "My head is pounding." "Of course," I reply. Mary takes Iris back to her bed. I sit at the edge and give my mother a hug. I tell her I'm sorry she isn't feeling well, and for a minute, I hold her tight as if I'm her mother. I don't understand what is happening.

Over the last few months, my sisters and I have become acquainted with my mother's physicians and her medications. We've reviewed her living will and have been in conversation with Maureen, the real estate broker. She told my mother that she could liquidate the furniture she no longer wanted to take when she moved and asked her to start stickering the pieces she wanted to keep. I think to myself, why put the cart before the horse? But I have learned over the years that there are moments when it is best not to interfere, and this is one of those moments.

In earlier weeks, we've helped my mother look at apartments and assisted living facilities and consulted with real estate brokers before Iris settled on Maureen. Then Iris decides she isn't going to move after all. Her erratic behavior reminds me of *King Lear* mad with dementia. "What place this is; and all the skill I have/Remembers not these garments; nor I know not/Where I did lodge last night. Do not laugh at me," says Lear. No, I'm not laughing. Inside I'm crying. What is happening to my mother?

Although I've long been anticipating this moment—when my mother would put the house up for sale and move into a place where she would not have to look after or worry about the cost and care of painting the house, the condition of the lawn and driveway—I don't want it to happen. Right now, I want to swoop in and tend to her needs, momentarily forgetting that I have an adolescent son, a husband, a full-time job, a book due to my publisher, and a home of my own in New York that demands my attention. I'm beginning to see the future that I've dreaded. How will we take care of our mother when she becomes infirm?

The migraine still hasn't passed. She lies back down and says she needs to sleep. She asks me to turn off the light and shut the door. "The light from the hallway is unbearable," she says. After I close the door, she calls out again. "Jill, will you call the doctor about my prescription?" "Yes," I say again. "I will, Mom."

In the kitchen, Mary and I discuss my mother's condition. My mother has been worried about the idea of the impending move; I suspect it may be causing some of her headaches. Mary sits on a chair with a pink Post-it stuck to its back. Pink Post-it Notes mark the furniture pieces that my mother wants to take with her when she moves. They adorn only a few items: her bed and a dresser, a small couch, and a square table with four chairs. Eventually, everything else will be gone. Mary says Iris is sleeping a lot and is confused. She barely gets out of bed. I return to Iris's room and sit at the foot of her bed again. I can hear the drip, drip of wet snow melting from the roof. "Are you sad about leaving the house?" I ask. This provokes a more upbeat tone than I expected. "It's time. I just hope I like it in the new place." But we haven't found a new place yet.

Mom sits up. She's groggy. She takes me by the hand. "Thank you, my darling, for all you do for me. Will you call the doctor about my prescription?" she asks again. I tell her that I've already called.

For so many years, I worried about my mother living in the house on her own; now I'm distressed at the thought of the perimeters of her life narrowing. It's hard to accept that her circumstances are not temporary or situational—that her inability to manage her health and finances independently, to oversee repairs on the house, or to drive are permanent. I haven't accepted the fact that she may not be able to come visit me in New York, where we'd go shopping together, out to dinner, or stroll through an art gallery or a museum, and where she'd spend time with her grandson. These days it is nearly impossible for her to travel.

I am unsure of how my mother will react when she is no longer in the home she's lived in for half a century, but surprisingly, she is not lost in a haze of nostalgia. I am the one who can't stop dwelling on the past and what this house signifies. From now on, returning for a visit will entail staying in a hotel, not in this cozy Colonial that my mother so meticulously cared for—the one that evokes so many memories I associate with the word "home." But she needs to move on—and I need to let her.

My visit is short. I sleep in one of the upstairs bedrooms across the narrow hall from my mother. She has hung curtains made from a thin lace antique cloth she must have found at one of the flea markets. The wind howls and whistles in the backyard. I hear the persistent cry of an owl that keeps me awake. The bed is a double, the mattress is too soft, the floors are wood, and there is a draft coming through the windows that reminds me of the chill of my childhood, how I used to lie in my bed at night, sometimes unable to sleep when my mother was out on a date. I pull the covers over my head to keep warm, buffing the rush of memories.

I'm tired and spent. Tears start in my eyes, but I make them stop. All I want is to sleep but the wheel of anxious thoughts and memories keeps me awake.

I remember playing red light–green light with my sisters and the neighbors on the front lawn in the summer, popping the violet flowerets of the hostas by the side of the driveway, the blinding yellow forsythia that blooms in March or April, the first sign of impending spring, building a snowman in the winter, school canceled. Rushing in the front door to ask Mom for money for push-ups or popsicles from Uncle Marty, the ice-cream truck that came every day in summer or coming in the house cold from the snow—on a blustery day much like this one—Mom in the kitchen in one of her good periods making us mugs of rich and velvety hot chocolate with mini marshmallows on top, or our housekeeper and babysitter, Olivia, serving us silver dollar pancakes for lunch while humming her hymns in our kitchen. She used to say jokingly under her breath while shaking her head, that our house was The House that Jack Built, from the nursery rhyme, "the Man all tattered and torn," "the Maiden all forlorn."

———

WEEKS LATER, MY mother fires Mary. "I don't need help," Mom tells me over the phone, irritation in her voice. More erratic behavior. I tell her she needs someone to drive her to her doctor's appointments, to the grocery store, or to the pharmacy. The agency sends over someone new, she's younger, Philomena. All seems well for a time, until we discover that Philomena takes my mother to bars at night and spends my mother's money on drinks. We let her go.

Cindy and I return for a visit to check on her a few days later. We enter the house, call out to our mother, but she doesn't hear us. We climb the stairs, and once we turn on the light, find her in bed in her bedroom with the shades drawn. Her pills and vitamins are in a plastic container with the days of the week for each slot, but she can't remember which pill she's taken and when. She won't get out of bed. She won't eat or drink or speak. Her eyes look funny. It's like peering into dark, hollow wells. It's hard to make out the iris from the pupil. Her coloring is pale. Her hair is unwashed. She's lost weight. There's a humid, tepid smell in the room. She pulls the blanket over her head and complains that her head is pounding. She lies in her bed, placed catty-cornered across the room, covered by the dark red floral duvet, and moans, saying she hurts all over. The bed faces her television. On the bed is a tray with a cup that holds a dried tea bag. Post-its with reminders tacked everywhere. I ask her to get out of bed, but she won't and tunnels further into her pillow.

And then it becomes clear. She's in the midst of a breakdown. It's as if everything holding her together has come loose. I have worried about this for most of my life, and now that it is happening, we don't know what to do. We call her psychiatrist, but he's hopeless; her visits with him amount to switching medications. He seems to have no idea about my mother's cognitive decline. I call Jewish social services to ask if they can send a nurse to the house to help us. A few hours later, the nurse arrives. After assessing Iris's condition, she calls us into the master bathroom where we can speak without my mother hearing. She suspects Iris has dementia and is experiencing emotional collapse. What do we do?

I ask. She suggests that we admit her into the emergency room of Lutheran Psychiatric Hospital so she can be properly diagnosed. Later, I learned that the agitation and fear associated with cognitive decline had paralyzed my mother. I'm terrified, as if I'm halfway across a shaky bridge and don't know what's next.

We take the nurse's advice and tag team. I return to New York and Cindy stays to admit our mother to the hospital. Cindy's fiancé flies in to help. Cindy slowly coaxes Mom out of bed—she's agitated, anxious, and uncooperative—by telling her that her doctor wants her to go to the emergency room to be evaluated. Eventually, they assist Iris into the car and drive her to the emergency room. A few days later, I return to Cleveland with my husband and son while Iris is in the hospital so that Cindy can return home to get back to work.

The geriatric psychiatrist who is assigned to Iris's care tells me he knew the minute he saw my mother that she had dementia by the hollow look in her eyes. I explained my mother was neurologically tested maybe a year ago and that the team's conclusion was "pseudo dementia." "I would call it pseudo-depression," he says. He's a saint. He's handsome dressed in his white coat and possesses a kind, midwestern demeanor. When he speaks, he stretches out his vowels in a Cleveland accent I'm accustomed to. He's not rushing to get to the next patient. He knows I'm concerned and upset about my mother. Finally, someone is telling us what is going on. He's compassionate, clear, straightforward. I trust him immediately.

To confirm his diagnosis, her doctor tells me that Iris will undergo a battery of neurological and cognitive tests to "evaluate executive function, judgment, attention and language."

The tests conclude that her cognitive skills are severely limited. She can't balance a checkbook, create a grocery list, or successfully cook breakfast (in the mock kitchen, she forgot to turn off the stove).

The vascular changes in the brain from an MRI show calcification that suggests Alzheimer's. "We'll have to wait and see how she is doing within the next year or two to be sure," her doctor says. He's surprised, too, that her psychiatrist hadn't suspected Iris's condition. He tells me that Nardil, the antidepressant she was last prescribed, was not helping, and perhaps was making things worse. "But what about the headaches and her not getting out of bed? And the last weeks when she was in and out of the emergency room? Did she have a breakdown?" "She was compensating for what was going on," he says. "And she must have realized she couldn't do it anymore. The physical symptoms were a way of deflecting the problem."

He tells me that Iris can't live alone. Since she doesn't have long-term insurance and can't afford a full-time round-the-clock aide, she'll need assisted living care. He assures me that Iris will do well with the scheduled activities. I tell him about Stone Gardens, the place where my aunt Harriet used to live once she became infirm. He thinks it would be a great place for her if we can afford it. We call Stone Gardens and luck out. They have an opening. I worry about how Iris will react to the news that she has dementia and needs to move into assisted living. When I mention how sorry I am that we had not known her diagnosis sooner, she says, "Let's not think about it. We're past that now."

———

DURING HER THREE-WEEK stay in the hospital, Iris has slowly weaned off the medication. The headaches no longer keep her a prisoner to her bed. The nurses slowly begin to draw her out. She goes to group twice a day and has meals with the other patients on the unit. She's responding well to the structured environment. She connects with the other patients, some younger. One is in for an eating disorder. Another has had a breakdown. I can tell my mother is feeling better. Color has come back to her face. The haunted, bewildered look in her eyes has, at least for a time, vanished. When I return to visit the next day, she introduces me to the nurses and other patients. "Your mother is so nice," the young woman on the floor suffering from an eating disorder tells me. Another woman says, "I love your mom." My mother has always been a sympathetic listener, and I suspect she's allowed the younger patients the space to share their stories. While I expected her to be subdued and withdrawn, she's surprisingly upbeat and content. She shows us her portioned-off space behind curtains where she sleeps, the pantry where one can make tea and coffee, and the common room where residents greet guests, have meetings, and hang out. She's dressed in dark jeans and a white button-down shirt, her brownish-red hair cut below her neck, and a touch of lipstick coloring her lips.

People with dementia often have periods of lucidity. In a study called "Understanding the Self of People with Dementia," the authors define two aspects of the self: "the remembering self and the experiencing self." "The experiencing self is the self with inner depth, mirroring the life history of the individual. Thus, the self of people with dementia is not unextended in time. Although people with dementia may have lost the ability to tell a story about their life, they are still able to express this story in their behavior . . . although the narrative self may be impaired in people with dementia, this does not mean that the self of people with dementia is a blank slate, a self without history or depth." The remembering self is the self that becomes impaired. "Dementia primarily affects the remembering self, i.e., the ability to put different experiences in context and to perceive different events as belonging to the same story, while the experiencing self remains largely unaffected." Iris's experiencing self is still intact. If she has her basic needs attended to, she can still experience the pleasures of daily living and aspects of her inner being are still available to her.

I wonder about the difference between dementia and Alzheimer's. I google and find an article from the Geffen School of Medicine. It explains that dementia "refers to a range of symptoms affecting cognitive abilities, while Alzheimer's disease is a specific type of dementia distinguished by progressive memory loss and cognitive deterioration." The presence of plaque in the brain is also a characteristic of Alzheimer's that is detected through brain imaging.

———

WHILE IRIS IS in the hospital, we pack up her possessions for the impending move to Stone Gardens, the assisted living community of Menorah Park. I walk through the rooms of the house that is now vacant of its owner. I walk upstairs to my mother's bedroom and feel her presence. I picture her hovered over the chipped turquoise sink in the master bathroom that has been in the house for fifty years to better see herself in the mirror. I sneak a peek at the two bedrooms that held our sleeping bodies, one with the posters covering the walls and the other now stripped of its once green carpet, to the second bathroom with the black and orange tiled backsplash over the beige tub, the cabinets underneath the sink with drawers still filled with our old shampoos, hairbrushes, curling wands, creams. I turn on the faucet and it still makes a rusty sound before spewing water. Downstairs the drafty den with its high-pitched cathedral ceiling resembling the high beams in a synagogue. The cabbage rose love seats across from each other as if in conversation and in between the brick fireplace where we hung our stockings on Christmas Eve. Then to the kitchen Mom designed, her greatest masterpiece. I trudge down to the cool and damp basement we sisters made into our girl-pad when we were teenagers.

I look at Mom's houseplants, like a tiny garden resting on a credenza in the dining room, and remember how my mother watered, spritzed, talked to, played music for them with care. Many of the jade and wandering plants have lived in the house as long as Iris has. The house immortalized and morphed with our memories, it grew up and aged with us, it bore the stamp of our temperaments, our anguish, it sighed and buckled when it needed relief. And when we had to clear out the house, sort through Iris's papers and belongings, drawers full of documents, her divorce decree, birth announcements, ripped-out obituaries, death notices, and bills, it was agony. We lay on the carpet for relief. When the movers came to load up the truck for Iris's move to Stone Gardens, and it was up to us to empty the rest to be sold to the liquidator to give Iris a few months' more rent, it was as if we were mourning a loved one's death. Packing up, I discover Post-it Notes Mom had written and attached to various folders and papers in her drawers as reminders: *Be Positive. Smile.*

7.

How did we get here, you may wonder. How did a life succumb to an illness so devastating that only the very soul and essence of a person remains? Grief and depression surely played their part. This is the hardest chapter in Iris's life I will ever write. Iris is fifty-seven years old. April 16, 1990, three days after my birthday, she calls me at my office to tell me my youngest sister, twenty-one, has taken her life. I'm thirty-one, newly married, four months pregnant, living in a five-story walk-up in New York City. The guardian of her beloved heroically calls each of her three remaining daughters and tells us, "Our baby is gone." It's unbearable, as if there are cymbals crushing the two sides of my head. The shock is like a physical assault. I can't take it in. The mind doesn't accept it. The words don't connect with their meaning.

Once outside my office building, David guides me by the hand (Iris phoned him first to ask him to come to my office to be by my side when she called), to find a cab on Forty-Second and Fifth Avenue and head to the airport. Suddenly, it hits me full force, like whiplash or a shot in the back. I crumble, and loud screams come out of me. David keeps me from falling.

The air is crisp and cool; cabs and cars zoom past, pedestrians dodge us as we wait for the light to turn. I hide my face in his coat. I can't bear it. I'm in agony. Tears fall unending and I know this is the worst day of my life. What did she look like? What was she wearing? Were there tears in her eyes? A dark phantom—the pain my sister must have suffered— has entered my body and won't leave. Her face is sealed in my mind. I won't let it go.

———

ON THE NIGHT she dies the facts are simple. She had broken up with her older boyfriend, Alan, or he had broken up with her. When he stopped by to pay his respects during shiva, he told us that Kim called him the night she died and said, "that she was going to a place far away." He said, he thought she meant that she was moving out of town. I'm sure Kim was asking him to come find her. I wanted to hit him. Scream. Instead, poor soul, I hugged him. I knew he loved her. He killed himself five years later.

Why, everyone wants to know. As if there's a quick answer. One narrative that will explain it all because we always need a story, an account, to make sense of the inexplicable. Every story must have a plot, an arc, and a denouement. Here's my attempt, my failure, my bewilderment. At the time of her death, Kim was stuck, struggling to find her way, going to college, then dropping out, waitressing, living with Alan, then back at home. She was having a hard time letting go. She had abandonment issues. Couldn't even bear overnight camp. Held her feelings and thoughts close to her. She was like a locked safe, unwilling to open up or share, not wanting to burden anyone. There were deeper hurts that had not been resolved. On the night she died, she was out partying with her friends. She arrived home, Mom asleep upstairs, wrote a note on a piece of notebook paper, left it on the counter telling us that she loved us, *dear mom, dear family*, maybe this is when she called Alan, then went into the garage, closed the garage door, slipped into Mom's car, a yellow Saab, turned on the ignition, and eventually fell asleep until the boy who mows Mom's lawn found her in the morning and called the police.

———

HOW COULD WE have missed it?

———

THE DAY BEFORE the funeral, Iris busies herself doing laundry, polishing silver, and getting the house ready for the shiva that will follow the next day. It's like she's walking in her sleep. She comes upstairs with Kim's jewelry box to the bedroom where David and I are staying (he's downstairs with my brother-in-law taking care of the funeral arrangements, calling relatives and friends, trying to hold our family of women together). I don't know what time it is, maybe eight o'clock. Mom sits down on the side of the twin bed where I am lying staring at the ceiling in disbelief. "She had so little," Iris says, holding Kim's bracelets and cheap jewelry. Then she breaks down. We hug. I'm nauseous and sick from being four months pregnant. All night, spooned next to David in the narrow bed, facing the wall, I can't stop thinking about Kim's unbearable suffering that would have caused her to take her life. I creep out of bed several times to vomit, but there is no food coming up, only bad tasting bile. Rain tambourines the window. The heavens are mourning, too.

The next morning, we dress for the funeral. It's still pouring rain, the darkest morning I can remember. *Ping, ping, ping* on the roof. *Pang* on the windows. The pain is physical. Lacerating. Unspeakable. Why did this happen to this beautiful, intelligent, sensitive young woman just at the age of becoming? Why to any child, to any person? I can't fathom it. Iris has chosen to believe that her baby is in the arms of loved ones who have passed. Months later, I, too, will lose a child. The baby I am carrying, Isabel, born at thirty-two weeks dies shortly after birth from undeveloped lungs. I can't help but wonder if the loss of my sister contributed to my premature labor. Again, there are no real answers. All of us are assaulted by the intense and surreal shock of my sister's death. Iris is mostly stoic. It's as if she wants to hoard the grief all to herself. She won't let her youngest daughter down, needs to keep her close. To revel in the marvel of her darling daughter. *At least she's no longer suffering*, is her mantra. Kim lives forever in her silences. But who knows? Iris may despair all through the night. We can't know the inner heart of anyone.

While we dress to go to the funeral, I go into my mother's room looking for a dress that will fit me now that I'm four months pregnant. She's in her nude bra, panties, and nylons in midstream of getting dressed, the phone cradled against her ear and shoulder and she's crying. When she hangs up, she tells me she was speaking to Kim's father. I ask why she called him. He's her father, she lashes out. They both had lost a daughter.

At the funeral I listen to the rabbi, but I can't really hear him. I'm trying to hold myself together. I turn around once and see relatives, Kim's friends, teachers, and Iris's friends. It's packed, and then I see a few rows back, Kim's father sitting in an aisle seat. He catches my eye, and the shame of it fills the air. At the graveside, Iris momentarily loses it and throws herself over her daughter's casket. "My baby, my baby," she cries, as if it's finally sunk in. I don't know how she will deal with this, how she will go on. Nick Cave, the musician and songwriter who lost two sons, said that in the dark place of grief the "idea of God feels more present or more essential. It actually feels like grief and God are intertwined." I sense Iris feels this closeness, but I'm raging at God, at my sister's world—all of us—who let her down. I don't believe God would take her from us. If so, I rail against Him. I think of Kim's early death as God's mistake, even though I'm not sure if I am a believer. And yet I must summon faith, especially for my mother. She needs to trust her daughter is finally at peace.

———

DURING THE WEEK of shiva, friends and family come in and out of the house, bring over casseroles, bagels, egg and tuna salad, muffins, kugel, and rugelach we place on the long farmhouse table in the kitchen and on the square table underneath the light fixture in the dining room. Iris has brought out the coffee urn from storage, and every now and then, one of us makes more coffee. All through the day and into the evening we chat, remember, eat. It's almost like a reunion, seeing people we haven't seen in years, Kim's friends, her teachers, and relatives, until we stop and remember why we're here, that the beloved is gone, and catch ourselves. The activity grounds us; it is a reprieve before the shade of darkness falls again, and we're alone, each with our own separate anguish and bewilderment. Our wish that we could have done more. I'm proud of my mother. It must be so hard to face her friends, Kim's teachers, and peers—a mother is supposed to protect her child—but she does it with dignity. All she wants now is to honor her daughter.

———

THE QUESTION IS how to push forward, how to live with the deep loss of losing someone who is precious to our sense of well-being. How to reconcile with suicide, its destabilization and bewilderment, the *if onlys* that creep in. Over time the acute malaise that grief and suffering bring becomes more bearable. Still, it catches us unaware. In *The Limits of My Language: Meditations on Depression*, Eva Meijer writes, "The edges eventually wear away, but they never vanish, just as grief never vanishes either, but simply changes form, and these traces carry on shaping everything that happens afterwards."

Many people believe and have suggested that suicide is an enactment of anger, a way of getting back at loved ones for damage they perceive has been done to them. This is not a belief I share. Anger keeps us alive; it is pain and hopelessness that sink us. I'm frustrated by the expectations society places upon us, the burdens to prove oneself, peer pressure, the shame of not feeling good enough, strong enough, capable enough. About how easy it is to miss the signs. About how the myths and lack of public knowledge of suicide prevent early detection. Everyone has struggles, but Kim felt alone in hers. At twenty-one how much can we know about ourselves, the nature of where we hurt, how to feel better, how to make the inner pain stop. I keep wondering about the missing piece, the strength or will that sustains us in our darkest moments. Why couldn't Kim find it? But maybe the answer is that she hadn't wanted to die. That she had hoped to be saved. Or that she didn't see that the impulse would be final. We go through all of it, again and again, and again, like a spinning wheel that doesn't land. In the end, we must live in bewilderment. For my mother, I can only imagine the worst. A parent is supposed to save and protect her child. While my mother tried her best to help Kim; comforting her when she was upset, encouraging her to go back to college, to get help when she glimpsed Kim's pain, she slipped through her hold. Love was not enough. I know that my leaving home when Kim was eight—Laura had already left for college and Cindy would leave a year later—was lonely for her and impacted her feelings of abandonment. Too, she must have felt, as the only child at home, that our mother was her responsibility. It's all so unbearable.

———

THE BELOVED'S BIRTHDAY passes in July. Then the anniversary of her death. The second year is worse. It's like living in a dull daze. Friends aren't always comfortable talking about suicide, afraid they'll say the wrong thing. They sometimes avoid you, or the subject, or urge you to move on when you're not ready. The loss becomes more private, lonelier. To go on with life makes my mother anxious as if she is leaving her daughter behind. And what is life now without her youngest daughter and steadfast companion. Sometimes, Iris believes her daughter will walk through the door, dressed in a jean jacket, blond hair bouncing on her shoulders, the clank of her keys on the shelf by the door. Other days, she thinks she spots her in a crowd. The mind won't let her quite believe yet that there is no chance for reconciliation. Going on means living two lives, one that wants to live and the other that has died. It's not all bleak. There are days when memories shine.

There's the phantom of the beloved tucked into the corner of the couch, tangled in her sheets after a disturbing night's sleep. There she is, making scrambled eggs in the morning. Phone cradled against her neck. Mom welcomes her into the cold, slippery day. She refuses to let go, like Demeter, who lost her daughter to the underworld, and bargains with Zeus to free her. Kim has become her shadow world. A friend calls to check in. There is nothing to say to offer comfort. There is no comfort. Iris is locked in grief's slumber. What to say. *I made tea. I washed my cup. I once held my daughter close.* Grief dislodges her from ordinary life. Nothing is ever the same again.

———

DAYS CREEP SLOWLY. Night settles into ash. Days turn to years. All life is reduced to this moment. The decision to forge ahead or slide away.

To Life, To Life, Le Chaim. When I come to visit, I see a vein I'd never seen before on the thin skin of my mother's forehead. What am I going to do without her? Iris says.

———

GRIEF SLIDES INTO depression. As the years progress, for the first time living permanently on her own, Iris grows insular, agoraphobic, rarely leaving the house. Kim's early death has robbed her of her future. The light in her eyes dwindles. The colors of the world disappear. In *The Limits of My Language*, Meijer describes depression as "more an absence than a presence. Everything worthwhile is slowly scraped away and all that remains is bare rock. Anxiety or grief often create a surplus of emotion, but depression, by contrast, weeds out the good feelings, making everything barer and emptier and giving negative feelings free rein. While anxiety or grief are often to do with things that are worth bothering about, depression shows you that nothing is worthwhile."

———

ON ONE VISIT I take my mother to a grief support group in Cleveland, but it's too much for her. She won't go back. She struggles to function with the help of several different antidepressants, none of which seems to prove effective. I keep hoping she'll get past this and find renewed purpose, but when depression takes hold, hopelessness, loss of pleasure and confidence, lethargy set in, and it is hard to find motivation. It's a double-edged sword. "Depression is the flaw in love. To be creatures who love, we must be creatures who can despair at what we lose, and depression is the mechanism of that despair," writes Andrew Solomon in *The Noonday Demon: An Atlas of Depression*.

———

AFTER THE LONG stupor of her grieving, eventually, Iris takes baby steps. Grief becomes part of her life as if her twin. She walks around the block of the neighborhood, finding sustenance in looking at the beautiful gardens—there's one house that she loves, a whole lawn filled with yellow and purple

crocuses and pansies. She picks up her favorite brown Bolog-
nese sauce from Aurora on Warrensville to rescue her appetite
and tends to her plants and the flowers in the backyard. Goes
to movies or out to dinner with friends. On Kim's birthday, I
call her. We reminisce about her kind and sweet temperament,
along with her dry wit that could catch you unaware, how much
she loved her cats—she had a mystical connection, especially
to her black and white cat, Gretel, who slept at the bottom of
her bed. We remember her favorite foods: grilled cheese sandwiches, tomato soup, Kraft macaroni and cheese. Bagels and
scrambled eggs. Her long blond hair, twinkling smile, inner life
that shined in her eyes. Her hourglass figure, and perfect legs.
How no one could tell her what to do. Her childhood birthday
parties. The day camp we sisters hosted in our backyard for
her and her friends in the neighborhood one summer. *Duck,
Duck, Goose, Red Rover, Come Over. What Time is it Mr. Fox?*
My mother tells me that Kim believed she had the best sisters
in the world. "How she looked up to you," she says. I remember
the time she cracked her head on the pavement, and we took
her to get stitches. I held her hand, and she did not cry. We
remember the delight in her blue marble eyes when she came
downstairs on her tiptoes Christmas morning into the living
room to witness stockings full, presents on the floor, Santa's
cookies eaten. How she crawled into my bed in the morning,
her cold toes against my thighs. Blond hair the color of the sun.
Good morning, Sunshine, Iris greeted her baby every morning.

———

ANOTHER YEAR PASSES. Iris decides to redecorate the
house. She tosses out the bed in the downstairs bedroom where

Kim slept and makes a den under its cathedral ceiling. Empties the closets. She asks us to clear out our old books, school papers, and memorabilia we've stored in boxes in the basement. She wants to begin a new chapter. She requests that we choose any clothes and artifacts of Kim's we want and gives the rest away. Why does she need Kim's possessions when her spirit resides within her, and in the house? I score the bridesmaid's dress Kim wore as maid of honor at my wedding, her Bugs Bunny sweatshirt, jean jacket, favorite stuffed animal—a replica of Curious George—the fabric on his toes wearing thin and showing its wire, hunched over, his hands clasped in prayer. One afternoon, Iris bequeaths me Kim's notebooks, diary, artwork, and papers from school. She doesn't want them. Does she want me to write her history? And indeed, months later I begin to write about Kim's suicide. Eventually, ten years later, hundreds of drafts coalesce into a book I publish called *History of a Suicide: My Sister's Unfinished Life.*

Iris hires a painter. She wants to wash away the old walls of the interior of the house and replenish with something new. Restoring beauty becomes consolation. For days and weeks, she plays with color swatches. She is nothing if not a perfectionist and I imagine she drives the poor painters crazy, asking them to try a certain color, then another, until she feels she's got it just right. Plum for the living room, dark burgundy in the den, her miracle kitchen mauve. The hallways are light gray. Dark garden green for the now guest-bedroom-former-beloved's-nursery, darker red for the master bedroom. She's single-minded and reckless in her mission to undo the past and restore it. Relies on Aunt Harriet's money for all the house repairs and painting and runs down her trust. The house is her creative canvas.

I feel her with me, Iris chants, and points to her heart. *She's right here. Kimmy would know how to fix this*, she'd say if the sink was clogged or she needed a light bulb changed.

———

EVENTUALLY SHE RECLAIMS the energy to attend dating parties for singles (this is before dating apps) with a friend, maybe meet a new man. And why shouldn't she? It's time to push out the cobwebs and scrub the floors. *To Chaim. To Life.* In her early sixties, she's still attractive, vibrant, yearning, hungry. There is still a self that demands pleasure, a libido that needs attending. When she's in this state her mantra is to keep moving, keep doing, as if she knows what's coming. It's always creeping in the background, waiting. The black hood suddenly pulled over the face. Those ominous ugly birds of grief pecking at the crumbs. One night I look at stars in the sky from my deck. There's Andromeda with her daughter, it looks like it's one star, but it is really two. Death cannot tear my mother apart from her daughter.

Painting of Iris by her friend Betti Franceschi

Iris at
Jill and David's
wedding
reception

Iris at Weinberg Unit,
Menorah Park

Family house on Lytle Road

Kim Elizabeth,
age two or three

From left to right, Iris
holding baby Kim; her
grandmother Gizella
Greenbaum, known as
Grandma Cookie; and Iris's
father, Eugene Greenbaum

Iris and Kim at the merry-go-round

Iris with her children from left to right: Laura, Cindy, and Jill

House on Lytle Road with Iris and Milt looking on as Laura pushes Jill in the stroller, Iris pregnant with Cindy

Iris and Milt in the den of their house on Lytle Road

Iris and Milt Bialosky, Wedding Day

Milt Bialosky

Iris, seventeen years old,
at the beach

Lillian and Eugene Greenbaum

Eugene Greenbaum holding his daughter Iris

Iris holding her baby brother, Larry

Iris and her father at the Statue of Liberty

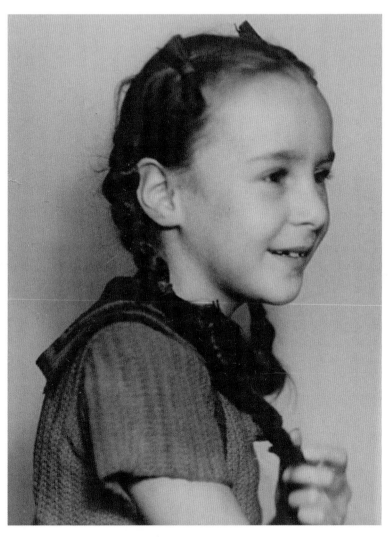

Iris Greenbaum, age seven or eight

8.

Mom is forty-three years old when I come home from my waitressing job and she's sunning in the small plot of her backyard. Her friend Rhoda is with her, both on lounge chairs, drinking cheap white wine, rubbing baby oil into their skin, and using a foil-wrapped reflector to drink in the rays. After all, this is the Aquarius of dark tans. Iris has her hair tied up in a ponytail, her cheeks are red and oily from the sun and she's wearing white balm on her lips so they don't crack or burn. She says there are no men. They only want young women. Rhoda is smoking a skinny cigarette. Her long super thin legs go up to her narrow waist. She's in a two-piece with the straps hanging down. She says she's given up on finding someone. *No more*, she says. *They just want to be taken care of.* Her husband divorced her and married a European model twenty years younger. The women in Iris's circle talk about it, outraged at his behavior. Now Rhoda works in a clothing store and lives in a tiny apartment. Iris has two sets of friends. One is the divorcées, and the other is those who are still married and financially supported by their husbands. Iris is a good friend to all of them. She likes to laugh and listen to other people's stories. Her friends open their hearts to her because no one has suffered more than she has. Iris and Rhoda talk about their kids and gossip about their friends.

The divorced set includes Ruth, the mother of Kim's best friend. Ruth is divorced, too, but after many years being single, she remarries. She's still devoted to Iris. And there's Eva, whom Iris went to high school with and roomed with during her first and only quarter of college. Eva's husband divorced her for a younger woman. Poor Eva. She's always struggled with her weight and, every six months, goes to a fat farm to shed pounds. She's not hoping to find a new love; she's too angry. She smokes her thin cigarettes and speaks in a deep, hoarse voice; when she laughs, it sounds more like a crackle. Iris's other friend from high school, Esther, is an artist; she divorced her husband and took her two kids to New York City. Iris's divorced friends are devoted to each other, women trying to make new lives for themselves and their children. Iris and her single friends dine together at restaurants, flock to the cinema, bring a picnic to flea markets on Sunday afternoons, offer decorating tips for their homes, bemoan their options, and talk endlessly on the phone when one is in a jam and needs advice. But there's no escaping the fact that when they came of age, validation for a woman's life meant having a husband. They bear that cross, bemoan their plight, sometimes feeling the scorn, snub, and shame from those in their wider social circles who are high-minded in their privilege—or luck—and think less of them.

The Vietnam War is over, Watergate ended and everyone's distrustful of the government. Long-standing norms begin to relax. Long hair and sex outside of marriage are in fashion.

Free love. Iris has a touch of the hippie in her. She's thin and youthful, and sometimes people mistake us for sisters, which thrills her. Macramé curtains slide down the living room windows crafted for her by her sister-in-law. Iris becomes a health freak. All kinds of vitamins, grains, sprouts, and raw nuts line the kitchen shelves. She allows no white bread, no more cookies or bakery treats, or Skippy peanut butter (only organic with an inch coat of oil on the top) in the house. She smokes a touch of weed from a stash her friend Esther brings her from New York. It's the era of going bra-less. The summer of love, uninhibited sexuality.

———

THIS WAS THE moment when Betty Friedan, Pauli Murray, and others established NOW, the National Organization for Women, to promote equal rights. The women's movement takes off, pushing for equality in education and the workplace, but Iris and her women friends are in their early forties, most of them had married in their early twenties, they are still raising kids and lack the time, education, and money to benefit from the new opportunities the movement is fighting for.

———

THESE ARE ALSO the years for Iris of perimenopause and menopause, making her irritable and suffer from hot flashes. *The house is too hot. Someone turn up the air conditioner. Who took my pantyhose? Where's my jacket?* It's hard for Iris to transition when she still feels so young. Tantrums erupt when anxiety catches up with her. She yells and slams her bedroom door. She spends a lot of time on her bed when she's in a low period. Thank goodness we still have Olivia who helps Iris around the house and cares for Kimmy like her own daughter.

———

IRIS LIKES STOUFFER'S Welsh Rarebit and Spinach Soufflé. Pasta with her favorite spaghetti sauce she picks up from an Italian restaurant to line her freezer. When she's had a bad day or just needs time alone, she carries her meals on a tray as if she is getting room service in a hotel. We older girls are teen-agers, running in and out of the house, working at waitressing jobs where we mostly have our meals in between our school schedules. In the summer, Iris will boil fresh corn from the farm stand, sprinkle it with salt, and take three cobs up to her room, and that will be her dinner. She does crossword puzzles on her bed. She plays solitaire, watches TV, talks on the phone, flips through magazines, and cuts out ads for things she likes or may want to buy. Perfume, lipstick, a fancy Chanel bag she can't afford. Skin firming cream. Once I find a copy of *Candy*, the pornographic novel, on her bed (I steal it and read it with my best friend, laughing out loud, half disgusted and half blushing at the sex parts) and a *Playboy* magazine. It confused me until I realized when I was older that Iris had a libido, too, and she's without a partner. Marriage is a matter of staying the course. For some women, that means bearing up and closing their eyes to unhappiness. Divorced women still bear a stigma, and after Iris divorced her second husband, she felt its double bind.

———

KIM IS SIX or seven and she has three teenage sisters to help look after her. She's growing up in a household of hippie teens, snubbing our noses at the circumscribed values and institutions of American society. The Kent State shootings during the protest of the US involvement in the Vietnam War brought the perils and reality of war closer to us. Now that we're older, we're more aware of the freedoms at stake outside our sheltered lives. It's the peace and love generation. We three teenagers have long hair parted in the middle and wear peasant blouses, low-cut hip-hugger bell-bottom jeans, and hiking boots. Kim looks up to all of us. We don't mention the fact that her dad has checked out; we don't talk about our own dad, who died when we were babies. We're all living in the moment. There's always chaos, one sister fighting with another, one of us upset, frustrated or angry, lots of eye-rolling at our mother who seems to us to be too into herself, superficial, who we are embarrassed by when she gets herself dressed up for a date or flirts with the plumber or landscaper to get a better deal. We don't have family dinners around the table. Kim doesn't seem to mind all the commotion and chaos. She likes hanging out with us when our boyfriends come over. Mine roughhouses with her on the lawn, and she yelps with laughter. Sometimes, we take her to the movies or get ice cream. If Iris's going out for dinner, we are on-call babysitters.

———

IT'S THE PERIOD when Iris's new refrain is *no one wants me.* Meaning men. The era when I begin to disapprove. When I want her to get it together and grow up. When I don't want to hear about her dates, she has a young child to tend to. But I still need her. I'm seventeen and want to get my driver's license.

She's impatient when she's asked to take me to the DMV. Why? Because she has her own worries to attend to. She's often agitated; it's hard for her to raise four girls on her own. We older, excitable, emotional girls, each month cycling through our periods—any one of us might be in bed with cramps—grow up quickly and we're not easy. But there are certain things I still need from her, though she makes me nervous for asking.

While I'm in the car with the driving examiner, I can almost hear her sighing in the waiting room. When I fail the parallel parking test, I never go back because I don't want to bother her. Without a driver's license, I must take the bus to get to my waitressing job at the mall after school. But even if I got my license, whose car would I drive? Mom is selfish about her things. Her room is off-limits. It's not our fault she had us, but she seems to resent us now that we sometimes talk back, get annoyed, and disapprove. A mother shouldn't be jealous of her daughters, but I wonder what Iris thinks about us. Unlike her, we haven't been raised with the expectation of being cared for by a man. We've witnessed the fallout. Was she at times envious of our freedom, wished she could walk out the door and leave us behind and start anew? Iris never speaks about her ambitions. I'm not sure she felt she was capable of ambition. Much later, one of my sisters found a journal Iris had started. She wrote that she hoped she had the confidence to get her real estate license. It must have been terrifying to her since she'd only gone to college for a semester. Hearing about her desire for confidence made me wish I'd understood her more when I was younger. This is the paradox of childhood: when we are children, absorbed in our own worlds, we can't fully appreciate and know our parents' struggles.

———

MY BOYFRIEND, WHOM I'm crazy about, is a year older and
has graduated high school. He's taking time off before college
working at the trotter track grooming horses. Horses are
his life, and I love his passion for them. On weekends, I stay
over in his one square window dusty tack room that smells
of horses and manure. I go to his softball games on Sunday
afternoons and read a novel in the stands. He doesn't mind
just as long as I'm there, watching when he's up to bat. I'm
devouring books by Jane Austen, the Brontë sisters, George
Eliot, and contemporary novels I find roaming the shelves
in the local bookstore. They offer an alternative reality of
intense relationships and conversations of worlds unknown
to me, peepholes into the mysteries of the human heart and
psyche. They make me restless and fill me with longing for a
different, more intellectual and passionate life.

———

IRIS NEVER TALKS directly to me about my future, though
it is all that I think about my last years of high school. She
doesn't instruct me how to be or tell me what to do. What
kind of person to marry. What kind of profession should I
want? What to study.

Iris never asks to see my grades. She doesn't iron or wash
my clothes. She rarely has food in the fridge. I am afraid to ask
her for anything. All of us are. She doesn't care if we sleep out
at night or if we've made the basement into a hangout where
we smoke cigarettes and drink beer. Friends and boyfriends
come and go through the back door while Iris is upstairs in

her bedroom. I'm not sure she even knows. Maybe she needs her own time, overwhelmed by four daughters and their heady emotional lives. Maybe because she lost her own mother when she was young and never had a road map for offering instruction. Perhaps more likely, she believes her daughters are more capable than she, but she has an uncanny ability to know when something is wrong and one of her daughters is unhappy, troubled, or suffering. She berates my boyfriend for not taking me to the prom when it isn't cool to go to it anymore, even though I have no interest in going. She gets impatient when one of her daughters won't open up and tell her what's wrong. Then she'll ask her other daughters, and then all of us are up in arms with speculation and worry. There are days I long to be released from the chaos of my home. And then suddenly Iris emerges from her own world, inviting our great aunts for brunch, and we all sit around our long table in the kitchen eating scrambled eggs and bagels while our aunts ask us questions about our lives and beam their love, and coo over Kimmy, just seven, who sits at the head of the table, and delights them. Aunt Florence entertains us with her vaudeville tunes, "My mother told me/ That she would buy me/A rubber dolly . . ." and we break into laughter and suddenly, we are a family again.

———

LOOKING BACK, IRIS felt more confident in us than we felt about ourselves. I'm not garnering pity. My mother made me who I am by preoccupation with her needs. She possessed few tools for survival as a single mother on her own. In *The Feminine Mystique*, published in 1963, a critique of women's roles in the era in which my mother came of age, Betty Friedan writes: "Over and over women heard in voices of tradition and of Freudian sophistication that they could desire no greater destiny than to glory in their own femininity . . . all they had to do was devote their lives from earliest girlhood to finding a husband and bearing children." Iris never got over the fact that fate had robbed her of the future she was raised to believe would be hers.

———

IRIS IS DATING again. But this time it is different. There's more of a sense of desperation as if time is running out. And the dates never seem worthy of her. There's one man, maybe a decade younger than her, who Iris is attracted to and glams up for, but we girls don't approve. He's never been married, lives in the carriage house of a couple my mother knows, he's a sports gambler, works in real estate. Who knows. Maybe they're in love. But he's sheepish and uncomfortable when he comes to pick Iris up, as if he knows he shouldn't be leading her on. Or perhaps Iris's world with her family of girls, one still a young child, is more than he bargained for.

I've graduated from the greasy spoon waitress job at the mall and have scored a waitress job at Charlie's Crab, which is more upscale, with better tips. One night, Iris surprises me, and when I check out my station, I see that the hostess has seated her and her date at one of my tables and I'm forced to wait on them. Lucky me. At least I get a good tip. Iris has been dating this man for a while. He's round, bald, with tan, crinkled skin and a gold ring on his pinkie finger. He's a Holocaust survivor originally from Poland with a thick accent, wealthy, and older than Iris. He's clearly in love with her, but though Iris likes him, he's kind and gentlemanly, she doesn't feel quite the same. She will not marry just to be financially cared for. Many divorced or widowed men want to marry her, but none seem to offer the kind of love she once had with my father.

I like a pharmacist from Coventry, the more down-to-earth, bohemian neighborhood in Cleveland Heights. He's intellectual, well-read, and talks to me and my sisters instead of leering at us, but Iris isn't attracted to him. I watch as she grows weary, first trying to impress her dates, and then her disappointment that none of them quite measure up. Iris complains that they all want younger women. Now that the adolescent plumpness has drained off my body and I have a figure, some of her dates lust after me with winks and inappropriate behavior. Cindy and I decide to move our bedroom down to the basement. We need our own space. There are two couches down there we sleep on. With the lights off, it's pitch black. When Iris comes home with a date, she sometimes turns on the stereo so loud it penetrates through the floor and wakes me. I picture them necking on the couch and it makes me ill. Does she not get that her lack of boundaries is inappropriate? Get a hotel, I think. I'm twisted. Part of me resents my mother, and the other part feels sorry for her. I understand that she needs attention from a man, but I wish she had more strength, more of a constitution, and didn't rely so much on finding a new husband to make her happy. I also know somewhere in my young mind that she's caught on the wrong side of history.

———

I'M LUCKY THAT we live in Shaker Heights where 99 percent of the high school student body goes to college. Otherwise, who knows what might have become of me. The guidance counselor instructs me to look at college brochures sprawled on the table in her office. I pick up one and it is a small college in Vermont called Windham College. I like the snowy mountains in the background. I like the idea of going to college in Vermont. I have good grades, graduate cum laude, win an academic award that comes with some money for college. I'm distracted and haven't yet learned how to advocate for myself. I'm not sure I know what that means. However, I know that education is my only way forward.

I chose a college because I like the snowy hilltop Vermont campus on the cover of the brochure and am offered a financial aid package with some scholarship money. I later discovered that most of the kids at the college are daughters or sons of diplomats, famous people who didn't quite have the grades to go to Harvard or Yale. Iris is supposed to drive me there with a friend of hers. It's a road trip. But the day before we're about to leave, she gets sick—pneumonia—and so I ship my trunk and fly to Vermont by myself. Later I wonder if it's because she's unhappy I'm leaving. I've always been her anchor. It isn't easy. Mom tells me she has no money, *what am I going to do* is her favorite refrain. It's hard to say goodbye to her and to Kimmy, who is only eight years old. I promise Kimmy I will write to her and call her every week.

It's the first time I've been away from home and I'm anxious until I find I like college. I love my literature and philosophy classes; studying grounds me; I can feel my mind expand. I make a few close friends. I have a work-study job at the library, and I'm finding my way. The snowy Vermont hills that surround the college gather us in. We are all, teachers and students, part of a small community. I succumb to my class schedule, at the end of the day hoofing it to the cafeteria and running my tray along the rail to gather dinner and sit with friends. For the first time, I'm oddly free, as if I can stuff my past in the closet and become a new person in this place where no one knows a single thing about me. I'm no longer one of poor Iris's girls.

———

IRIS IS WORKING at a European retail clothing store. She's her best self when she is engaged in the world that exists outside her home. She likes helping customers find the right outfit and making sales. And now she purchases elegant clothes to wear at a discount, and she looks spiffy with her manicured nails and blow-dried hair. When I'm home for a break, I visit her at the mall, and she shows me off to the staff. That Christmas, she surprises us and to our delight uses her discount to buy each of her daughters an expensive outfit from the store.

Iris's life is different from her married friends in Cleveland, a handful of couples who were close friends of my mother and father and whom she still sees on occasion, ensconced in their modern kitchens, with their walk-in closets and plush furniture, their homes surrounded by too-perfect lawns and gardens. They don't have to worry about spending money on new clothes or budgeting for the beauty parlor or hiring some-one to cut the lawn or plow the driveway. Sure, their husbands might be having affairs or are grumpy and demanding, but they prove it's better to stay married. It usually comes with a fancy vacation. They have the life Iris always wanted, the life promised to her, not the life of her and Rhoda, who works in retail, too, and are living with financial burdens always plaguing them. Eva's lucky. She received a good settlement in her divorce and opens her own antiques shop.

These are all women who, like Iris, were raised to be wives and mothers inspired by 1940s and '50s beauty queens and debutantes and the rules of dating, which required that they were given the burden of being desirable to men. Dating was about finding the man you were going to marry. Women were supposed to have an aura of intelligence but not enough to challenge men and scare them away. They were not brought up to lead independent lives or have an identity outside the opposite sex. Their job was to cater to men, to be the perfect housewife and put domestic duties first, to keep up appearances and to repress their own desires. To be an object of desire was an aspiration! In *The Feminine Mystique*, Betty Friedan cites a psychiatrist at the Margaret Sanger marriage counseling clinic: "We have made woman a sex creature . . . She has no identity except as wife and mother. She does not know who she is herself. She waits all day for her husband to come home at night to make her feel alive." Even though Iris does not now have a husband, having a man is a priority and a validation of her womanhood. No wonder she's obsessed.

———

SOMETIME DURING MY first year at Windham, we learned it was going bankrupt and I transferred. Years pass. I graduate from college with a Bachelor of Arts in English from Ohio University. It's where I discover poetry, and it's like a beam of hope lighting my way. Iris is hosting an informal get-together with close friends to celebrate. She's made her famous strawberry and sour cream Jell-O mold, a salmon mousse, chicken marsala, roasted potatoes, vegetables, and a huge, tossed salad. Once we have our glasses of wine in hand, I sit down on the couch to talk with Iris and Rhoda. Rhoda asks me about grad school—in the fall, I'll be going to Johns Hopkins University to get a Master of Arts in Poetry. I receive a scholarship to cover my tuition and a work-study job at the Johns Hopkins University Press. I ask about her kids and how they are doing. I'm waitressing at a fancy restaurant for the summer. I learn about fine wine and food and the tips are good—I'm saving money for grad school and living in an apartment with a friend. Iris has gotten used to us older kids being away from home. Kimmy is now eleven. With just one young daughter to care for, Iris is more present and engaged. I think about how lucky I am, to have the education and opportunities that Iris and Rhoda didn't have. I have an entire life in my mind and ambition to make something of myself that nobody knows about. The private life is mostly about books and writing. Lodged inside are works by Virginia Woolf, Colette, Anaïs Nin, and Marguerite Duras, women writers I want to emulate. Let's not forget the Russians: Tolstoy, Dostoevsky, Chekhov, and Akhmatova. There is, of course, poetry; it is the mountaintop on which I live. Poems by Sylvia Plath, Anne Sexton, Robert Lowell, The Confessionals. I, too, have lots to confess, many secrets and unconscious pain from the death of my father and my fraught coming of age that I hope to hone and transform in my art. Writing poems deadens the pain and sadness in my being. My great heroes are Emily Dickinson, Wallace Stevens, Robert Frost, Elizabeth Bishop, James Wright, and then further back, the Romantics, Keats and Shelley, and even further back, Shakespeare. *A poet?* People reply when I tell them what

I'm doing. It's embarrassing, but it's the only thing I care about besides wanting to fall in love. But love is dangerous. I know this from observing my mother. I must be careful.

IRIS IS LONELY. She's still hoping to find a new husband. I wish she'd stop thinking about it and focus on supporting herself and Kim, find pleasures in her own life to sustain her. I know I should be sympathetic but loneliness is a pit she falls into and sometimes can't crawl out. The men she dates don't seem to help, and a few of them are not like the more put-together and financially stable men she dated in the past. Dear lord. *The good ones are taken*, she tells me. She must be relieved to have her three older daughters mostly out of the house. We've become critical of her. We can't understand why she relies so much on wanting a man and fear she's setting a bad example for Kim. We're judgmental. We're part of the free-love generation and are less enamored with the idea of marriage. Many of our friends' parents are unhappy. And we've experienced the fallout of those who are divorced, especially the women. When we're all home for vacation from school, my sisters and I talk for hours about our mother. We dissect every aspect of her personality, trying to figure out why she can't get it together and be a grown-up, it's like an ongoing reel, or a puzzle with a piece missing, but there are no solutions, nothing to be done.

KIM AND IRIS share a close and symbiotic relationship. When they need cheering up, they order pizzas and get take-out sundaes from Draeger's. Their favorite is called Marvin's Mistake, chock-full of chocolate and vanilla ice cream, creamy thick hot fudge, nuts, marshmallow syrup, a swirl of whipped cream with a cherry on top. Iris takes her youngest daughter to parks, movies, and birthday parties, sometimes on these outings with Kim's friends' parents. She's a good, attentive mother to Kim. Kim adores her mother. She's cool. She lets her have friends over for slumber parties. Trusts her. Iris always has her back. Oprah offers a Mother's Day contest, asking daughters and sons to nominate their mother for the best mother ever. Kim sends in a nomination for Iris, and Iris brags about it. But there's also a downside to being the only daughter living with our mother, when she falls into a dark place. When Iris is in the dumps, Kim will say, "Why can't you make yourself happy?"

———

IRIS IS ON a decoupage kick. She's collected hundreds of old postcards from flea markets. She buys wooden boxes the size to hold jewelry and decoupages the cards onto the top of the boxes. The kitchen smells like glue. She's engrossed, obsessed. Her absorption is spectacular. I think she might have been an artist in another life. I wish she had gone to college and had a formal education and found her ambition. I imagine, too, that she'd make a great social worker as she cares about people and has the uncanny ability to search into their souls. I encourage her to sell her creations. She could try some of the shops in town or set up a booth at a fair, but she shook me away. She doesn't have the gumption or the confidence and soon loses interest. She decides to get her real estate license, passes, and joins a real estate agency run by two women; one is the fancy mother of a friend of mine from high school. Both women have husbands and nice homes. I'm so proud of my mother. She sells two or three houses, then the real estate market bottoms out, and she gets frustrated and quits.

———

TIME IS MEANINGLESS if not marked by the passing of a day. I know we're moving back in time. I know I'm not exactly following chronology. Kim's thirteen, and the cat is out of the bag. It's the age when one begins to wonder. She wants to know about her father, who she has not seen since she was three. I'm ashamed that we were too afraid of her hurt to have discussed the fact that her father never reached out to see her since my mother divorced him. Nevertheless, his absence was always there in the shadows. Did we think our love, care, and attention could compensate for the lack of a father's love? And it's a mystery why her father hasn't ever tried to see her when he lives only a few hours from Cleveland. Maybe it's something he pushed out of his mind, buried, forgetting he ever had a daughter, ever married my mother, had ever been a stepfather to three young girls.

Iris consults a psychologist for advice. She encourages Iris to track down Kim's father to determine whether he wants to see his daughter. She tells Iris that Kim needs to decide who her father is for herself. I'm home when Kim's father picks her up for the first time in his shiny black Cadillac. Kim's ecstatic and nervous. She's at that awkward age, thirteen, not yet a woman, but no longer a child, where she hasn't quite grown into her curves and still has a baby face. Her blond hair is parted in the middle, sometimes in pigtails or pinned back in barrettes. She's dressed in white shorts, a polo shirt and tennis shoes. How could he not fall in love with her? Kim answers the doorbell. Kim's father strides into the house with his wide, unabridged smile, gives her a big hug and holds her tight. He's wearing a polo shirt, too, lime green pants and a V-neck sweater tied loosely around his neck. He looks like a golf pro, and most likely spends most of his time on the golf course, as he did when married to Iris. The family resemblance is striking. Both blond with blue twinkly eyes. He's tan, which makes his two front teeth with a space between them brighter. I greet him and he mentions how grown up I've become. I feel like I'm in the twilight zone. There's *Dad* who used to squeeze my knees to make me laugh when I was a kid. Who tussled my hair on the top of my head and presided over our table. Who, for a short time, made Iris feel special and taken care of. He chats with Iris for a few minutes, then leaves the house with his arm around Kim. With a sick feeling, I slip into the downstairs bedroom and look through the blinds as he escorts Kim to his car and opens the passenger door for her. I want to run out and take her back, fearful of what this encounter will mean to her. I feel for a moment as if my childhood ghost came back to visit, and I shut my eyes to make it pass.

They're going to Mentor-on-the-Lake, where he has a boat. When she comes home from the weekend, she's elated. He makes all kinds of promises. Spoils her with new clothes and presents. Tells her that he'll help fix up our house because he noticed when he came to pick her up that the couches in the living room were fading and torn at the arms. Is Dad feeling a little guilty? Kim has stars in her eyes. He takes her on extravagant dates. To fancy restaurants. One weekend, Kim brings her best friend, and they go boating and partying on Lake Erie. He's married his secretary, the woman he had an affair with that caused his marriage with my mother to break up. When I asked about her, Kim said she was nice. Next, it's to his fancy club on Rattlesnake Island on the shores of Lake Erie. Kim brings her first cousin. It's a party! Sunning, beach, boating. Fine dining and tons of drinking. The girls have a blast. They go weekend after weekend. But then Dad checks out again— who knows why—maybe he's having another affair (indeed, later we discover he divorces his secretary and marries again). Maybe the fifth time's the charm. Iris doesn't know what to do. She feels like she's opened a can of worms and can't put the lid back on. "All he thinks about is himself," Iris tells me. When I catch my sister twirling her hair with her finger, staring out the window with a forlorn look on her face, it occurs to me how little one can do to make someone else's hurt go away. If we map where childhood ends, it finished for her here. She was always happy and carefree as a child. Maybe this is when her secret self, the one who says *you're no good, you're not lovable, everyone will eventually leave you*, begins to form.

———

IRIS HAS HUNG a bulletin board in the kitchen where she posts with thumbtacks phrases or jokes she likes. Lines of poetry and inspiration.

"Just one small positive thought can change your day."

"No one can make you feel inferior without your consent."
—Eleanor Roosevelt

"Trust your dreams for in them is hidden the gate to eternity."
—Kahlil Gibran

And funny cartoons, *Peanuts*, *Garfield*, *Cathy*, and clips from the Cleveland *Plain Dealer*. She puts a full-length mirror on the refrigerator to keep her weight in check and to remind her even if she's *really hungry*, does she need to eat that leftover slice of pizza? That last slice of pumpkin pie?

———

IRIS REMINDS ME of female characters from the literature I'm reading, women in Tennessee Williams's plays, or characters from Jean Rhys's and Edith Wharton's novels whose desperation cripples them and robs them of dignity. Emma Bovary in *Madame Bovary*, Daisy Buchanan in *The Great Gatsby*, and Anna in Tolstoy's *Anna Karenina*. I see my mother in these characters, weakened by desire, diminished by the patriarchy, with no real means of their own. I now possess a paradigm with which to view her more objectively, and it makes me sad. I don't want my life to be defined by dependence on a man or be enfeebled by longing and desperation. I want to be the actor of my own life. I want Iris to be stronger. To set a good example. I secretly wish she was a librarian or a teacher, like the women I admire in my community who are, at least from the outside, independent and not reliant on others for happiness and stability. The problem is that I don't want to care for or worry about her. I want my own life.

———

SOON THE DATES stop coming. Again, Iris falls into the dark well of depression. These are the days before Prozac, before William Styron's *Darkness Visible: A Memoir of Madness*, about the devastation of the disease when the manifestations of clinical depression are not readily known. When I'm away at school, I worry about Kim living alone with Iris when she's in a dark place and call often to check in and say hello. I check in on my mother, too, though always with a sense of dread, wondering what her mood will be like when I call. I talk to her about her current medication and encourage her to look for a new job now that Kim's in school all day, but it's hard for her to find motivation when she's depressed. The calls make me anxious and give me stomachaches; I don't know what to do to help. Neither do my sisters. We are struggling, too.

Iris shares her financial worries. Says she has no money. I don't know exactly what she means. My sisters and I all work and pay for our own expenses, including college and we are barely scraping by. I know she receives some child support for Kim, and that Aunt Harriet gives her money for household repairs. She still gets social security from my father's death and occasionally is employed. It's not a lot, but it's something. I'm trying to concentrate on poetry, literature, and writing. I want to pursue it, but I have no idea how I'll eventually make a living. I hope that my leaving home, along with my sisters and us becoming financially independent, means Iris can now focus on caring for herself and Kim, but I'm conflicted and guilt-ridden. I worry Kimmy will be lonely without me. My sister Laura has already left home, and Cindy will leave for college the following year. (Later, after Kim ends her life, I wonder if her fears of abandonment that began when her father left manifested again after my sisters and I left home and am plagued by insufferable guilt.) I wish our mother would set a better example for my sister, be stronger, and understand the worries she's placing on her children, but she appears not to understand the burden her disclosures bear. I long to forget about my mother and her problems. I know that all Iris wants is to be taken care of. She's made of fantasies and dreams.

———

YEARS PASS. KIM is struggling in high school, is dating an older boyfriend, coming home high, skipping school. Her father is in and out of the picture, depending on his schedule, on what he approves and disapproves of. He has high expectations for Kim, even though he hasn't parented her. I wonder if Kim's sudden problems at school are meant to seek her distant father's attention, test his love. If she is having problems, she tells herself that he'll have to step in and help; but instead, after a meeting with my mother and the guidance counselor at Kim's school—she's failing some of her classes and not showing up—he criticizes, shames, ostracizes her, and stops paying for her braces and car payments. Tells her she'll never amount to anything. When all her friends leave for college, she's stuck. I used to think it was because she was too attached to our mother to leave, but now I wonder, too, if she feared what would happen if she left our mother on her own. Sometimes, thinking about what Kim shouldered as a teenager and a young adult while I was away building my own life in New York is unendurable.

———

AT COLLEGE, I support myself with part-time jobs— work-study, cafeteria duty, taking orders at a sub shop, and working at a literary magazine as a work-study job. In grad school at Johns Hopkins, I work as a proofreader at a university press. After I graduate, I'm at loose ends. I move back to Cleveland and renew my waitress job at the same upscale restaurant where I used to work. I've grown close with the two owners and the other waiters and work on my poems when I'm not on a shift. Occasionally, one of my poems is accepted by a literary journal, which gives me hope. A year later, I applied to get my MFA at the University of Iowa's Writers' Workshop and receive a work-study job in a program for international writers. I also secured a job at the Iowa University Hospital, where I made the surgery schedule and wondered if I should train to be a nurse; at least, it's a reliable profession. I live in the attic of a three-story house whose owners take in students. I'm always worried about money and there's no one to fall back on. How am I going to make a living on poetry? I don't mind working. I like it. I like earning my own money for my education, being able to buy thrift store vintage clothes, and not having to answer to anybody for my wants and needs. This is what my mother taught me without ever saying it. But I'm anxious about my future. I tell myself I can always waitress if worse comes to worst.

———

THERE'S A COST to all this anxiety. This young woman, who is me, is in trouble. In grad school, she has many friends and boys who want to sleep with her, even a professor or two, but she keeps her distance. She's lonely. Timid. Hides her emotions. She doesn't know what's going on. Sometimes, she can't bear herself. She binge eats until she's sick, and the next day, she starves herself. This is a pattern, not every day and not even every week, only when she needs to punish or numb herself, to stuff her feelings. Her childhood was fraught with fears and insecurities, and she has no idea how these unprocessed feelings will turn on her or how they will manifest. When things are too painful, she disassociates. She has issues with intimacy and attachment, afraid of getting too close to anyone. Later, she will wonder if it all concerns her childhood, but now she's just trying to get through. Poetry saves her. If she can find the words, if she believes she can sublimate suffering through imagination and art, if she can continue to try to live up to her predecessors she reads and admires, then even though she hasn't quite yet found her voice, she knows she'll survive.

Eventually this girl, after she graduates with a Master of Arts Degree in Poetry at twenty-four, moves to New York City and finds a job as an editorial assistant in a publishing house and writes her poems in the off-hours. She's determined and driven. She doesn't quite know yet that she sees herself as the bad one, the one who got away, that maybe another kind of daughter would have moved back to Cleveland to look after her mother because, though her mother would never say it, she felt her mother needed looking after. She wanted to forget her mother and get her out of her system. So many times, when she is in New York struggling to make something of herself, she wonders why she didn't choose a simple, normal life. Not a life of striving for her own ambitions. Not a life of leaving her mother behind.

9.

ris is 33 years old. Wild joy. A new husband. It's 1966. I'm eight years old. Iris comes home with a luminescent glow on her face and a gold and opal wedding ring she shows off, holding out her pretty left hand with her painted pink nails. She sits us down on her bed and tells us we are going to have a new father. Iris and her new husband, George, were married privately a few hours ago before the justice of the peace, unbeknownst to anyone. How had we never met him before? The new husband comes to pick my mother up later that afternoon to take her on a honeymoon trip to Acapulco, and a babysitter is coming to take care of us. All the while, Iris is packing and primping in the mirror. She's so excited she can barely focus or sit still. We girls are stunned and don't know what to think. His name is George, she tells us. He's Irish Catholic, tall and broad with a gap between his two front teeth. George had been married twice before. He works in the food sector, or so we think. There's so much we don't know about him. My mother has never left us before. We don't know what to do when the new husband rings the doorbell. Mom rushes us down the stairs and introduces us. I'm unbearably, self-consciously, almost pathologically shy, and hide behind my sisters. I do not remember if he hugged us. I remember that the house seemed smaller the minute he entered.

Mrs. Toich, the babysitter, is a mean old woman (we call her The Witch in private) with a crown of tightly pin-curled gray hair around her head, stout, a slow walker with a limp, and stockings that rub together and make a swishing sound. A terrible cook, she once lit a towel on fire on the stove and nearly burned down our kitchen. I'm not sure how my mother found her. All our previous babysitters have been teenage girls we idolize from the neighborhood. Why this old bat? I lean next to my bedroom window each night to see if I can glimpse the plane bringing my mother home across the dark starlight sky. I'm heartsick. What if she never comes home? Who cares if we don't have a father? We've had our mother all to ourselves for six years and soon there will be a six-foot-tall man with broad shoulders, blond hair in a classic sweep over his forehead, sides combed back behind his ears, with blue evasive eyes, and shiny manicured nails living with us. Good grief.

They make a handsome couple, the attraction between them thick enough you could stir it. I never asked my mother how she met George or how long they had known each other before they wed. At the time, I was too young to consider it all. Their marriage must have been impulsive since we'd never met or even heard of George before, nor had Iris's family. I know Iris had plenty of potential husbands to consider and that to have chosen George she must have been truly smitten. The photos from their honeymoon in Acapulco present a sunny and romantic picture. It must have been a treat for Iris since we rarely went on vacation, only once I remember we piled into

my mother's car, and she drove us to Detroit to stay with her
artist friend from high school and her two children. In photos
from Iris's honeymoon with her new husband, she wears a
white bikini and sits on the steps of an aqua kidney-shaped
pool, tan legs dangling in the water, sipping a drink with a
pineapple garnish that looks like a piña colada. In another,
she is breakfasting at a café table, her ample bosom held up
by the cups, the straps of her bikini top fallen to beneath her
shoulders so she doesn't get a tan line. Another enjoying cocktails at a bar by the pool, new husband's arm around her. In
another Iris wears white cropped pants to her ankles and a
white eyelet top, her face bronzed by the sun, her eyes staring
at the camera in a love stupor. George is wearing white pants
and navy polo shirt. With dark sunglasses on, they look like
movie stars. My mother saves a postcard from a bullfight they
attended, Corrida de la Temporada, starring César Girón, and
another one at the Caletilla Bullfight, Sunday, April 3, 1966,
starring Antonio Sánches competing with Armando Soares
"defying ferocious bulls" from Santa Rosa De Lima. Her new
husband likes bullfights; they are gory, competitive, manly. I
imagine my mother gasping, hiding her face in her husband's
chest when the bull attacks. I imagine he's dazzled by the bull-
fighting performance and wants to show off his bravery to Iris.

The last photo in Iris's honeymoon album is of the newly
married couple standing in front of the American Airlines
plane to bring them home. Iris is handsomely dressed in black
pumps and a white knit shift, with a black straw sun hat in
one hand and a burst of colorful handmade cloth flowers in
the other. She's bronzed from the sun, and her head is tilted
to the side, and she kicks one leg up, posing for the camera.

She looks like Audrey Hepburn. On the ground next to them is a woven colorful basket from Mexico, filled with trinkets and gifts no doubt for us kids. George is standing behind Iris, sporting navy pants and a navy short-sleeved collared shirt, holding her arm. I'm not kidding; he looks like George Peppard in *Breakfast at Tiffany's*. I suppose it is a disappointment, leaving their fancy and romantic Acapulco trip to come back to Cleveland with three girls waiting for them.

―――

ONE OF THEM steals the do not disturb sign written in Spanish from the hotel and hangs it on their bedroom door back home. The bedroom is off-limits. A cocktail of alcohol, perfume, pheromones, aftershave fills the air when their door opens. We're supposed to call the new husband *Dad*. It's hard to wrap my mind around it all. Destroyed is the notion that we have our mother all to ourselves. Now, we must share her with a stranger.

My mother is determined to make it work. Good lord. Now, she can be a real housewife, taking care of her husband and children and tending to their home. Why shouldn't she be hopeful? During the week, George vacates the house to go traveling—he is a man with many interests and business schemes. One is an investment in a vending machine company, which I find rather glamorous; every time I see a vending machine filled with sandwiches, chips, Cheetos and Milky Ways it inspires a peculiar sort of pride. On the weekend, he loads up his golf clubs in his trunk and goes golfing. *This is my dad. Is it really true?* I don't know. I'm tentative about it, but try to buy into the performance and utter that three-letter word. I've never called anyone Dad before, at least that I can remember. I was two years old when my father died. Now Iris wakes up every morning on a new mission with a smile on her face and a bounce to her step. Before she remarried, she barely got out of bed in time to see us off to school. What if he doesn't like us? Still, it's a joy to see my mother happy. It's what she's always wanted, what she grew up to wish for, someone to love who would take care of her.

The best thing the new husband brings with him, along with his clothes—now my mother has to divide her closet— and a black Eames chair, is Olivia, our new housekeeper and babysitter. She cleaned his apartment for him and became our caregiver and housekeeper, eventually my mother's confidante, and our second mother. I like to retreat down in the basement while Olivia is ironing. She has black hair she oils and styles with pin curls, an apron around her stout waist, dark skin so soft that when she hugs me, she engulfs my entire body with her big, plump arms and soft chest. There's a portable TV down in the basement and we watch her stories while she irons our sheets and clothes. Sometimes she tells me tales about her daughter, Van, and her two foster boys. Even though the basement is damp and dark, there is nowhere I'd rather be than close to her. When we say or do something she doesn't like or approve of, like leaving our dirty clothes on the floor or eating peanut butter out of the container with a spoon, she says, "I'm not studying you," and turns her back to us. We instantly pick up our clothes and put them down the laundry chute, and put our spoon in the dishwasher. She takes me on a trip with her church group to Disneyland in California. On the tour bus, I'm the only white girl. I feel so special I could burst. I stay with her in her hotel room with her daughter. Sometimes, I pretend I'm her daughter. But when all the lights go out and everyone has fallen asleep and the hotel room is dark, I'm lonely and suddenly afraid. How to describe fear. It's like every nerve in my body is at attention. But then morning comes, and we are off to have breakfast with Mickey Mouse and my heart fills with new blood.

———

AT HOME FOR a while everything feels safe and calm, and Iris is happy. And so is our new dad. He comes home from work or a business trip, kisses Iris's neck and snuggles her. What is happiness? I suppose for my mother, it is the flip side of depression, a feeling of being taken care of and protected. She'd been deprived of that for a decade after my father died when she worried about how she would financially support all of us. George is so different from Iris's father, Eugene Greenbaum, son of Hungarian immigrants, with deep depressions under his melancholy eyes, reading glasses dangling from his neck, quiet, modest, and entirely devoted to his family. I don't remember him ever having a cocktail or even a glass of wine unless it was Manischewitz for Shabbat or Passover. The new husband has a loud booming voice and a boisterous laugh. He takes up all the space in a room. Sometimes, he's a little too gruff, squeezes my leg just above my knee too hard to make me laugh. He drives a black Cadillac and has several country club memberships. He loves to go on shopping sprees and has a huge appetite. His mantra is fun and adventure, but there's anger lurking in the shadows and I'm afraid of him. He does everything in excess. He won't just buy a dozen donuts, instead he brings home two dozen in all assorted flavors. His favorites are the jelly donuts he pops in his mouth like candy. One Saturday Iris and George come home with sixty or so empty jars in a big crate and a barrel of small Kirby cucumbers. They take them down to the basement to the big sink, and for hours, they work on canning the cucumbers with brine to make dill pickles, Iris preparing the jars and the liquid concoction, George doing the scrubbing. Once they're finished, they store the jars of pickles on the shelves in the little storage room in the basement we call the locker room that soon smells of garlic. Apparently, George is a pickle guy. He likes to eat them with his thick roast beef sandwiches on rye.

———

EVERY MORNING IRIS gets up, starts the coffee, spritzes and talks to her plants, she says it keeps them healthy. No more mornings in bed. She's out the door to grocery shop or go to the beauty parlor. Her new mission, forming a new family for all of us; finally, she enjoys the luxuries that her still-married classmates and friends seemed to have, or at least that is the façade. She has expensive new clothes that make her look glamorous when George takes her out to a fancy dinner every Saturday night. She now doesn't have to worry about paying the bills, is redecorating our house with a brand-new kitchen so she can make George the elaborate gourmet dinners he likes when he's home.

Iris is agitated when George goes away on business trips and she doesn't hear from him, but their magnetic attraction holds them together. Though he has fathered two children of his own in a previous marriage, he isn't what you could call a family man. He likes the idea of family, when there are no preteens causing a fuss, or a wife wondering when he is coming home. His routine is to work, play golf, and dine out with expensive wines, whiskeys, and after-dinner drinks. Suddenly, we have a well-stocked liquor cabinet. A man who enjoys a beautiful woman on his arm. A few times, his two children, who live in Philadelphia with their mother, come for the weekend. His daughter, with clear pink cat eye glasses, is a year or two older than me, and his son, with a cowlick in his hair, is a few years younger than Cindy. George makes fun of his daughter, tells her she's gaining weight, and she cries. I think she's jealous that her father now has three stepdaughters who are prettier than she is and get to live with him (sort of) when he's around and feel sorry for her. Iris is shy and uncomfortable around George's children from his first marriage and stays in the kitchen. I confront her and tell her she must go talk to them. She looks at me skeptically and then reluctantly agrees. Her voice goes into high-pitch mode when she asks them about school, their favorite foods, and other pleasantries as if to compensate for her discomfort.

———

THERE IS ONE photo of us girls all dressed alike in black and white checkered dresses with a red scoop neck George bought for us at Saks Fifth Avenue at the mall. George's son is tucked in a suit with a white shirt and red bow tie, all five of us standing in front of the brick fireplace on our way to dinner at the Country Club, where George is a member, as if by dressing us alike we magically belong together. George likes showing us all off. At the club, we sit at a long table, and he orders us

Shirley Temples, with a maraschino cherry so sweet it makes my teeth hurt while they sip their cocktails.

Going out to dinner was a rarity before my mother got married unless she gave us money to walk to the corner and get hamburgers at Mawby's, where we sat at the counter on red swivel stools, or in a booth at Manners Big Boy when she wasn't up for cooking her specialties, sloppy joes, tuna noodle casseroles, and wiener goulash, or on the special occasions when she took us to the Hong Kong where all the Jews go for Chinese food on Sundays. At the Hong Kong, we'd devour bowls of pastel-colored shrimp chips along with cold glasses of water. My mother would order egg foo young. We girls preferred the egg rolls with sweet and sour sauce and fried rice we blackened with soy sauce. Now, with our new dad at the country club, we don't know what to order. Lobster, salmon, steaks, roast beef, food we've never eaten before are on the menu. Luckily, they have a children's menu with small pizzas and grilled cheese sandwiches and hamburgers. They prolong the night with after-dinner drink concoctions, a green frothy drink in a martini glass for Iris and a bourbon or whiskey for George and conversation with other members of George's club who stop by our table. George likes to show off his harem. By the end of the evening, we are restless and tired, and our cheeks hurt from smiling, and Iris and George are woozy from all the drinks.

———

IN ANOTHER PHOTO, George and Iris are sitting on the couch, George in white khakis and a white T-shirt clinging to his muscular arms and chest, and when he sits down, his pants hike up and we can see he's wearing sports socks with red and blue stripes at the top. Everything about him is unique because we've never had a man living with us and because he takes up a lot of space. On the arm of the couch is balanced a cocktail glass no doubt filled with scotch on the rocks, his go-to cocktail, or a Manhattan. We are on the floor with the new husky puppy George brings home on one of his children's visits, hoping a new puppy will bridge any discomfort between us. He names the puppy Moishe, a Yiddish name that means Moses. I suppose he thinks it's funny now that he's married to a Jewish woman. On Easter, he brings home two black and white bunnies, and we name them Georgie and Georgie Girl, a hat tip to our new dad's name. They live in a cage in the garage.

———

FOR THE FIRST time we get a Christmas tree. George brings the evergreen home strung on top of his Cadillac along with boxes of colored lights and bulbs and ornaments. Iris insists we string the tree with cranberries and popcorn. She's not a tinsel gal, she thinks tinsel looks cheap. We play along with the festivities even though we're Jewish and we don't believe in Christ. But we like the Christmas spirit, the carols we learn at school for the Xmas pageant, the stockings and the presents. Even though we are Jewish and celebrate Hanukkah by lighting the menorah, spinning the dreidel, and eating potato latkes, our mother didn't deny us the spectacular fantasy of Santa Claus when we were young. We hung our stockings over the fireplace and left a plate of cookies and a glass of milk for Santa. On the cold, snowy morning, we'd come down the stairs starstruck by all the gifts and stocking stuffers. Iris played a good Santa. One year she gave us a mini kitchenette set and a mini bake oven on which we happily and proudly baked mini cakes for her. I think she was trying to make up for what we had lost. But now I don't know how to feel about a Christmas tree. Have we crossed the line? Will God punish us? I turn on the colored lights and stare at the tree with a golden angel on top hoping the angel will keep us safe, even though I know in my bones that soon, like the Christmas tree if we don't watch out, everything is going to topple.

———

IT IS A swell time, until it isn't. George's temper can be quick. A sister might get a kick in the butt or a shove. Once he dragged one of us kicking and screaming out of her room because she refused to come down for dinner. I try to stay out of his way and play the good girl role so as not to cause any trouble.

There are some perks. Once, he brings us on vacation to Wildwood, New Jersey, an ocean resort town. The three of us crowd in the backseat of his brand-new black Cadillac for the drive (I'm nauseous the entire way from the smell of leather), and my mother scoots next to him, his arm around her shoulder, her hand on his thigh. We learn how to ride the waves in the ocean where we get pounds of sand in the bottom of our bathing suits. We sleep in a motel, us girls all together on a king bed in our own room. We eat hot dogs and cotton candy, attend a sad and tired carnival where Dad shows us how to shoot a rifle at a target. He plays until he wins each of us a stuffed animal. I take home a giant stuffed dalmatian. Though I'm cautious and tentative, I'm slowly becoming attached to him.

———

THERE ARE A few Saturday trips to look at new houses once
we discover Iris is pregnant and a new baby is on the way.
Whether it was planned or not, I don't know. Nine months
seems a long time; I can barely wait. I can't imagine having
a baby in our house. Mom says she'll be like our little doll.
I walk through these newly constructed homes, peering in
and out of rooms, wondering if a new house with fresh wood
beams and sturdy walls and more bedrooms will hold us all
together. In the end, they decide to stay in our house on Lytle
Road, expand and remodel. Iris works with the architect to
design the new kitchen with the larger dining area, a kitchen so
pleasing that whenever someone new comes over, they marvel
at it, and Iris glows from admiration. Now she has two ovens
to cook her recipes from the cordon bleu school she attends
once a week to learn to satisfy George's wish for gourmet feasts.
Suddenly, instead of the easy meals of mac and cheese, tuna
noodle casseroles, and sloppy joes Iris used to cook on the days
when she was in the mood for cooking, there are lavish meals
of chicken and lamb stews and fresh almond cakes. From the
ceiling hangs a huge pot rack with all new copper pots in different sizes and shapes dangling from hooks. The countertops
are made of butcher block. On a small corner shelf, small glass
jars of spices stand like a line of toy soldiers, all neatly labeled
in Mom's perfect cursive. On a side counter, a handy built-in
knife rack with knives shoved blade side down into the wood.
When George is in one of his rages, I fear he might use one
on us or my mother. Beautiful ceramic tiles stretch across the
kitchen floor. In the new extension step-down dining area is a
long dark wood farmhouse table and open shelves for Iris to
show off her colorful casserole dishes and bowls. We gather

around the farmhouse table for weekend dinners that Iris cooks; sometimes, she spends all day in the kitchen. George likes meat and potatoes on his plate. We help our mother dry each lettuce leaf for the salad with paper towels, and if she sees one leaf that isn't perfectly dry, she picks it out of the bowl and makes us do it over. She even makes her own salad dressing. No more store-bought. George likes roast beef, lamb chops, steaks so rare that when you cut one open, it is the same color as human blood. I cut the meat into little pieces and stow them away in my napkin; I've discovered that meat comes from animals. Because I want my mother to remain happy, I do everything I can to please Dad. When he comes home from the road, I give him a smiling welcome and kiss him on the cheek. He likes it when I call him Dad. He needs constant approval.

———

ONE WEEKEND, I'M the daughter chosen to go with him to visit his mother in Philadelphia. Lucky me. On the plane I sit next to him, and he playfully squeezes my knee, something he does to make me laugh. He puts his arm around me and pulls me close. Secretly I fantasize about what it would be like to be living alone with him, having him all to myself. A Freudian complex at the age of nine. I worry that somehow my mother is going to push him away when she gets annoyed that he travels too much or doesn't return her calls. When she pesters him for answers, he calls her a nag and I pray Mom will not test him further. And then I feel guilty for my fantasy, for x-ing my mother and my sisters out. My job, I believe, is to make a good impression on Dad's mother since I'm the only stepdaughter she'll meet. She greets us and George gives her a peck on the cheek. We sit down in the lavish living room with heavy velvet curtains darkening the windows for cocktails. George's mother is nothing like my relatives who are warm and loving, our aunts who slobber us with kisses and hugs. She has gold chains and pearls draped around her neck, her face is thin and taut and looks as if it might break. She tilts her head to the side, still sitting in her chair so that George can kiss one side of her cheek. She holds her cocktail in her freckled and bony hand. The image of Miss Havisham pops into my head when I now think of her. I remember that George's brother had an accident when he was young, and maybe died, and I feel sad for him as he tries to cheer and impress his stoic mother. Clearly, he has his own phantoms to bear. Perhaps it is his own insecurity and hurt he hides behind his anger. Whatever it is, I'm beginning to learn that you can't really make anyone happy or fix things when they're not right.

———

IN PREGNANCY, IRIS'S abdomen expands into the shape of a large basketball, while the rest of her remains trim and pretty. She outlines her eyes with kohl, wears bangs across her face, and has shoulder-length, shiny dark brown hair and looks like she's in her twenties. I can't believe a live baby is growing inside. Mom lets me put my hand on her tummy to feel the baby move. Dressed in black stretch pants and a long shirt, hair streaming to her shoulders, she bustles around the house preparing for the new baby. Upstairs are three bedrooms, including the master. Cindy and I share a room; Laura has her own room. But now we need a nursery for the new baby. They convert the den downstairs into a bedroom for Cindy and me and turn our old room upstairs into a nursery. The walls of our new bedroom are wallpapered with gold embossed butterflies. In my imagination, they come alive, flitting around the room.

> *Three little butterflies resting in the sun. One flew off, then there were two. Two little butterflies resting in the sun; one flew off, and then there was one. One little butterfly, now the only one, flew off, and then there were none.*

The room fits twin beds with a storage table in the center and a chest of drawers between two closets. Iris decides that the new baby's room must look like a garden. Memories become mythologized and stamped in the brain. Iris lays down green shag carpeting, paints the ceiling and walls blue, and asks my older sister, who has an artistic flair, to draw wild sunflowers on the walls. We paint them yellow and orange. The nursery's grand finale: the carpenter installs a short white picket fence around the lower walls of the room. Iris insists on buying a wooden cradle she finds in an antiques store because she reads babies like to be in confined spaces. She picks out a white crib for when the baby gets older and a white bassinet to match. Iris reads in a magazine about a bedroom wallpapered with posters and decides it is perfect for her eldest daughter's room. She picks out black-and-white posters of movie stars, rock bands, and political figures, meticulously choosing where each poster should go, creating a work of original collage on the walls and ceiling. Bright pink shag carpet gives the bedroom a disco vibe. Perfect for her soon-to-be teenage daughter, who is enamored with her cool new room.

———

ON JULY 19, 1968, two years after her second wedding, my mother gives birth. A baby girl as bright and sturdy as a hibiscus, and a late bloomer. I turned ten that April. George is out of town when Iris goes into labor. Eventually the hospital reaches him by phone. Two days later they come home with the new baby cradled in Iris's arms wrapped in a flannel blanket. Mom is glowing and I'm besotted with this purest of creatures, touched only by two days of life. I almost feel my heart burst from my chest. Happy tears cloud my eyes. Iris wants to name the baby Elizabeth. George prefers Kim. My mother gives in, and they name her Kim Elizabeth. She has shiny blue eyes and the softest skin I've ever touched. Olivia calls Kimmy baldie, since she hasn't yet grown hair on her head, only a cover of peach fuzz. She's a healthy baby, with little dimples in her cheeks and knowing old-soul eyes. Isn't every newborn perfect until the world eventually, hour by hour, day by day, presses itself upon her?

Shortly after Kim is born, we all go to our grandfather's house to introduce baby Kimmy to Grandpa Eugene and his mother, Grandma Cookie, and his new wife, Bea, who gives us saliva kisses we don't like and walks with a hobble. We call her Grandma Bea Bea. For Hanukkah she gifted us used perfume with tin foil wrapped over the top and gives my mother a chipped teacup, and we all pretend we like our gifts to please her. George is cheerful and friendly, maybe a bit too brash, and I can tell that Iris's solemn and quiet father doesn't quite know what to make of him. Iris lavishes kisses on her father's cheek and lets him hold baby Kim. George doesn't know quite what to do with himself in their small, modest home; before long, he's anxious to go. I look at my grandfather with his sorrowful eyes, and suddenly, my heart feels too big in my chest. I know in my soul that something isn't right.

———

AT HOME, IRIS shows us how to diaper Kim. Once the diaper is folded between her legs, she instructs us to keep our finger under the diaper pin when we fasten it, so we don't accidentally poke her. She hires a service that brings fresh cotton diapers and removes the dirty ones; no Pampers for her baby. We learn to heat up her bottles, hold her so that we don't touch her fragile fontanel, and cradle her in the rocking chair before we put her down for naps. I like the solid weight of holding her sweaty, warm body in my arms when she awakes in the middle of the night. I feed her while quietly playing "Bye, Baby Bunting," from an album of lullabies on the record player Iris has placed on a nightstand by her cradle. When I'm older and remember the lyrics I'm haunted by the lines, "Daddy's gone a-hunting/Gone to get a rabbit skin/To wrap the baby Bunting in," that Kim listened to every night before bed.

We are built-in babysitters when Iris and George go out on a Saturday night. On these nights when they are out late and have been drinking, Mom sometimes can't hear the baby cry for her midnight feeding. I don't mind. I creep downstairs and heat up a bottle in a saucepan of water on the burner, with baby Kim on one hip. Mom has taught me how to test how hot the milk is by putting a drop on the inside of my wrist. Once it's ready, I take Kimmy back upstairs to her room and feed her in my arms, her body warm and sweaty, careful not to touch the soft fontanel when I kiss her sweaty head. During the day, I take her for walks in her stroller. My best friend's mother miraculously also has a new baby, too, and when our little sisters are toddlers, we take them to the playground together, wheeling our strollers side by side on the sidewalk. At twelve years old, Kim just two, suddenly I'm responsible for caring for someone besides my uncomfortable, self-conscious adolescent self. With this new responsibility, I can feel my shy awkwardness slipping away and in its place a strong desire to protect my baby sister.

———

DESPITE THE UNDERTOW of anxiety and conflict George occupies when he's home—sometimes they fight, and we hear them shouting in their bedroom (sometimes I wonder if George and Iris would be happier had they shipped us older girls off to boarding school once they got married), but baby Kimmy inspires hope and new purpose. Just to see her laugh, learn to crawl (Mom makes us get down on our hands and knees and teach her because she reads that crawling is important for a baby's eyesight), then stand on two feet we deem miraculous. Iris can now turn her whole focus on Kim, different from when she had three girls, one after the other, to care for on her own, and she is rapturously in love. Once, when their bedroom door is open, I see baby Kimmy lying on the bed, George kissing her feet, and Iris watching and laughing. For a minute, I can breathe without the fear that something's about to break. When George comes home from work, he pours himself a scotch, puts on the stereo, and plays Frank Sinatra albums or Burt Bacharach singing "Raindrops keep fallin' on my head" and takes Kimmy in his arms and dances with her. He tickles her and kisses and blows raspberries in her tummy, throws her up in the air and catches her while we hold our breath. He reclines in his black Eames chair with her in his lap and twirls it around in a circle. Kimmy has inherited his fair complexion and his blue eyes. Eventually, he hands the baby to Iris so he can read the sports section of the newspaper with his cocktail. He isn't the kind of father to walk his baby in her buggy, change her diaper, feed her a bottle, or wake up in the middle of the night when she cries. He's out the door quickly when Monday morning arrives.

———

THERE'S AN ELEPHANT in the room. George isn't Jewish. Is this why, for a time we stopped going to Grandpa Eugene's house for Shabbat? Maybe in secret he's unhappy that Iris married a gentile, but he'll allow anything for his daughter to make her happy.

Suddenly Eugene is fighting colon cancer. Iris goes to see him in the hospital. The cancer comes on quickly, or perhaps it had been growing for years without Eugene being aware, and a few weeks later Iris is rushing to the hospital to say goodbye to her father. Eugene's death devastates Iris.

We are sad, too. Everything is changing. After the funeral, she goes directly upstairs to her room and crawls into bed. Her father was her childhood protector after Iris lost her mother. Eugene took a new wife, Bea, after Iris got married to her first husband. Bea never fully embraced Iris. She was jealous of her husband's devotion to his only daughter. My mother learned after her father died that Bea had asked to change his will so that all would be left to her. Perhaps she convinced Eugene that his daughter no longer needed any money now that she had remarried. Who knows why people do the things they do, or what unhappiness or envy does to a person. She'll never say a bad word about her father. From outside her bedroom door, we can hear Iris sobbing. One loss remembers others and reopens old wounds. Her father was her only means of security, and now she's lost him, too. George goes up to comfort her, and then once she's asleep, maybe he gave her a sleeping pill, he tells us not to bother her. It might be the first time he fixes us dinner. At the table, we eat in awkward silence. An uncomfortable hush has gone over the house. After dinner I tiptoe upstairs to see my mother. When I open the door, with the blinds drawn, it's pitch black in the room, and I hear my mother moaning into her pillow. I climb onto the bed. She turns over, sits up, and gives me a hug. I feel her wet, hot tears on my face. For weeks, she's listless and filled with grief.

————

KIM IS NEARLY three when the arguments between Iris and George erupt more violently than before. I'm not sure what they fight about; maybe Iris wants him home more or is suspicious of his time away. My sisters and I retreat to our bedrooms or down to the basement and take Kimmy with us. Sometimes, we hear yelling and screaming and doors slamming shut. Furniture gets knocked over. George's loud stamping feet make the basement ceiling quake. We are terrified. Once, during one of their entanglements, Cindy and I colored an entire wall in the basement with crayons, hoping to cheer our mother up. It doesn't work. Or maybe we did it to get noticed. We are punished and sent to our room. One morning, after they've been fighting, we discover Iris's eye is black-and-blue. She says she accidentally walked into a door, but we know what happened. George disappears for days. We sisters are like houseplants absorbing the air and atmosphere of their rocky union. We don't have the words for it then, but George has a drinking problem, which we later learn exacerbates his rages and abusive tongue. No wonder his cheeks are always red. I'm beginning to see into the secret truth inside him and my dreams for happiness slip through my fingers.

——

GEORGE IS AWAY when Kim's fever spikes to 104 and Olivia drives us to the hospital in the darkness of night. I sit in the backseat with my mother, who is holding her baby wrapped in a flannel blanket. Laura is instructed to look after Cindy at home. In the car, Iris is in a panic. She says Kim's whole body is on fire with the heat of her fever, and her body is limpid. When we arrive at the hospital, I sit with Olivia in the waiting room, and I'm afraid my baby sister might die. She's so fragile. Kim is given a spinal tap, and we learn she has meningitis. Bacterial meningitis can be deadly if not treated immediately with antibiotics. Iris is beside herself with worry. She refuses to leave her baby's bedside and sleeps in the hospital next to her for days while Olivia cares for us girls at home. While they're at the hospital, there is a pit in my stomach. I pray that baby Kim will survive. Slowly, the antibiotics do their magic, and Kim's fever and hacking cough diminish.

Eventually, George turns up at the hospital with a string of balloons that fill the hospital room and a dozen red roses for Iris. Who knows where he's been? When he's done something he later feels bad about, he tries to make up for it with presents, apologies, and good cheer, and my mother typically gives in. When they bring Kimmy home from the hospital, Iris constantly fears that she'll get sick again and can't pull herself away from Kim's room, even when she's napping. I hope and pray the tension between Iris and George will break now that Kimmy is better, but my prayers don't work.

———

MAYBE IRIS SMELLED perfume on him. Maybe he skipped coming home one weekend. Maybe Iris was too tired to have sex. After he's been gone a week or so, Iris receives a call from the hospital that he has suffered a near-fatal car accident driving while intoxicated. His secretary was in the car with him. When George comes home from the hospital, he's got a wired halo brace all around his head, his jaw wired shut, scratches and cuts over his face, black and blue underneath his eyes, lips bruised and puffy. It's as if he turned into a darker, more terrifying version of himself. Maybe that's when Iris gives up. The experiment failed. Shortly after, Iris and George sit us down in the living room and tell us they are getting a divorce. George's been having an affair with his secretary. It's like an episode from one of the soaps I watch with Olivia while she's ironing in the basement. Mom is done. She wants him out of the house. George breaks down and cries like a baby. I feel sorry for him; toggling between wanting him to stay and go. I don't understand his tears. Does he *really* not want to leave us? But I also know in my young heart that their marriage is unsustainable. George packs his suitcase upstairs, and drives off in his black Cadillac. I don't know if once upstairs, he went into his baby daughter's room, where she is napping, to kiss her and say goodbye. Once he's out the door, my mother comes to the three of us sitting frozen on the couch, bewildered and in shock. *We'll be okay,* she says, stoically. I'm proud of my mother for protecting us and herself. It must have taken a lot of strength, since she now has four girls to raise on her own. Our family returns to a tribe of females. Kim is three years old. I look at the empty Eames chair and feel the dark shadow George leaves over our house.

Rock a bye, baby, on the treetop, when the wind blows the cradle will rock, when the bough breaks the cradle will fall, and down will come baby, cradle and all.

———

AFTER THE DIVORCE Iris is plagued by frequent migraines and debilitating periods of anxiety and depression. George is erased. X-ed out. I go down to the basement to put some clothes in the washing machine and for some reason the locker room calls out to me. I open it and see the shelves of jars and jars of dill pickles in their cloudy brine. It was the abundance, the adventure, the impetus he craved and at the bottom of it, emptiness. I know now that individuals are not one thing or another but made up of a kaleidoscope of complicated colors. For a minute my heart catches and a deep sadness that comes with the end of love overtakes. I sense that I have climbed out of childhood.

———

IRIS IS ANGRY. In desperate moments she calls George a sociopath—a man who only cares about himself. She says she does not understand how she could have married him and berates herself. Her pride's been hurt, too. She is just nearing forty, though still young looking and beautiful. Nevertheless, she feels her options closing in on her. I tell her that she did the right thing and try to boost her ego. We all do. She's jealous of her former social circle, a set that had prospered in Cleveland during the post-war boom, whose lives are more stable. And now she's a widow and a divorcée. Living again in the shadow of that once promised and now lost life grates on her. *Of course they have nice things, they have money*, she might say about a friend. Iris goes through a brutal divorce battle and ends up, unconscionably, with a small alimony settlement and child support for their daughter. For the first time, I notice a change in her. She's become bitter and resentful. She blames herself for not seeing through George's polished façade that masked his demons. Then she says that we'd never have had baby Kim if she hadn't married him. Later, when I'm older, I wonder if, after losing my father, so different from George, Iris did not want to replicate her true love and unconsciously became attracted to a darker, more charismatic personality. Did she want to punish herself for betraying her beloved?

After all these years, I still don't completely understand George's impact on my own life. My mother's regrets and disappointments are wound deep inside me, as familiar as my own skin. What will happen to baby Kim? Years go by. Iris says her baby has four mothers. We hope it will be enough.

———

A FEW YEARS ago, curious, I googled Kim's father to see what has become of this man whose bad temper, drinking, abusive rages, and abandonment of his young daughter shaped the lives of my family, and I discovered he'd died. Turns out you can find out things you didn't know about a person, even after they've expired. His obituary says that he passed away in 2018, was an honorably discharged veteran of the US Army, and had been a resident of Naples, Florida, for the past twenty-one years. "His passions were offshore powerboat racing, in which he was a participant, gourmet cooking, golf, tennis and his rose gardens." His survivors include his current "loving wife," his daughter, son, grandchildren, and this phrase that cuts into my heart: "he was preceded in death by his daughter, Kimberly." The obituary includes a photo of him looking at the camera dressed in a blue suit jacket, white shirt, tie, with hairline receding, slightly balding, yellow-whiteish hair combed back on the sides, puffy face, the characteristic gap between his two front teeth, but instead of sparkling white as I remembered, slightly brownish, crumbling, brittle. How could one man be capable of wrecking so many lives? I note two things in his obituary. There is no mention of what he did for a living; and two, his daughter was named Kim Elizabeth, never Kimberly.

10.

Milton, Iris's husband, my father, dies at thirty years old. Iris is twenty-five years old. All this is before Iris marries George, before Kim is born, but you know this already. Iris is raising three girls on her own, Cindy is nine months, I'm two, Laura is three. We are fifteen months apart, and Iris is a young widow who is unequipped emotionally and financially to support a family of young children. Iris is in shock and can barely function from the immensity of her grief, it's almost as if all the walls of her house have blown apart and she's left to put it all together. Iris's doctor prescribes Valium to calm her nerves, relieve anxiety and stress, and tranquilizers to help her sleep, amphetamines to keep her functioning during the day—the sudden shock of her husband's unexpected death is unfathomable—her loving, sturdy husband won't be here to support her family, to see her girls grow up. Poor Iris. Her babies crying and wailing, wanting to be fed, the toddler pulling at her skirt, baby Cindy needing to be diapered, night after night, the screams she cannot fully quell, one baby on her hip, the other crying in her crib, and the three-year-old staring at her in bewilderment. *What will happen to all of us*, screams in her head. How can she do it? How can she manage caring for three babies alone when she's barely a grown-up. What about the days when her children are sick, chicken pox, mumps, measles, taking us to doctor appointments or dentist appointments? It seems inconceivable. Iris's relatives come to step in and help, but they have their own families to care for, too. I don't know how Iris managed these early years before her babies could have a level of independence, which typically doesn't happen until five or six years old when a child begins school. Luckily, we three young girls have each other to help take care of ourselves.

———

MILTON DIES BEFORE he has even considered the necessity for a life insurance policy or has accrued savings. We live off the social security check Iris receives in the mail each month and some help from relatives. For a time, Iris has a part-time job as a receptionist at a doctor's office, but the job doesn't last long. It's hard for her to juggle a job with three girls underfoot, constantly worried about how to make ends meet.

———

WE LIVE IN a white house with black shutters and a black door. I share a bedroom with Cindy, and Laura has her own room and our mother now sleeps alone in the master bedroom with a king-sized bed where on one side, the ghost of her dead husband resides. There is a wall of white dressers, each with three large drawers, beneath two windows, and an attached bathroom with its own dressing room. When we're toddlers, we find it a good hiding place for hide and seek. Downstairs in the living room sprawls a bright yellow rug we name the scrambled egg rug because that is exactly what it looks like. A framed print of Van Gogh's sunflowers is on an easel on one side of the room and a portrait of one of Modigliani's long-necked women over the mantel.

In the early years, when our mother has a part-time job, we are sent from one relative's house to another. We like going to Aunt Harriet and Uncle Joe's two-bedroom apartment in University Heights, where they take us to the playground, and afterward, we bake cookies. We sometimes sleep over at the apartment of my father's mother, Grandma Sonia, camping out on the long couches in her living room. But I don't like to leave our mother. Even at a young age, I sensed that she was fragile and vulnerable. We do whatever we can to make our mother happy. While she's still sleeping and we are now five, six, and seven we go on a mission to clean the house so that when she wakes up and comes down the stairs, we will hear her call us her darling daughters and say, look what you've done and clasp her hands in delight and wonder. Sometimes the pressure is too great, and our mother loses it and yells at us, breaks down in tears, whether in the middle of fixing us dinners of scrambled eggs or wiener goulash, and then she turns to us ashamed by her behavior and gives us a hug. We are afraid of her grief, how the tide of it catches her unaware and everything is dim. In those hours, the world dims for us, too. As young girls, we sense our mother's despair and desperation.

A plant grows to the ceiling in a corner of the living room. It's our own Jack and the Beanstalk. I wish I was Jack, with five magic beans, who had climbed up the stalk to save his mother and had been greeted by the Giant.

Fee Fi Fo Fum I smell the blood of an Englishman.

I want to find a golden egg to make us rich, so our mother won't have to worry.

I want to be by my mother's side always; if I'm with her I know she will not fall apart. I love when we drive in the car, and I claim the front seat and can lay my head on her lap while she's driving, and she strokes my hair. I notice everything about her. For instance, how she lifts her hands on the steering wheel to admire her manicure or stretches her neck when we are stopped at a traffic light to see into the rearview mirror, and dabs fresh lipstick on her lips. I love everything about her. She's so warm and sweet to us when she's not afraid. When I'm home sick it's the best day of my life. I'm allowed to sleep in her king-sized bed, and she makes me tomato and butter sandwiches on white bread, and we watch TV and I get my mother all to myself. I want to grow up to be just like her. She has long tan legs and long slim arms and big brown eyes that get misty with emotion. I'm so proud when she comes to our school assemblies, and I see her in the rows with the other parents and I think I have the prettiest mother of all my friends. At night, she tucks us in before bed and covers me with the scratchy burnt-red blanket and kisses my forehead. Even though our father's ghost lives in our house, when we are all together there are days when I don't long for more. Sometimes Mom stretches alongside me in bed, and tired, she strokes my hair, kisses the top of my head and whispers, *what am I going to do?* And I hold her close.

———

WE HAVE A big tree by the side door of our house that I love to hug when I come home from school, as if this tree is a true being. On one side of the driveway is a row of super large hostas that separates our house from the neighbors. We love to pop the purple pods when they bloom. In the backyard we have a swing set that likely one of Iris's admirers bought us. We pump and pump our legs to see who can swing highest until we get cherry bumps, because the poles are popping out of the holes in the ground. We play outdoors almost all day in the summer with friends on our block. Red Light–Green Light, Kick the Can, Red Rover, Red Rover while our mother talks on the telephone to one of our relatives or friends, the receiver cradled on her shoulder while she makes our dinner. On her birthday we clean the house and make her breakfast in bed, because we feel so sad she doesn't have a husband, and she says she can't believe how lucky she is to have three wonderful girls. For the holidays, Aunt Harriet takes us downtown to the Twigbee store in the Terminal Tower in downtown Cleveland where kids go to buy presents for their parents. We buy our mother candles and perfume and when she opens our presents tears appear in her eyes. Who else is going to buy her a present?

———

ONCE I'M A mother myself, with just one child to raise, and a supportive, loving husband to help, I can't imagine how my mother managed. I know how lucky I was to be raised in a good neighborhood where every house looks solid, and neighbors seem to vie for the most beautiful well-tended lawn and garden and our house belonging to a sad widow and three fatherless daughters doesn't seem to stick out. From the outside we can pretend we fit in. I feel a lump of sadness for my mother who had to discover so young, before so many others, that no matter what one does, happiness isn't permanent, when really nothing is. Even though lovely Iris goes through the motions of life, death does not take her husband away. He is immortalized in her heart, her soul, her carriage. When I first fall in love with Emily Dickinson's poetry, and my own experience shudders through her words, I come to understand my mother's deep lasting bond even though she was still here on the earth and her beloved was in heaven.

> Because I could not stop for Death—
> He kindly stopped for me—
> The Carriage held but just Ourselves—
> And Immortality.

———

DURING THE SEASON-TO-BE-JOLLY, we pile into our mother's yellow Comet and drive through the streets of our suburb, cross the Rapid Transit tracks to the glitzy side of Shaker Heights with sprawling brick mansions built during the era of the Van Sweringen Company after they designed Shaker Heights as a community in the early 1900s. Any property owner was required to build according to strict regulations that favored traditional English, French, and Colonial designs. As we drive through the neighborhood we *ooh* and *ahh* at the spectacle of colored lights wrapped around rooftops and trees and Iris points to her favorite houses in the neighborhood. Where we live, on the other side of the tracks east of Warrensville Center Road, are the homes built after the 1930s, when the architectural requirements were less stringent and more modest. In the summer, our mother buys us a splash pool for the backyard and while we play in the tepid water on a good day, she suns herself on the lounge chair, browning her skin to the coppery color of a penny.

Sometimes we talk back. If our mother doesn't do what we ask, we tell her we hate her. She gets furious, pulls us by the arm, takes us into the bathroom and washes our mouths out with soap and sends us to our room. I fear she wishes we were never born. She rarely mentions our father and it is only when a relative or a friend who knew my father comes to the house and looks at us with cloudy emotional eyes that I remember I'm a fatherless daughter. Perhaps she felt that by talking about our father she would hurt us? Or it was too painful for her? Nevertheless, we intuited her dark fear and bitter loss even as she remained our only hope for the future. Like a young lovely cherry tree whose blooming blossoms weigh down its branches, she bravely bore our sweet burden.

———

WE'RE ALL IN the drafty den with the big cathedral ceiling. We have a big cozy chair with a matching footrest where we watch TV sprawled on the carpeted floor with our pillows and blankets, if someone else has called the chair. On this day Iris is sitting in the big chair, and we're camped on the floor still in our pajamas. It is the day of John F. Kennedy's funeral, our president, Mom tells us. We watch the motorcade pass by and then see images of Jackie Kennedy with gloves on and a black hat and long veil over her face getting out of the car. She is holding the hand of her son John Jr. on one side and her daughter, Caroline's

hand on the other. It is November 25, 1963, and I am six years
old. Jackie looks a little like Iris with her dark hair and petite,
feminine physique and suddenly I make the connection. Mom
has a handkerchief in her hand and is crying and I'm upset,
too. How could someone shoot our president. And now like
me, Caroline and John Jr. no longer have a father. I creep up on
my mother's lap and hug her. I feel so sorry for her. It's the first
time my consciousness has truly registered her enormous loss.
I think of my father's death as more my mother's loss because
all I really know and remember is our mother taking care of us
even though I sense my father in her shadow. But really, I have
come to think of my father as someone in heaven watching over
us. My mother must have told this to me, or my imagination
must have invented it, but on this day, I feel my mother's grief
and it's like it is inside me now, growing like a weed threatening
to overwhelm. It is a part of me and will never dissipate. It is the
day I realize I must take care of her, protect her, she's so sad, and
like Jackie she has lost her husband. How will she ever recover?
She is bound to a world where she might not flourish.

———

IRIS'S AUNTS AND her father encourage her to try to marry
again, hopefully to a Jewish man who can offer her stability in
exchange for her taking care of the home and the children. We
go to Grandpa's house every Friday night for Shabbat and my
aunts cook matzoh ball soup, chicken paprika, boiled potatoes,
and carrots, and Grandpa Eugene always puts a coin in each of
our hands. He has bags underneath his eyes. He always has a
small leather case in the pocket of his white shirt containing a
pen and reading glasses and wears a bow tie. Sometimes, over

dinner and dessert, the relatives squabble. As soon as the plates are cleared, Grandpa Eugene goes to the closet and takes out the vacuum and zooms it underneath the table and over the carpeted floors and we are carted off to the living room and offered a sour ball from the candy bowl on the coffee table before we say goodbye.

With his short mustache and big belly laugh, Uncle Joe takes us girls to the circus every year with his lodge group wearing his Masonic lodge hat with its tassel hanging. I am terrified of the flying trapeze, even in its splendor, and the hush that goes over the crowd when one trapeze artist flies into the hands of another, and I worry one of the lions will escape from the cage and kill the lion-tamer. The clowns look sad. The circus tent stinks of elephants, one trunk hooked to the tail of the next as they parade around the circus ring. I look around me at all the children who seem to be enjoying the spectacles and am sure there is something deeply wrong with me.

Sometimes, on Sundays, we go to our great aunt Harriet and uncle Joe's apartment for Sunday lunch. Aunt Harriet never had children, and she cares for Mom like a daughter. Uncle Joe makes us laugh by telling his silly jokes. He's the one who laughs the hardest, making his big belly shake. Before he eats, he tucks a napkin in the collar of his white shirt so as not to dribble on it. Aunt Harriet playfully scolds him. She makes lavish lunches for us. A plate piled with radishes cut like roses, carrot and celery sticks, olives, and slices of dill pickles is always on the table. Then comes the homemade chopped liver we spread on mini slices of rye bread. Sometimes it's potato latkes with applesauce and tender brisket. Uncle Joe used to be in the Navy and now is a dentist, and we get our teeth cleaned and cavities filled for free. At lunch, Aunt Harriet asks who Mom is dating, and once Iris replies, she asks if the man is Jewish or gentile. Mom's still young, not yet thirty, but can she really find a new husband when she's saddled with three young girls? It's a conundrum no one knows how to solve.

————

MOM'S MARRIED FRIENDS and sisters-in-law fix Iris up on dates. It's like a new career, this dating life. Iris must manage it perfectly. She spends her mornings in bed, sometimes recovering from a late night out, her afternoons shopping, then making dinner for us; sometimes it's Stouffer's frozen food or TV dinners, and if time is on her side, sloppy joes, tuna noodle casserole, or wiener goulash. Once a week she fries up liver, says it's good for us, but it's rubbery and tastes funny. I put mine in my napkin and throw it out. Mom tries to hide her qualms, but she's often distracted and absent even when she's home with us.

On occasion, she'll pick us up from school in her yellow Comet and drag us to the beauty shop, where she sits underneath the hair dryer with curlers in her hair. If there's an empty dryer, we fight over who gets to use it. When she gets a manicure, the manicurists sometimes give us one for free. They all know Iris and that she lost her husband. Now that she's a widow, we receive many things for free. For instance, when the repairmen come, if the furnace is broken or the sink is stopped up, Iris puts on her charm, and the handyman says, "no charge."

After dinner, we trudge upstairs and watch our mother prepare for one of her dates—it could take hours—collapsed on her bed watching *Gilligan's Island* (which one of us wants to be Ginger or Mary Ann) or *The Patty Duke Show*. Her pillowcases are satin, so that when she sleeps, she doesn't mess up her hairstyle or get wrinkles from the pillow creases. While Iris dresses up, we sometimes play a game called Giant. The giant waves a pillowcase in the air, and the other two run across the king-sized bed and around and hop up again, hoping not to get swatted by the giant. (Once I fall and the side of my face close to my eye hits the corner of the dressing table, and it's off to the emergency room to get stitches, and Iris must cancel her date.) It's as if Iris turns her bedroom and bath into a beauty salon or fashion show. Rollers are everywhere: hair dryers, drawers full of makeup and lipsticks, not to mention perfumes, and fancy lingerie, high-heeled shoes stacked in neat little rows in her walk-in closet. I watch her try on outfit after outfit and look at herself scrupulously in the mirror as if she can't find herself. One can't help but admire the perfectionism she puts into caring for her too-expensive clothes, her lacy double cup bras, sheer pantyhose, and panties she washes by hand and are always drying on a rack in her bedroom.

She looks at herself, with puckered lips in the mirror, trying out poses, chest thrust out, slim waist, hand on hip. This is the era where Marilyn Monroe and Jayne Mansfield served as the epitome of beauty. We sisters sort of enjoy the dress-up show (until we don't), and certainly, Iris deserves the fun and enjoyment of going out, having fun, and being desired. But she takes too long getting ready, and when the date rings the doorbell, she shoos us downstairs and makes us greet him. Sometimes she lets the date wait a good half hour—is this intentional?—and we're forced to entertain. We can't help but admire how dazzling she looks when she finally walks down

the stairs for her entrance as if she's an actress on the red carpet. Still, there are nights when I don't want her to go out. I
look out the window and follow the date, escorting Iris into
his car and shutting her inside. As the car eventually pulls out
of the driveway, the sky is already dark, and I feel a sour pit
in my stomach.

————

THERE ARE BENEFITS. For a while, Iris dates Johnny Brewer,
who is a football player for the Browns, and gives us a signed
photo of himself. Another time, a kind friend called Joel presents us with a miniature gray poodle we name Poggy. Poggy
sleeps in the hallway between two doors. I wake up in the
morning and snuggle him. My sisters and I crack up when he
does his zoomies through the living room, hallway, kitchen, and
around again. Mom says even dogs need to let off steam. One
day, Poggy runs away, and it's my fault. He slipped out the door
when I was leaving for school. I can't forgive myself. Iris drives
us around the neighborhood with all the windows open so we
can search for him, but we never find him. Heartbroken, we
watch the Animal Protective League show for weeks, hoping
he'll be one of the lost puppies they showcase, but to no avail.
His shadow lives in our house, too.

————

WHEN IRIS HAS a date, we are sometimes allowed to pick
who we want to babysit for us from the teenage girls in the
neighborhood. Our favorite is Maddie, who plays Go Fish and
Old Maid with us. Before bed she brings us into a circle on the
floor to recite our prayers together.

Star light, star bright, first star I see tonight, I wish I may I wish I might. God bless . . . and we recite a litany of names of our family members, friends at school, our teachers, hoping to stall for time before she tucks us into our beds. When Maddie switches off the light and closes the door and leaves, I will myself not to fall asleep until I hear our mother come home safely through the door. I worry about her when she goes out.

Dating distracts Iris from loneliness, from the practical worries about how she will pay the bills. It gives her a break from a house full of girls, with the hope, of course, that she'll fall in love and remarry. She enjoys dining in expensive restaurants. It's like her dating life back in high school, when she was very popular; only this time, more is at stake. Sometimes she comes home late with a date, turns on the music too loud, and it pounds through the house, keeping us awake. In the mornings, we sometimes find her in bed suffering from a hangover, and she tells us to shut the door; she can't bear the light. On the weekends, when we are not at school, while she's still sleeping, we make houses with cards on the coffee table and have contests to see whose house of cards stands up the longest. We stack boxes of cigarettes from a carton she keeps in a bowl on the coffee table, too. She may sleep until one or two in the afternoon if she's been out late. She'll eventually come down the stairs with her hair matted and makeup in the corner of her eyes, her robe bundled around her, and sleepily slap down slices of white Wonder Bread on the counter and take out the peanut butter and jelly to make us sandwiches. Sometimes we catch her standing by the window, with a cigarette in her hand, blowing smoke out the screen door, hand on her hip, looking into the blankness.

Occasionally our mother falls asleep on the couch after her date leaves when she's had too much to drink. The next morning, we'll find her curled up still in her dress and nylons, and when we wake her, she tells us she has a raging headache. She'll shoo us out of the house to sleep it off. Once, on a snow day from school, we are outside building a snowman on the front lawn, and by accident, when we want to come in, we find we are locked out of the house. We're cold, our cheeks burning, and our fingers wet and frozen inside our mittens. We ring and ring the doorbell, but locked in a dark sleep, our mother doesn't hear the doorbell for hours. Maybe she'd taken a pill.

———

WE LEARN TO make our own breakfast, popping into the toaster a Pop-Tart, or shoveling down a bowl of cereal. My favorite is Cocoa Puffs. Cindy likes Lucky Charms and Laura goes for the snap-crackle-pop of Rice Krispies. We sometimes fight over the prize at the bottom of the box. When we come home for lunch from school, sometimes our mother is still in bed, and we make our own peanut butter and jelly sandwiches, heat up a can of SpaghettiOs, or pop in the oven out of the freezer some crumbly Fish Stick fingers. All this seems normal, except when I have lunch at my girlfriend Karen's house and see the spread of soup and sandwiches laid out on the table once we rush into the door, notice the perfectly cleaned kitchen and living room. My friend's mother wears an apron over her dress, yes, a red and white checkered apron, a mother straight out of *Leave It to Beaver*, and greets us cheerfully as if our coming for lunch is the highlight of her day. I never bring my friends home for lunch. Iris might still be in bed.

———

WE SLOWLY UNDERSTAND that the dates signify that Iris is hunting for a husband and father for us. She's like Cinderella waiting for the prince with the right slipper to fit. Some dates want more than Iris is willing to give. Some are divorced or have never been married. They come into our house mostly dressed in suits and ties and ogle our mother. One who is older than Iris, he's rich, we learn, and wears a gold ring on his pinky finger and takes her to fancy restaurants and wants to marry her. Iris says she doesn't love him. He's too old for her. Then there's another so tall he must hunch his shoulders to come through our door. He's dutiful, but Iris says there's no chemistry. Iris reconnects with Bob, one of her high school beaus she dated before my father. Her relatives call him a "mensch," a doctor, Jewish, smart, loving, also a widower. But Iris doesn't know what to do. Is she afraid if she marries someone as kind and good as my father, he'll die, too? Or that she is replacing him? She talks to one of her close friends from high school who is newly divorced and perhaps a little jealous. Mom looks up to this friend. What sounds like jealousy creeps into her friend's words. She tells Iris she thinks she should wait, that it's too soon. Does she not want Iris to be happy? Much later, when Iris is ill, at the care home and regretting what could have come to pass, she doesn't forgive her.

———

IRIS SIGNS US up for ballet lessons. An etiquette class in
the school gym where we must walk diagonally across the
floor with a book balanced on our heads. It's important that
we learn balance and poise to grow up to be graceful girls.
I think she imagines we'll grow up to be just like her. She
enrolls us in after-school programs, theater classes, and day
camps in the summer. She tells us we are ungrateful if we
don't want to go. We have to go to Hebrew school we call
temple every Saturday, which we hate, especially because our
mother is always the last car to pick us up. We're so hungry
waiting, we steal pastries from the Bar Mitzvah reception
being set up outside the synagogue chapel. Iris never goes to
services in the synagogue; maybe she lost her faith after her
husband died. We tell her she's a hypocrite, making us when
she doesn't have to go. She says it is important that we have
a Jewish education.

———

I CAN'T TELL my fears to my mother. She has her own problems. I am like Eurydice who has lost her voice. I am afraid
of birds that swoop too low. I'm afraid to talk to boys. I am
afraid to speak in class in case I am wrong, and blush from
embarrassment. On Father's Day we are supposed to make
cards for our fathers at school. My teacher comes to my desk,
leans over my shoulder and tells me I can make a card for my
grandfather. I'm so embarrassed, afraid the other kids might
hear, that I feel my cheeks turning bright red. I'm superstitious.
I am afraid to walk on the cracks in the sidewalk out of fear
of breaking my mother's back. I admire the more courageous

and confident girls in my class, prettier ones with new clothes instead of hand-me-downs, and who are not afraid to speak up. I feel an emptiness and a detachment from myself. Sometimes, I have the strangest feeling that I don't exist. Maybe all children feel they are second fiddle in the orchestra of their parents' dramatic and sometimes careless lives.

11.

Surely Iris knows or has heard about Milt Bialosky since they both attended the same high school when her friend Irene, later to be her sister-in-law, sets her up with her brother. Iris is eighteen and Milt is in his early twenties. He was a star athlete and quarterback of their high school football team and later played football for Miami University in Ohio.

They double with Irene and her boyfriend Dick while Milt's home from college on a break and Iris is a senior in high school. Irene is in Iris's class, and Dick is one of the guys from the tight athletic gang that Milt played sports with. Milt and Iris dated all that summer before my mother leaves for her first quarter at Ohio State University. Milt is five years older than Iris, tall, broad-shouldered, bright, and solid, and though Iris is tentative, she feels what she's never quite felt before with any other boy she's dated: a sense of safety when she folds into his arms. What words pass between them? Maybe Milt talks about the real estate business he plans to start. Maybe they share secrets of their pasts, their families, their friends, as Milt looks at Iris with his brown eyes with sprinkles of gold that twinkle when he smiles, sending butterflies through

Iris's stomach. Late at night, she'll remember his smile, and it inspires unspeakable thoughts.

We can only imagine the chemistry between the motherless daughter and the first son of Jewish immigrants. Iris and Milt, both raised in the shadow of fear, versed in the history passed down to them, instilled in them, never to stand out, protect one's own, family comes first, the silent knowledge lived and felt in the hinterland of silence, never to be talked about or discussed, *kinehora*, lest it happen again.

Milt's parents, Isadore and Sonia, are Russian Jews from Vilna on the border of Lithuania and Poland. After World War I, hundreds of thousands of Jews left Europe. Isadore and Sonia immigrated before Milt was born and, because Isadore had a cousin in Cleveland, they joined him to establish a new life. Izzy and his brother, Abe, who also immigrated, opened a pawnshop that later would become more of a jewelry store. Economic stability and survival were the immediate challenge of Jews immigrating to the United States. Izzy did well and eventually transitioned into real estate, buying apartment buildings in Cleveland proper. Sonia and Izzy never lost their accents or their ties to the old country in which they were born. It was a silent thread sewn into the fabric of their very being.

While pregnant Sonia visited her sister Bertha in Hoboken and while there gave birth to Milton Abraham Bialosky on May 29, 1928, Sonia's and Isadore's first-born American son, a mitzvah, they can't believe their good luck. Milt is the bright, shining star of their new lives in America. Sonia and Bertha left behind a sister, Jenny, and her family in the old country, who were lost in the pogroms. Jenny and her husband taught at the university or had some sort of connection to the university and stayed behind. No one spoke of her. No one talks about those who died or endured hardships. It is as though the tragedy is wiped clean, too painful to remember or articulate in words. Izzy is short and stocky. He speaks broken English with a European accent and smokes cigars. He's never not dressed in a suit and tie. He eats European-style with his fork blade turned around using his knife to slide the food onto the back of his fork. Sonia is short, too.

Milt and his sisters embrace the American pastimes of driving around in cars, drive-ins, the beginning of rock 'n' roll. They're embarrassed by their parents' thick accents and old-world ways. They're young and free, stepping into each day anew, frustrated by their family's extreme claustrophobia and overprotectiveness. Suburban life proliferated in this era, and, along with it, the expectation of marrying young was a nine-to-five job for men while women tended the home and children. It was the period of green grass lawns, early marriages, and young families with more than one child, which meant that being a teenager came with the responsibility and pressure to be more like an adult.

Iris attends Ohio State for a quarter, and Milt visits her on weekends. Another weekend Iris comes home to visit her family, but really, she just wants to see Milt. No. He can't wait any longer. It's too hard to be away from Iris when she is all that he can think about. He's fallen in love with her modesty and polite manners, her femininity and warmth, how easily she laughs, unabashedly, even when he's being corny, how everyone seems to like her (*I can't believe he chose me*, Iris will tell me again and again). He has made up his mind. Milt kneels on the floor before Iris who is sitting on

the thread-worn couch, the left-over smell of the evening's
roasted chicken coming from the kitchen.

Let's imagine it's snowing outside and they're in Iris's living
room, her relatives giving the young lovers some privacy. Perhaps
he's already asked Eugene for his daughter's hand. Milt is wearing
wool trousers, a sports jacket, and loafers, with his hair swept
back in a pompadour like a movie star. Iris is in a skirt flowing
between her knees and ankles, a lacy blouse and cardigan, bobby
socks, and loafers. Her hair is cut just above her neck. Her cheeks
are pink from the little spot of lipstick she creams into them.
"Will you marry me?" Milt says and slips a rectangular diamond
ring that catches the light and sparkles on Iris's slender finger.
He surely purchased it at his father's pawn shop and likely got a
good deal. Iris can't believe her good fortune. Of course, she says,
with a little laugh. They embrace. They are completely absorbed
in each other, in the moment, in the absolute silence in the house.
Can they even hear the gusts of the wind and the snow lapping
the windows? It's the most monumental event in their young lives
and they both want it to last forever, to hold back anything that
might come between them. For a minute, Iris thinks it can't be
true. When will the floor drop? In the Greenbaum home where
Iris grew up, tragedy is always around the corner. The future is
hopeful. Milt lifts Iris's chin and kisses her. Tells her he's never
loved anyone but her. She looks into his damp eyes, then at the
ring shining on her finger, the same diamond set in platinum,
she will admire for the next seventy years.

Should Iris have stayed in college? Postponed the wedding? What would her fate have looked like if she'd received
an education? Begun a career? Milt has already graduated.
Perhaps if she waits, she'll lose him. Iris breathes in the scent

of her betrothed, a mix of soap, aftershave, and perspiration. She devours the scent of him when she kisses him on his sometimes-bristled cheek. In his arms she's never felt so protected and loved. For we've learned that love is essential, but it does not stop terrible things from happening. Iris won't ever forget this moment. Her betrothed still on his knees and Iris clinging to his shoulders. She will rehearse it in her mind until the day she expires. Sometimes she can't breathe out of happiness. It's like a fairy tale. She's so overpowered by emotion it hurts. And Milt. He can't believe his good fortune. He's found the woman he wants to build a life with. Everyone loves and admires Milt, but he, too, has suffered. His mother, god love her, smothers him. His father is critical and fearful. He knows what it takes to build a life. Milt feels the pressure to make it up to them and it's no small thing and now he has found the woman who fits, a young woman with no airs, who is humble and kind and radiates warmth. There's no façade, no mask, no *I'll do anything to please you* about her. He's dated those kinds of girls. And many young men have dated Iris. She was one of the most popular girls at school, he's been told. And now she's his.

Mr. Eugene J. Greenbaum
announces the marriage of his daughter
Iris Yvonne
to
Mr. Milton A. Bialosky
Sunday, the seventeenth of January
Nineteen hundred and fifty-four
Cleveland, Ohio

They have a small wedding in the rabbi's chambers, with a family dinner afterward at the Hollenden Hotel; there isn't money for a big wedding (Iris's father works as a bank teller). There's Iris's father, Eugene, with too-long trousers that hang over his shoes, and deep lines around his mouth, dark bags underneath his eyes. Larry, Iris's younger brother, standing beside his father. Eugene's mother; his four siblings: Harriet, who is betrothed to Joe; brother Jimmy and his wife, Margaret; sister Horty and her husband, Charlie; and sister Florence, who has never married. Milt's family is here, too. His parents, Sonia and Izzy; his two sisters, Irene (and her now husband, Dick) and Rita. Iris's aunts have handkerchiefs in their white-gloved hands to wipe their teary eyes and wear hats with hairpins and greet each other with hugs and kisses. It's cozy in the Rabbi's chambers filled with shelves of books and a big desk and the *hum, hum, hum* of love. The morning light beams through the stained-glass window. Everyone is standing as Milt and Iris walk in, followed by the sound of *oohs* and *aahs* over Iris's satin dress that falls to her ankles and a modest veil draped to her shoulders. A kiss curl on her forehead, and her bright, searching eyes reached out to all of them with love.

Milt is clothed in a dark suit and white tie with a white corsage pinned to the lapel of his suit jacket and a white kippah on the back of his head. *What a beautiful couple,* a whisper that travels from one relative to the other. A shower of white lilies scents the room. There's a moment's hush, and the ceremony begins. Under a makeshift chuppah braided with white flowers, Rabbi Brickner, the new reform Rabbi at the temple on Euclid Avenue, in a black suit, balding, with gentle eyes and a commanding voice asks the bride and groom to repeat the blessing.

*I am my beloved's and my beloved is mine. Harey at
mekuddeshet li b'taba'at zo k'dat Moshe V'israel. Behold,
thou art consecrated unto me with this ring according to
the law of Moses and of Israel.*

A profound silence and then a few murmurs and sighs fill
the chambers. Milt chokes up when he places the gold wedding band on Iris's finger, Iris slips a gold band on Milt's. She
is shaking from happiness, and a little laugh escapes from her
mouth to temper her nerves. Milt smiles at her, humbled by
the responsibility that awaits him. For a moment, he closes
his eyes and squeezes his bride's hand. Tears of happiness fill
their eyes. "In the name of God, I, Iris, take you, Milt, to be
my husband, to have and to hold from this day forward, for
better, for worse, for richer, for poorer, in sickness and in health,
to love and to cherish, until parted by death." And then Milt
recites the same vow.

You'll never see a smile on Eugene Greenbaum's somber
face until this moment. His eyes water, and he takes a handkerchief from his pocket and removes his glasses to dab them
before he blows his nose. He lets out a long, melancholy sigh.
How he wishes his wife, Lillian, Iris's mother, was here to see
their daughter marry. He's dressed handsomely in his best
suit, white shirt, and white tie, black shoes he polished that
morning shine brightly for the occasion. He's both proud and
relieved his daughter is marrying such a mensch and joining a
family a step up from his in terms of prosperity. Does he for a
moment give a nod of thanks to his benevolent God who he
has let back into his heart? Maybe now he can breathe a sigh
without worrying about his beloved daughter.

Everyone is beaming at the young couple with damp eyes. Milt smashes the glass underneath his polished shoes, a gesture that represents the destruction of the temple in Jerusalem and announces a new beginning. Even in times of joy, we must remember our history. The breaking of the glass symbolizes that what is private is now made public as the world rushes in.

They kiss. And then they break away and look at their families and embrace again. *Mazel tov, mazel tov,* the families chant. Iris's heart is bounding in her chest so hard; she can barely breathe. Packets of rice unleash and rain on the newlyweds. The cake is cut.

Milt gives Iris the first bite from his fork. It's the sweetest frosting ever. The afternoon light floods the room, celebrating the warmth of thousands of days sure to follow.

———

IN A PHOTO taken of the lovely couple in the backseat of a car as they are off on their honeymoon, Iris's smile stretches so wide her cheeks must hurt. Milt's arm holds her close, he's so very handsome, with sparkling brown eyes, dark red hair, high cheekbones, fair skin with faint freckles, and a square chin. For their honeymoon, they fly to Bermuda, the first time Iris has been out of the country. I imagine Iris doing her nails and rolling pink sponge-soft curlers in her hair to hold her hairstyle in place before getting ready for dinner at the hotel the first night after they've landed. Putting that little dab of perfume behind her ears and on the soft part of the inside of her wrists, pinching her cheeks for color. Milt kissing her neck then helping Iris fasten the white pearl necklace Aunt Harriet gave to her after the wedding, so she'd have something special and new to wear for the honeymoon. They've booked a table at the hotel restaurant because what newlyweds want to travel too far from the bedroom on their honeymoon? Champagne popped at the dinner table, afterward up to the Honeymoon Suite at the hotel. Maybe there is no air-conditioning, the fan overhead moving to their lovemaking, the room pitch black. They sleep wrapped in each other's arms. Have they ever slept in a bed together until this night? The next morning, breakfast brought up and the table laid on the balcony, fresh orange juice, coffee, sunny-side-up eggs, toast and muffins in a little basket, the happy couple wrapped in their matching white hotel robes, Iris still admiring the way the Bermuda sunlight catches on her diamond engagement ring, the feel of the warm, silky Caribbean air. Maybe they've just opened the wedding gift envelopes from relatives they plan to deposit in their now joint savings account. Are they talking about starting a family? Milt's new job in real estate? Perhaps they are doing a play-by-play of the wedding ceremony and the guests, laughing at nervous Aunt Florence who told them to make sure they buckled their seat belts on the plane.

The morning is long in the hotel room because who wants to leave when this is the first time they've been alone together without the fear of being caught? Maybe it's noon before they change into their swimsuits, Iris a two-piece with the bottom that goes just over her belly button and a cover-up, Milt in his trunks and a long button-down white shirt. There is a photo of Milt in his bathing shorts standing in the sea. I imagine Iris on a blanket in the sand or on a lounge chair, or perhaps she's getting her feet wet in the crystal-clear water, looking out admiringly (she never learned to swim) at her tanned and charming husband and then snapping the photo. Let's stop here for a moment and linger. Let's not take this moment of bliss for granted.

———

IRIS IS NEWLY married to Milt. She's twenty-one. Soon, like the friends in their social group and Milt's sister, Irene, they will start a family. It is 1954. When they first marry, they live in an apartment while a new house is being built for them on Lytle Road in Shaker Heights, Ohio. I imagine Iris going to her bowling league once a week and afterward getting a salad or a tuna salad sandwich with the women on her team, sitting on stools at the luncheonette counter at the bowling alley while Milt is at work at the real estate office. Once a week, she plays mahjong in the afternoon with a steady group of friends, each host laying out bowls of chocolate-covered raisins and bridge mix, along with bottles of Coke. She goes to the beauty parlor on Friday to have her hair done for the weekend.

Iris waits in anticipation for Milt to come home from work. She makes dinner for them, simple meals of roasted chicken or brisket with potatoes and carrots, or stuffed cabbage Aunt Harriet taught her how to make. Cozying up on the couch after supper to watch *The Honeymooners* before going to bed, laughing when Ralph Kramden sends Alice to the moon. This is the era, too, of *The Dick Van Dyke Show* and *I Love Lucy*, a world where young wives take care of the house and husbands work. Milt and Iris belong to the temple where they got married. Being Jewish in America means it is best to assimilate, but the family's soul is still informed by the traditions of centuries of the Eastern European ghetto. Their ambitions are to secure a prosperous future for their children based on their Jewish heritage and to take care of their elders. Not to make themselves stand out, just in case.

Both families are close-knit and have their own private ways of being. My mother's family is humbler and more modest than my father's. Every Friday night, they're invited to Iris's father's house for Shabbat. At Passover each year, Eugene leads the seder. He recites the blessing for the candles. Next the blessing over the wine. *Baruch Atah Adonai Eloheinu Melech ha-olam, boreh p'ri ha-gafen, Blessed are you, eternal one, our God, ruler of the universe, Creator of the vine* and everyone takes a sip of Manischewitz's overly sweet wine that tastes like grape juice. The Hebrew Haggadahs from the old country, illustrated in color with smudges and fingerprints from previous Passovers on the pages, sit on each plate. Eugene states that salt water represents the tears that were shared and the hardships the Hebrew slaves endured, and the hard-boiled egg, slimy to pick up, represents rebirth, the circle of life. The matzoh, the unleavened bread the Jews took on their exodus. Snap, snap, snap. The matzoh is passed, and everyone takes a bite.

How is this night different from all other nights? Larry, the youngest, recites. All weepy eyes go to the newly married couple sitting next to each other, Milt's hand on Iris's thigh, who will carry on the traditions of the family and eventually have their own children.

After the long drawn out seder and the hearty meal in Eugene's small dining room with Iris's brother, aunts and uncles, and Grandma Cookie, sitting so close their elbows touch, so there's room for everyone around the table covered in white cloth, set with the best china and silver. The air is warm and stuffy from all the cooking, the scent of brisket which will last for days. Iris and Milt can't wait to get back home to snuggle in their own marriage bed.

———

ON SATURDAY NIGHTS they go to dinner parties hosted by other newly married friends. On the weekends the young couple sometimes go to Northfield Lanes to bowl together in a couples league. Then Iris, at twenty-two years old is pregnant with her first child. They are out of their minds with joy. But three months later, Iris begins to cramp and has a miscarriage. Iris cries into Milt's chest, and her tears soak his shirt. She's heartbroken, already attached to the embryo that, in her mind, has become the dream of a baby. What if it happens again? What if she can't have a child? But they're young. They have their entire lives stretched out before them. Milt reassures her they can wait. A few months later, a new life forms in her belly, a little seed that grows into a bump. Milt kisses Iris's belly, rubs it, and feels the baby move. Soon, their own lives will take a turn. This is what they want, what they've been hoping for. What they've grown up to believe in. It's time for nesting, getting ready for the newborn baby. Milt keeps his eye attuned to his pregnant wife, constantly making sure she's comfortable, propping her legs up with a pillow to prevent her legs from swelling when she's lying on the couch, and bringing her cool glasses of water. He gently holds her arm when they go out to make sure she doesn't trip or fall.

———

WITHIN A YEAR, Laura is born. They can't believe they've been blessed with this beautiful baby with chubby arms and legs, and skin as soft as butter. They're still in their cozy modest apartment where Iris feeds and diapers baby Laura and Milt can't wait to get home after a long day at work. Sometimes he returns at lunch to help Iris cuddle his baby daughter, kiss the top of her head. Months later, they move into the brand-new house on Lytle Road in Shaker Heights, Ohio. The street is so fresh that there are barely any trees along the sidewalk. The house smells of shaved wood from the new floors and fresh paint. When Laura is six months old, Iris is pregnant with me. The ritual begins again: the embryo planted and forming a bump, Iris aglow in pregnancy, Milt taking baby Laura out in the stroller so Iris can nap because pregnancy and caring for a one-year-old is tiring, but they are in love and nothing else matters except for the sound of baby Laura laughing when Milt tickles her and Iris giving her husband a kiss on the cheek because she can't believe how lucky she is and then on a cool April morning, right after the forsythia in the backyard have bloomed, I am born, and named after my great-grandfather, Jerome.

Iris is pregnant again! Will this one be a boy or a girl? They don't know. They laugh, because they've conceived again, one baby after another. Poor Milt. Did he pray for a boy? The house is now filled with Jill's cries for milk in the middle of the night, along with baby Laura, who is only fifteen months old when Jill is born. Is that a new milk tooth coming up? It's no wonder she's been crying and is hard to soothe. Iris applies pressure with her finger on her gums to stop the pain. Milt and Iris are so tired they can barely breathe. One baby is up, and then another, and in the middle of the night, both their baby daughters are in their bed between them. And a third on the way. The next day is the same. And the day after and the next. Who cares. Their blessings make them buoyant.

———

IRIS AND MILT take baby Jill for a stroller ride. Laura, dressed in a snowsuit with bunny ears, perhaps a warmer day in Cleveland as the snow begins to thaw, pushes the stroller, the cool wind slipping down their collars. Iris is newly pregnant with baby Cindy. Iris wears a skirt that clings to her calves, loafers with bobby socks, and a light jacket. Milt's arm is around her shoulder; he's in beige khakis and a zip-up light jacket. Laura has his smile. All during Iris's labor, Milt's at the hospital waiting, pacing the floors, cigars in the inside of his jacket pocket, ready to be passed around, as he has for his two other daughters. Cindy is born on a beautiful day in late June. They stare at baby Cindy in disbelief. Another beautiful girl. Iris has her hands full. "I don't know how I did it," she'll laugh. "We used to tumble you all in our bed to diaper you one after the other like we were on an assembly line. An entire evening could amount only to giving you girls a bath." Something must have gone wrong. Maybe they had little fights or arguments—*can you get the baby, no too tired, you go*—prayed for a moment's peace, but Iris doesn't recall any of that. It's like they're floating in their own private oasis. Does Milt mind that Iris is too tired on some nights to make love?

———

THEIR EXTENDED FAMILIES are growing. Birthday parties and holidays with Aunt Irene and Uncle Dick and their children, close to the ages of their daughters. Iris holds baby Cindy in her arms; on one of Milt's knees sits one-year-old Jill; on the other, Laura, at the table with aunts, uncles, and cousins; for cousin Bruce's birthday. Birthday balloons float to the ceiling, candles are blown out, and Aunt Irene cuts the birthday cake. Grandma Sonia and Grampa Izzy blow kisses. Sonia has a lump in her throat. Is it really true that in this new world, we all may be safe? She thinks, and then, afraid of the evil eye, lets the thought escape.

In the five years that Iris and Milt have been married, they've shared wedding anniversaries, birthdays, Passovers, High Holy Days, and thousands of memories sewn into their bodies and souls. So many mornings lying in bed with the bassinet at their side to hold their infant daughter, ears peeled to hear if the other two in their cribs in the next room are awake. Days welcoming the first blossoms of spring, winters where the endless snow locks them inside the house for days. They're absorbed wholly in their own world. Nothing outside can penetrate their bubble. How many times have they made love? Kissed? Cried from fatigue and happiness? Thanked God for what they've created?

———

I DON'T WANT to go here, but I must, even after days and weeks of avoiding it as if I could turn the clock and see into a future that might have been, but the past can't be changed or wiped clean. Or forgotten. On a late cold afternoon, March 5, 1959, Milt and Iris drop off their girls at Grandma Sonia's house

to go to their couples bowling league at Northfield Lanes.
Iris is a good bowler. I imagine her lobbing a strike down the
shiny waxed lane, the pins kicking back one after the other,
and then coming over to receive a hug from her husband. I
imagine they're laughing and joking, drinking rum and Cokes
or highballs with their friends; maybe someone's drinking a
beer, talking about their kids, what kind of counter to put in
the new kitchen, the occasional sex joke, the sounds of balls
crashing and pins toppling, and from the food stand the rising
smell of hot dogs roasting on the spinner and fresh popped
popcorn. Iris is dressed in a long blue mohair sweater and black
stretch pants, bowling shoes. Milt brushes his hand across
Iris's bottom, and pulls her close. *Milt stop*, Iris teases and
settles into his embrace. They must admit, it's nice to spend
time together without their daughters. Then it's Milt's turn. He
locates his black bowling ball with shiny blue specks amid the
others, steadies it in his hand, anchors it, and collapses just as
he is about to drill it down the lane. Everyone huddles around
him. The lanes go quiet. Someone calls the EMT. Iris leans
over Milt. Her face has turned white. A scream forms in her
mouth. It's impossible to imagine what happens next and to
realize this moment in words—what Iris is experiencing is too
painful. Too much of a shock to bear. She doesn't even hear the
cacophony of panic around her. The walls shut in. The world
has suddenly stopped. Milt's had a heart attack. Iris faints. At
the hospital, they can't revive him. He's only thirty years old.

———

MY MOTHER IS twenty-five years old when Milton Abraham
Bialosky dies from sudden heart failure in 1959. He was Iris's

hero, the love of her life, her soulmate who rescued her from the stifling two-story house in Cleveland Heights where she lived with her father, grandmother, younger brother, and a boarder. What will happen to their three girls? How will Iris manage? She's barely a grown-up herself.

Iris hoards her memories of my father and keeps them close to herself so they will not fly away. Milt's death is a shock to his family, to Iris's family, and to their friends. Izzy, Milt's father, dies in September 1961, a year and a half after Milt died. Everyone says it was from a broken heart. Milton is immortalized as a tragic hero. Why did he need to die? What did the gods have in mind? To make Iris stronger? To instill bravery and survival skills in his young daughters? Milt's death marks all of us. Iris is now a poor widow, and we are her poor fatherless daughters. And, worse, Milt does not get to spend his adult life alongside his beloved wife and witness his children growing up. He does not get to have a single gray hair. He will never realize his professional dreams, never again watch a football game with his buddies, kiss his wife's cheek, or snuggle his babies.

———

RECENTLY, I LEARNED—and why no one ever told me this before, I don't know—that my father had rheumatic fever as a child and that it can cause damage to the heart later in life. One of my paternal aunts explained that my grandmother had been worried about his health since he was three years old. I wonder if my mother ever knew that his health was fragile. I wonder if my father knew.

———

EVERY WORD, EVERY sound is a stab of anguish. Oh, how Iris must have wanted it all back, railed against God, her strong, protective young husband; how can he be gone? It isn't possible; it must be a bad dream; when will she awaken from it, her future emptied out like sand in an hourglass? She's sealed the trauma in a box never to be opened. Never to be remembered. There are times you must shut your eyes to pain. I am just shy of two when tragedy strikes. Down in the cellar of my childhood, this moment—the death of my father—has informed all that I am and will ever be.

————

IT'S MARCH 5, 1959. It's always cold in March. The trees are naked, the sky gray as the face of death. The wind outside howls. What happens next? Who comes to take Iris from the hospital where her beloved's heart has stopped, his breath extinguished. Perhaps one of Milt's friends in their bowling league has called to inform Eugene, Iris's father, and Sonia and Izzy, Milt's parents, and now they're all congregated in the hospital lounge. Iris is heavily sedated and folds into her father's chest leaving makeup smears from her tears on his white button-down shirt. Sonia is broken, too. How can this happen to her baby? Her only son.

What can be said, what words? *I'm sorry, Iris, how can this be? What kind of God would do this? A man in his prime, just beginning.* "I want Milt," Iris hysterically cries, breaking away from her father to try to get back through the hospital's swinging doors to see her husband. Eugene grabs her wrists to hold her back and calm her down. "Let me see him again," she cries. Maybe she thinks she can will him alive. Eugene brings

Iris back to the hospital room where her husband lies with a white sheet over everything but his face, still hooked up to a bank of monitors. Iris weeps over his still-warm body, "No, no, no," she cries until, eventually, Eugene pulls her away. Perhaps this is when Iris decides never to go visit a body in a grave.

———

EUGENE KEEPS HIS arm around Iris to hold her from collapsing as he guides her from his car over the dirty chunks of old snow on the walkway to the new Colonial white house with black shutters that Milt bought just two years before with a mortgage. The door opens into sparkling white rooms and wall-to-wall cream-colored carpet stretched on the living room floor.

Aunt Harriet is inside looking after the babies. Sonia and Izzy dropped them over when they heard the news before rushing to the hospital. Nine-month-old baby Cindy is in the playpen in the living room. Just barely three in January, Laura is drawing on the floor in a coloring book. Jill, two next month, is sprawled on the carpet with her thumb in her mouth. The minute they see their mother they know something's different. Eugene takes off Iris's coat. She's still in her blue mohair sweater and slim black slacks she wore to bowl, her eyes red and puffy, her hair tussled, her drawn face collapsed. Iris picks up baby Cindy, who is suddenly crying from her playpen, and holds her tight, "my baby, my baby," she says and ravenously kisses her forehead, her cheeks, her neck. She sits down on the sofa with the baby in her arms and Jill crawls up and comes into her mother's lap and Laura stands in front of her mother, she wants a piece of her, too. "My poor girls," Iris says and cries.

"My poor, poor babies." Aunt Harriet, dressed neatly in a cardigan and gray wool slacks, takes baby Cindy from Iris and tells her niece she needs to go and lie down; she's upsetting the girls. She's the stoic in the family, but her emotion pulses through her blue eyes that, at this moment, look as if they'll crack from anguish. Control, logic, reason, and discipline are how she mines her emotions, her own disappointments and hurts, but Iris, Iris, how will her niece survive this? Nothing happens without a reason.

"*Baruch dayan emet*, may you be consoled from heaven," she wishes upon her beloved niece.

Eugene, with his melancholy eyes, escorts Iris by the arm up to the bedroom where she and Milt made their love nest. Eugene gives his daughter a sedative the doctor prescribed at the hospital. Downstairs, the mirrors are covered. Aunt Harriet eventually comes upstairs holding a tray with a bowl of hot chicken soup and toast. Iris is half-awake, lying on the bed curled in the fetal position, her eyes gazing out. "You need to eat something," Aunt Harriet says, but Iris won't eat. "My Milt," Iris moans, "what am I going to do?" Aunt Harriet takes Iris's hand in hers. "Look at me, I," she says, using her pet name for Iris. "Hold on to Milt's love, and don't let it go. He will always be with you." She rises, goes into the master bathroom, takes a tea towel, wets it with cool water, folds it, brings it back to Iris, and presses it over her forehead. "I'm so sorry, I," she says, almost breaking, but holds her composure, rubbing Iris's back. She must be the strong one in the family.

The funeral is the darkest day of Iris's young life. The chapel is filled with Milt and Iris's family and friends, all dressed in black, handkerchiefs or Kleenexes rolled in palms. Everyone is somber. Milt's life was just beginning. This isn't supposed to happen. Iris sits in the first row; she does not bring her babies to the funeral; next to her is her father and her brother on the other side of her, her father's arms around her shoulder. Psalms are sung, prayers recited, the rabbi speaks. Iris cannot hear any of it. She's already lost in mourning the happiness of all her days. "I knew it was too good to be true," she says to one of her friends who embraces her after the funeral service, before they go to the graveside where the coffin will be lowered to the ground.

———

SOON, THE RABBI will come to say the Kaddish. Shiva will begin. The house is flooded with friends and family who come to console Iris. One of her friends from high school overhears Bea, Eugene's new wife, forever jealous of Eugene's devotion to his daughter, in the kitchen talking to her sister. "Good for her," she whispered. "Iris was too happy." When Iris's close friend tells me this, as I'm working on this book, I don't doubt a word of it. Jealousy makes people cruel.

As days pass, the aunts rotate to help care for the children. Iris will not leave her bed. She's sick with unbearable grief. Her blank eyes and hollow face put fear in Aunt Harriet, who loves Iris like a daughter. She pleads with her niece to get out of bed, even for an hour or two, but Iris refuses. If she gets up, she knows that what happened will be true. Day after day, Aunt Florence, Aunt Horty, and Aunt Harriet, the bossy one who runs the house like a ship, cook the girls' dinner, give baby Cindy her bottle, change diapers, and tidy the house. Iris is heavily sedated. In bed, she remembers Milt's body next to hers, the shape of his lips, his eyes, the feel of every tendon and muscle in his body; she must hold on to every detail until she slowly begins to absorb what has happened. It's like layers of protection she needs to peel off one by one because the pain is too great to let it seep in all at once. Iris curls in the fetal position, memories running through her mind like a slow-moving film; it's been weeks and she's barely gotten out of bed, only to use the toilet. And then, one morning, she hears one of her babies crying, and she rises, tightens the strap of her robe around her waist, follows the sound, and walks down the stairs, the sun so bright she can barely stand it. But somehow, she does.

———

LIKE NAOMI IN the Book of Ruth, Iris is instantly stripped of the future that she imagined. Does Iris feel that God abandoned her? Naomi (which means sweet and pleasant) changed her name to Mara (which means bitter), after she lost her husband and two sons. Iris is not bitter. She's heartbroken. To be bitter would be to insult Milt's spirit and generosity. To deny that he had chosen her, that they were one.

12.

Every morning offers the possibility of hope. Is it fate or chance who one meets, who one becomes? Iris, sixteen, upstairs in her room, fastening her navy skirt that flows between her knee and her ankles, buttoning a red cardigan sweater with pearl buttons straining to open, pulling up white bobby socks, slipping into loafers. She combs her hair (cut like Joan of Arc's) and admires her figure in the mirror, grabs her satchel of books, climbs downstairs to the kitchen that smells of coffee and toast and scrambled eggs. There's the Greenbaum family around the aluminum breakfast table with olive-green padded aluminum chairs that scrape the lino-leum tiled floor. Good morning, Daddy, Iris says and kisses her father on the cheek. He's dressed in his suit. Today, it's the blue one; he only has two, and the other is brown. He switches from one suit to the other throughout the work week. Now you can hear the ruffle of the Cleveland *Plain Dealer* he neatly folds as he reads it, the front page is news about the signing of the NATO Treaty. It's the beginning of the Cold War and there's threat of Soviet aggression. Her brother Larry is seven and is eating a stack of pancakes, one hand holding his fork, the other poking an ear into his Mr. Potato Head. Iris ruffles the top of his black curly hair. Eugene's sister Harriet with her high aristocratic forehead and sparkling blue eyes, Iris's favorite aunt, always wearing a pair of clip-on earrings, is by the stove hovering over the eggs. Eugene's mother, Iris's grandmother, Grandma Cookie, her silver thinning hair pulled back in a bun, in a house dress with an apron tied around her waist is at the sink washing dishes. She's sad, meek, and heartsick. Because the family is poor, she checks the icebox daily to see if she can make the weekly food supply last another day or two. Her husband, Iris's grandfather, Jerome, whom I am named after, took his life on a cold March day of that year, when old snow was frozen solid and coated with black ice. Iris, eager to leave the family fold and the sadness that hovers over all of them even when they try to be cheerful, takes a bite of cold toast saturated with butter that is already on a plate laid out for her and says she's late, she'll miss the bus. *Won't you have a little egg*, begs Aunt Harriet, who is staying over to help take care of Iris and her younger brother while she waits for her husband to return from the navy. Iris looks at her father with pleading eyes, and he tells Harriet not to fuss and to let her go. He'll allow his precious daughter anything. Don't forget your coat and scarf, says Grandma Cookie, wiping her hands on her apron and following Iris to the hall closet, and then watching from the window as Iris leaves the house. Iris should be used to all the attention, but as much as she loves them, they brood over her like she's still a child. Is it the warm, stuffy air in the small kitchen, the smell of mothballs that rises from her grandmother's sweater that makes her want to escape? Is it because she can still see her mother's shadow in the same spot near the stove where Aunt Harriet is standing?

Iris was only twelve when World War II ended, but she is living in the shadow of her family's grief over the six million Jews exterminated in the camps and their own personal losses. *If it can happen once, it can happen again.* Perhaps that is why her family is so overprotective and wants only for Iris to find a good Jewish man to marry. I imagine that she, too, dreams of falling in love to escape the somber worry and dread in the air at home. Two of her uncles fought in World War II and, luckily, came home safe. Several thousand Holocaust survivors settled in Cleveland after the war was over. The rabbi at Iris's temple, Rabbi Barnett Brickner, was chosen by the Committee on Army and Navy Religious Activities to travel through the war theaters in Europe. He advocated for the rescue of refugees in Europe. He later received a Medal of Merit in 1947 from President Truman.

On June 3, 1949, when Iris is sixteen, she finishes a nine-year course of Jewish study and is confirmed in the presence of the congregation of the Ansche Chesed Euclid Avenue Temple. With the rest of her confirmation class, she reads from the Haftorah from "Akdamus" and "Sayings of the Fathers," a collection of wisdom from the Jewish Talmudic sages which says, in one translation, "you are not required to finish your work, yet neither are you permitted to desist from it," so apt for the last day of her religious studies. An interesting conundrum. A cutout from *The Social Swirl* in Iris's scrapbook reads:

> Iris Greenbaum, daughter of Mr. Eugene J. Greenbaum, 13346 Cedar Road, will be among the confirmands of the Euclid Avenue Temple on June 3.

After the confirmation, the family has a dinner in Iris's honor.

There's Iris after the family dinner celebration retreating to her bedroom, her bed covered with the light pink soft wool blanket her mother knit for her. She turns on her nightstand light and pastes a photo of the ark of the temple with its menorahs, scrolls, and Jewish Star into her scrapbook. She didn't love Hebrew school, but she has learned to respect the traditions and now she's graduated. But something more has happened. She's passed a milestone and in doing so, possesses an enduring faith in the Jewish belief in the immortality of the soul that will be a mainstay throughout her life.

In Cleveland many Jewish families have simplified or anglicized their names from the more Jewish sounding Russian, Polish, and Hungarian names in response to American anti-Semitism.

With so many decades of Jewish history behind them and the long shadow of the atrocities to remember, what if they, too, are unsafe? The Greenbaums instill in Iris what it means to live under the burdens of history and her connection to the Jewish tradition. She feels the burden of being the center of attention, the one person her family can dote on for their moments of joy and laughter. As a young girl she was their Shirley Temple. They dressed her up in coats with matching hats and gloves and tied ribbons in her hair. Now she is becoming a young woman and slowly moving out of their grasp. They want Iris to forget the past but to also remember it. Who wants to burden a sixteen-year-old girl with fear? Every corsage she receives, every honor, all the dances and parties she attends, the boys that come to pick her up to take her out, they drink from like a soothing beverage. Their hope is that Iris will marry a nice Jewish man and be taken care of.

———

ONCE IRIS CLOSES the door of the brick family house with white shutters where she lives with her father, brother Larry, grandmother, a rotating set of aunts, and a boarder named Max on the third floor, she's able to let go of the utterly bewildering, smothering weight of it all, sip in the spring air, and breathe again. *To life!* The sky is gray; she can feel the dampness on her skin, and somehow, the just blossoming trees and their greenery spring hope. At home it's hard to dodge her squabbling aunts who come in and out of the house to help their brother Eugene take care of little Larry, this one, that one, telling her what to do, speaking in Yiddish when they're angry or don't want Iris to know what they are saying, afraid she stays out too late, isn't dressed properly, doesn't eat enough. The look of her mournful father gazing into nothingness lingers. Her love for him is unwieldy and enormous. She must do all she can to please him. He calls her his darling. She's embarrassed that he has taped the frame of one wing of his broken eyeglasses, not wanting to spend money to get a new pair because anything extra should go to his only daughter. Her sometimes-annoying brother horsing around, running through the narrow hallways of the house until someone tells him to settle down. What are her thoughts about this brother nine years younger than her? Does she have time for him? Is she resentful? She walks to the bus stop in her skirt that sashays to her ankles pulling her light coat close, her books pressed against her chest.

When the bus arrives, its door squeaking open, she climbs

the steps and is swung into another world. There's Millie and Irene and Sandra. She scoots in next to Sandra. They're gossiping about some of the boys in their brother's frat. How one wanted to go to second base when they were at the cinema. Iris blushes. She's a member of numerous clubs and societies and seems (at least from what she posts in her scrapbook) to be on top of the world. She's popular and likable. What is it that attracts others to her? It's more than her slim figure and wide smile. Maybe it's that cloud of sadness she tries to hide. She exudes a craving for openness, the ability to laugh and feel joy, and an intimate and empathetic knowledge of other people's needs. She never has a bad word to say about anyone. She's aware of other people's suffering. There is a girl in her class who has a terrible stutter she's befriended. Sometimes it takes more than a few minutes for a sentence to emerge and her classmates are not as patient as Iris. Iris claims her as one of her best friends. Iris believes in kindness to all and the innocence of love and is always quick to put herself second. No, she's not a top student; shies away from the terrible world of competition among her peers, of constantly measuring herself against others. She's not loud or a show-off like some of her classmates. She's modest and wants to be liked. What is fun if not an escape? What is joy but the flip side of misery?

———

LUCKY FOR ME, her documentarian, she has kept a scrapbook of her junior and high school years where she logs in every outing, every date. In a cutout from the high school paper dated

June 6, 1949, called "The Long and Short of It" is a column that
reads *You'll Never See* followed by a listicle:

> The boys without squirt guns.
>   The members of the Reflector Staff, the school paper,
> not wanting their names mentioned in this column (satis-
> fied, Iris)!;
>   Tom Jacobs without his mother.

The Perfect 9Am, another school newspaper cutout, lists
seventeen characteristics such as voice, personality, clothes,
ability to speak French, or play sports, and then which girl or
boy it is applied to. Iris nails it for her figure!

Girl		Boy
Shirley K.	hair	Jerry S.
Phyllis A.	Eyes.	Victor K.
Beth R.	Nose.	Eddy K.
Iris Greenbaum.	Figure and physique	Stan G.

Another column *Last Will and Testament* records what
each graduating student is passing on to the next class.

> Tom J, leaves his sports writing ability to—he just leaves it!
>   Phyllis A, and Ailene B. leave their big, beautiful eyes to
> Judy H.
>   Iris Greenbaum leaves that "Miss America Figure" of
> hers to Carol K.

Does Iris like all the attention paid to her figure? I'm sure it
awakens feelings of pride and who doesn't want to be desired or
told she has a knockout body? But there's more to her than just

her shape. She's soulful, warm, a bit of a dreamer, always has a smile for everyone. Her aim is to please and make others happy.

She's a member of the school sorority, S.O.T. The boys of BAT (Milt's fraternity) wait on the lawn for their meetings to end so they can mingle with the S.O.T. girls. In her scrapbook Iris pastes her pledge badge. On November 27, she's invited to a Stag and Date dance with Nortie G. In July she travels to Daytona Beach, Florida, for a visit with Aunt Horty and Uncle Charlie in their small apartment. Iris pastes in her scrapbook a fake newspaper clip someone, surely a date, must have made for her in *The Beach Daily News*: "Iris Greenbaum Arrives in Daytona—Boys Go Wild!" I'm awestruck when I discover it as a kid thumbing through Iris's scrapbook. It isn't until I'm older that I learn that anyone can get a fake newspaper made for them in one of the kiosks on the beach. In Florida, Iris dates Morty S. Then on July 17, Ralph D. takes her to a beach party. Aunt Horty must be fixing her up. When she's not out, she fills time by filing her nails, neatly folding her clothes and arranging them in the dresser, flipping through magazines and catalogues, careful not to be a bother. She senses something like repressed anger born out of routine underneath the bond between her aunt and uncle. Iris feels sad for them stuck alone together in the small apartment with no kids of their own and tries to make it up to them by showering them with attention. She asks Uncle Charlie about his golf game, and lets Aunt Horty style her hair.

All her relatives want a piece of her. In 1949 she travels to San Antonio, Texas, to visit her mother's family. Into her scrapbook she tapes a cut out picture of the airplane she flew on and an invitation illustrated with three kitties with bows on their collars for a Sweet Sixteen party for a friend named

Barbara. She plays mini golf with Richard G. at the Cool Crest. Visits the Alamo and Indian Village, dines at Luby's Cafeterias and is taken by Richard to the Plaza Hotel to dance, memorialized by a pink corsage. Her aunt, her mother's older sister, wears the same lavender scent her mother used to wear. She gifts Iris a gold locket and when Iris opens it there is a cameo photo of her mother inside. Her aunt tells her that she looks exactly like her mother, bringing a sting of tears to Iris's eyes. She can sometimes hear her mother's soft voice in her mind telling her to sit up straight and to keep her napkin in her lap when she's at her aunt's dinner table.

———

ON AUGUST 10, back home, Freddie invites her to a drive-in to see *She Wore a Yellow Ribbon* with John Wayne. Two or three times a week that month, she's out with Sandy, Eddie, Jimmy, sometimes going to drive-in movies, confirmed by theater tickets cut in half, *Adam's Rib*, starring Katharine Hepburn and Spencer Tracy, *On the Town*, with Gene Kelly. On August 12 Iris and Sandy double with Melvin A. and Frances to play mini golf immortalized by a junior golf scorecard in her scrapbook along with matchbooks from an assortment of restaurants where she dined. Sometimes she pastes the entire menu in her scrapbook. When her dates come to pick her up, she feels ashamed of the dim brown furniture in the living room, the faded drapes, and the worn carpet of her modest home. But then she pushes away her shame. She's proud of her father who does his best to take care of the family.

———

NOW YELLOWED AND fraying at the edges, the paper about to crumble after seven decades, a card in Iris's scrapbook certifies that Iris Greenbaum, then a freshman soon to advance to the high school which is for sophomores, juniors, and seniors, "is a member of the staff of the *Reflector*, the Roosevelt Junior High school paper and is in good standing as a reporter. We bespeak for her the courtesies usually extended the press." A cutout from a newspaper shows that on April 23, eight members of the *Reflector* staff including Iris attended an event at Kent State for all junior and senior high school newspapers from Ohio. They interviewed the Judge and Chief Justice of the Supreme Court of Ohio. Iris is also a member of the Euclid Avenue Temple where she is a reporter for the Temple newsletter. In the Cleveland *Plain Dealer* on Saturday, March 26, a headline reads:

'Teen Town' Delights Students
of Roosevelt Junior High School

Iris is pictured holding two balloons, wearing a Peter Pan collar dress, ankle socks and black loafers, her head tilted back as if the camera caught her in a laugh with Jerry C., who is in a suit and tie and is tying another balloon around her ankle. On this page is a photo of the Heights High School building and a card that says "Sigma Delta Rho" along with an invitation to a formal Dinner Dance at the Hotel Alcazar. Does Iris like being pressed up against her date in a slow dance, or does she prefer the jitterbug and swing, or the stroll and bunny hop? I suppose it depends on the guy. In a photo of the Cleveland Heights High School class of girls, Iris is in the top row wearing a checkered jacket and smiling her signature broad smile, her hair longer now, in a bob. She's a member of the Friendship club from 1949–1950 and a member of the Athletic Service club. She's invited to attend the Science club for her interest and success in the study of science, and to join the Junior Literary Club. "The members of the Junior Literary club would like very much for Iris Greenbaum to join their group. It has always been considered an honor to be extended this invitation. You have been chosen because of your grades in English and your appreciation of good literature. Signed by Abbie Sabin, President." On Valentine's Day, the school paper announces Iris participated with the Soph Friendship Club in a skit entitled "In Loveland." As I continue to turn the pages, I can't help but feel a tug of regret. Iris had so many interests in high school, and writing was one of them. What might Iris have become if she had grown up in a different era and pursued some of her talents?

Iris's artful scrapbook qualifies as master class. She includes illustrations of a couple in a tux and evening gown dancing with hearts around them. A cigar someone gave her. Postcards and business cards, ribbons and tinsel.

On November 4, "Don't Forget the K.D.G. Dance Tonight at Fosters" with Jerry.

With Phil to the Vogue theatre and then to a double A House party on Oct. 15.

On Oct. 17, a date with Burt and then to get pizza with Barbara and Mort.

What fun! December 24, a date with Marv S. to the Playhouse to see "Life with Mother" and then to a Sig Phi Dinner Dance!

———

SOME NIGHTS I imagine Iris stumbles home late and tiptoes up the stairs so as not to wake her family. In her bedroom, she turns on the little desk lamp and pastes in a rose corsage that still gives off its sweet scent. It's important for her to record, to not forget. To remember.

Sometimes she can't sleep—the house is so quiet—and she wishes she had her mother to talk to and share her secret thoughts. She's envious of many of her girlfriends at school who seem so carefree, without carrying the weight of their childhoods on their backs, as if they do not secretly wish that their mother had never wanted another child because it is a sin to curse one's brother, and because deep down she loves him, as if childhood is over when it never is. Finally, sleep comes, and it is a relief. The next morning, a lazy Sunday, she awakes to the sound of her little brother pounding on her door to come down for breakfast, the smell of blintzes rising from the kitchen. She climbs out of bed, puts on her slippers and robe in the house, drafty to save on heating bills, puts on her cheery face with her wide grin and greets her father at the breakfast table with a hug around his shoulders. She tugs on her brother's ear to tease him, and he brushes her hand away.

———

IT'S 1950, IRIS is seventeen. In Iris's Yearbook Bob writes:

Never have I had such trouble before with any one girl. But no kidding, it's been worth it. I hope it keeps up for a while. Take care of yourself and luck always, Bob.

What does Iris make of this? What kind of trouble is he referring to? They go to the Palace theater to see *Cinderella*, then to a dance at a hotel where they double with Chuck B. and Helen S. Next a Saint Patrick's Day party with Bob, the night memorialized by a green three leaf clover and party hat. Off with Bob to the Allen theater to see *Frances* then to a Friar King and Queen Dance. Another night they see *Our Town* by Thornton Wilder. On April 5 Bob escorts Iris to the Western Reserve Freshman, Sophomore, Junior/Semi-Formal at a hotel. Then a Spring formal from Kappa Chapter of Phi Sigma Delta. Bob is a star athlete and linebacker for the Cleveland Heights High School team. Iris has pasted in her scrapbook dozens of cut out articles from the *Plain Dealer* that report the details of every game, underlining Bob's name from each newspaper clipping. Bob's the one Iris thinks about when she's in the care home, regrets she didn't marry him when he proposed to her years after Milt died. I wonder what other regrets she bore.

———

ON JUNE 8, 1950, another date with Bob to attend his graduation and then a dance at Fosters, and then Manners Big Boy after for a late-night bite to eat. Oh, look, there's the red toothpick from Bob's sandwich. On June 29, Bob takes her to the Palace Theater to see Ella Fitzgerald and Jimmy Durante! On July 22 she pastes a letter in her scrapbook that says:

> Please report for work on Sat. July 22 at 9:30 for work at the May Company department store.

The beginning of Iris's retail career at seventeen.

——

I LOVE IRIS'S obsessive and meticulous desire to record the good times, the constant dating and going out, the joining of clubs, societies, and groups decorating her scrapbook with napkins and corsages, matchbooks and ticket stubs. Surely, it's partly the post-war mentality that drives all the social activities in Iris's cohort. It's a time of peace and healing. For her, it is a world where she can forget the weight of what her humble family has endured. In some of her photos of this time, she is with a few of her girlfriends, all in two-piece bathing suits, sunning on the banks of Lake Erie laughing; in others, she's with one of her beaus, an arm casually slung over her shoulder, her head tossed back, looking flirty and fun.

——

MAYBE BOB'S THE one who will know who she really is even though she's a closed book, keeping everything locked up, always presenting the best side of herself. In her junior year she's dating him exclusively. In her scrapbook shines a photo of him, good-looking, with blond hair parted to the side, high cheekbones, square chin. They venture to the Fairmount Theatre to see *Summer Stock*. Iris tapes a napkin from "Bob's Sandwich" in her scrapbook. Later to the Richmond theater to see *My Blue Heaven* on October 21, 1950. On November 4, 1950, to All School Party and out for spaghetti. Iris records a newspaper heading called "Dept. of Congratulations." It's a contract for Bob after he graduates to play with the Cleveland Browns. He has scored eleven out of the twenty-one Heights touchdowns.

On Nov. 3, Iris writes, *went out after the Heights Shaker Game to the Theta Dance at Fosters and then to Jake Draw restaurant* (there's a cutout from the menu). Iris receives a *corsage of 4 white carnations with a white bow from Bob.* On November 18, they go to the Vogue Theatre to see *Mister 880* and then to an I.A.T. Barn Dance at Wiegand's lake. *Bob gave me this orchid he won for being 'football star of the week,'* she pens. A little round handful of hay is taped to the black scrapbook board: *date with Bob—went to the Esquire Hayride.*

November and December are filled with matchboxes, menus, restaurant napkins, torn cinema tickets—more excursions with Bob. On November 29, she wrote:

> *Date with Bob, went to Mary Seigel's house with Bob and Jed W., then the four of us walked to Cedar Center and ate at Harvey's, and then Bob came back to my house. The Big Snow!!!!*

Bob takes her to see *I'll Get By* at the Fairmount Theatre. For Christmas, they attend a formal at the Alcazar Hotel,

the merriest of Christmas,

a cutout Iris pastes from the event. On December 23 to the Richmond theater to see *Convicted.* They watch a hockey game together at the Cleveland Arena. Bob is chosen for the Lake Erie League all-star team. In January of 1951 they venture to *The Toast of New Orleans* at the Vogue Theatre. Jan 5,

date with Bob. I went to a meeting, and then Bob called for me. Went to my house.

I turn the page to a photo of the two of them in tux and ballgown for a reunion dance at Fosters Ball Room. Iris breathless in her long silk gown. Bob tall and athletic. They attend a New Year's Eve dance together remembered by red glittered

New Year's hats. A ribbon from a "Pink Camellias" corsage from Bob decorates the same page.

"You'll Never See" from the school paper:

Sonna B.	without short hair
Barbara B.	without pep
Sue D.	without looking twice
Judy G.	Not joking
Iris Greenbaum	with a sour disposition

Song Titles

Donna B.	Temptation
Barbara B.	Sweet and Lovely
Sue D.	Charleston
Mary F.	I can't stop Talking
Sandy F.	Smoke, Smoke, Smoke that Cigarette
Iris Greenbaum	You'd Be so Nice to Come Home to.

———

DOES IRIS HAVE time for herself, working weekends at the May Company and going out most nights, to wonder if there is anything else she wants to make of her life outside the expectation of marriage and children? She harbors a heavy sorrow for her father who works so hard and whose unhappiness breaks her heart. Her aunts prod her with questions: Is he Jewish or Gentile, what does his father do, is he related to the Shapiros? She can see her aunts peek out the window when a date comes to pick her up. Aunt Florence says that a man can take all the time he needs to decide who to marry because he doesn't need to be supported. Aunt Harriet says she doesn't know what she's talking about, that a man is nothing without a good woman to take care of him. Iris knows what is expected of her.

———

A CLIP FROM the "Black & Gold" on May 4, 1951:

———

You're used to seeing all the guys throwing the balls and catching the flies. Should the "girls" take over the team, we'll try to show you how it would seem. "You're out,: she cried in a timid voice, for the umpire's job, Judy Miller's our choice. Our pitcher is the gal with the deceptive curve. Greenbaum strikes em all out with nerve . . .

———

I KNOW IT is time to stop recording from Iris's scrapbooks, there are pages and pages and pages, but I don't want to stop. It makes me happy to imagine a time when Iris was popular among her peers, studying, reporting for the school paper, taking her first job, so innocent and outgoing, falling in love, just becoming the lead player in her own life. Her family doesn't have the money to take her to fancy restaurants, to the theater or the movies, to hear music and she's clearly having a ball. Soon she will graduate and has been accepted at Ohio State, the first person in her family to attend college. What will all these memories amount to? How will they coalesce? What does Iris dream of?

———

ON JUNE 5, 1952, she is honored with her diploma from Cleveland Heights High School, which naturally makes its way into her scrapbook. Underneath it she proudly writes, "my diploma" in her neat cursive hand. Taped on the opposite page is a white tassel from her graduation hat and a ribbon from a bouquet of a dozen American Beauty peonies gifted from her proud father. Is the adoration she receives from her many admirers a precursor of future happiness or a curse? Another friend from Iris's cohort tells me that the boys groped at the girls every chance they got, but I'm not sure that Iris minded if it was a boy she was attracted to. Is what we're given early in our lives a signal of what's to come? I turn the page of her scrapbook. Something's happened. The dates with Bob have stopped. If only Iris were still here for me to ask. I feel, somehow in writing about her, I'm drawing closer to some kind of secret that will explain everything to me, as if a life can ever be fully understood or known.

———

I FIND THE page with her first date with Milt Bialosky on May 16, 1952. Milt has graduated from Miami University in Ohio with a Bachelor of Science Degree in Business on February 4, 1951, and has returned to live in Cleveland. My heart stops. This is the moment in Iris's life where everything turns but she doesn't know it yet. Doubling with Irene and Dick, Iris and Milt have tickets to the Cleveland Indians game (in her scrapbook, she pastes the face of the Cleveland Indians logo), and after, they sit at the swiveling stools at the counter of Mawby's (there's the napkin!) for the best hamburger and milkshake in town. What's different about Milt? He doesn't babble like a never-to-be-stopped stream about the weather, the football game, who's going with whom, who's driving what kind of car. He asks Iris about her family and wants to know if she'd like a slice of apple pie for dessert. What does she like to do? He radiates kindness and restraint.

In one of Iris's scrapbooks there is an article from the

newspaper with a headline that reads, **Cage, Tank Stars.**
Milt was the star of the Cage, meaning the basketball team of
Heights High School. The reporter writes:

> Red-headed, athletic and friendly describes Milt Bialosky to a T. Playing his second season as guard, Milt may bring added punch needed for a successful season.

Perhaps Iris had an eye for him, even before they dated.

———

WHEN MILT PULLS up Iris's driveway to bring her home from
a date, he walks her to the front door, takes her hand. Always
a gentleman, she told me. She feels the heat of his body and
her heart begins to pound. He's one of the first that doesn't
try to immediately kiss her on the first date. Iris surprises
herself by giving him a good night kiss on the cheek. She's
never done that before. Milt asks if he can take her out again.
And they date for months. Milt gives Iris his ID bracelet,
which means they are going steady. Iris said she knew he was
the one on their very first date. "It felt like a bell was ringing
inside me," she said.

That's not all that's changing. On June 9, 1952, Iris glues a
cutout of a woman wearing a telephone headset in her scrapbook along with a note that says she begins work at Ohio Bell
as a telephone operator for the summer before Ohio State. Her
days are spent at Ohio Bell, sitting side by side in close quarters
with other female telephone operators, inserting the appropriate
plug into its jack on the switchboard, plugging and unplugging
several hundred connections per hour. She saves the money she
earns for clothes and shoes and spending money for college. All

day she inserts the plugs and tries not to let her mind wander thinking about Milt, otherwise she'll make a mistake and get fired. After one date with Milt, she sees no one else.

———

ON JUNE TENTH just when the forsythia have shed their last yellow blossoms, Iris takes Milt's arm as he buys tickets at the Mayland Theatre box office to see *Tap Roots*. Did she wear one of those swanky neck scarfs tied to one side, cresting her chin? On June 13, they drive to Geneva. June 20 to the Heights Theater to see *Flesh and Fury*. On June 28, to a beach party in Painesville. Iris cuts out from a newspaper a man with a bandana around his neck playing the guitar on the beach along with two other beachgoers singing by the campfire. On July 2 they see *The Well* at the Fairmount Theatre. On the next page is a list of the names of the guys in the fraternity with their nicknames. Milt's nickname is Muftie. His favorite last words are, "Yes, but." On July 5, Milt escorts Iris to the BAT reunion at the Lake Shore Club. On July 6 they attend Renee and Bernard's wedding and then after to Manners Big Boy. On July 14 they go for a ride. On the sixteenth, "Milt Bialosky came over!" On July 18 they see *Clash by Night*. On July 23 they venture to Howard Johnson's, famous for their fried clams. (In Iris's scrapbook is a cutout of an ice-cream cone next to the Howard Johnson logo.) Iris sits across from Milt in a booth, he's telling her a joke and she laughs.

Yes, she's taking in his hair the color of an Irish setter and light freckles, fair skin. He's older and more mature than the boys she's been dating. There's something about him that exudes comfort. How he asks her what she'd like, making sure she orders first. He's well-mannered, kind, and selfless, always opening the car door for her, taking her hand, and holding an umbrella over her head when it rains. Hayrides, Cedar Point, Geneva on the Lake. On August 6, a drive to the Mayland to see *King Kong*. Iris cuts out a picture of the gorilla from the newspaper for her scrapbook. Does she curl into Milt's arms when King Kong threatens? Does Milt cup her breast in the dark? Wrap Iris in the broad sweep of his arms? After the show, they eat hamburgers again at Mawby's. *Tell me about yourself*, I imagine Milt asks. Iris is confounded. *What's there to tell*, she teases.

Iris pastes in her scrapbook Milt's first business card he must have given to her:

MILT BIALOSKY
Realtor The Elliot-Guest Co., Cleveland Heights Ohio.

On Saturday Iris is invited to Milt's house where they "ate ribs." This is monumental. She can't remember if she's ever been invited to the home of a boy she's dating. She's nervous about meeting his parents. Why should she be? Milt won't leave her side for a minute. And Iris, too, is raised with good manners. She feels Milt's mother's eyes on her and senses approval. Milt's father is quiet, but his brimming eyes show her that he approves, too. They see *The Wild Heart*. Afterward they slip into Milt's car. She trusts the outline of his long sturdy nose, his warm chocolate-colored eyes, and strong shoulders underneath his V-neck sweater, can smell the pomade in his hair and Aqua Velva coming from his freshly shaved face.

Is this when Milt tells Iris he loves her? Or is he toggling between wanting to say it and restraint. He's moved on from his first job in real estate to form his own real estate company business with a partner. It's called Summit-Bailey, Bailey instead of Bialosky because Milt can't use a Jewish name when selling real estate in gentile neighborhoods. Milt is a real catch, his face already pressed to the glass of success. Like Iris, he, too, wants to escape his smothering family, his mother who always worries about him because of the rheumatic fever he had as a child, the guilt he bears for his father who works so hard in the pawnshop later turned jewelry store to support the family and send him to college. What the young couple don't understand is that to their parents, they offer hope for the future. When Milt comes for dinner, Iris's aunts lather his plate with more brisket and potatoes, convince him to take one more slice of honey cake one more piece of apricot rugelach. Earlier they made sure the table was laid with their finest linens, china, and silver. Iris beams as she hears Milt speak to her father about his new business venture. Later when Milt leaves, reserved Aunt Harriet is giddy with happiness, but she won't say one word out of fear of jinxing it.

———

ALL THAT SUMMER Milt and Iris have dated and now she's off to her first quarter of college at Ohio State. Milt can't bear to be apart from her. Iris said he used to drive all the way there to see her. Sometimes just to pick her up from class in his leather bomber jacket to take her for ice cream. She's dressed in either her plaid pleated skirt or a full swing skirt over layers of crinolines with a button-up blouse or sweater, and Milt's eyes move from the top of her head all the way down to her ankles as if starstruck. It elicits that indescribable feeling in Iris's chest, that can't-stop-thinking-of-you smile. Milt loves that Iris makes him feel special. She never holds back her appreciation. It's one of her best qualities.

Perhaps when Iris comes home for the weekend, they park near Shaker Lakes to witness the stars and the crescent moon over the lapping water. They drive to the Mayflower, to Dairy Queen, to the Navy vs. Notre Dame game. Navy wins 17 to 6. Off to Morocco's and the vast Vogue with its smell of buttered popcorn and spilled Coke on the theater floor. A cutout of a martini glass. A Life Savers candy wrapper she wins playing a game called Toyland at a party at Joe and Sylvia's.

How long will Milt wait? The end of the war has spawned "a rush of young Americans into marriage, parenthood, and traditional gender roles," as *Time* magazine says in an article analyzing post–World War II teens' social norms. Is this what's on the horizon for Iris? No one brings a date home for dinner with the family otherwise. Maybe it's true. He really does love her. The excitement sends her stomach into turmoil. It's where she holds her trauma and anticipation. When she feels this way, it's hard for her to concentrate on Milt's words. She's never witnessed a man look at her as if he could see into the very being of her soul. Sometimes it scares her—to be seen. Milt makes her laugh, and laughing with someone is deep. Iris doesn't yet know that falling in love is like a precious dream. Later she will learn that if it happens once in a lifetime, you are lucky. "I can't believe he chose me," Iris says, again, and again, and again.

13.

Iris Yvonne Greenbaum is born on December 31, 1933, just an hour short of being a New Year's Day baby. Iris is born during the Great Depression. Hitler rises to power in Germany and becomes führer in August of the following year. Lillian and Eugene Greenbaum are from Hungarian descent. Cleveland is known for its Hungarian Jewish community, and the area in which they live, once nicknamed Little Hungary with the largest population of Hungarians outside Budapest, is the neighborhood that my relatives called home.

Eugene married his much younger wife Lilian Hurwitz, originally from San Antonio, Texas, in Cleveland on August 16, 1931. He was thirty-three years old. I wish I knew how they met and how Lillian ended up in Cleveland, but it is a story I was never told, only that they were deeply in love and that Eugene would do anything his young wife asked.

Eugene is a bank teller, and Lillian is studying to become a teacher, but she puts that aside to build her family. In one photo, Eugene has his pipe in his mouth, and he is wearing pantaloons, suspenders, and a white shirt. Lillian's arm is swung around his neck, clutching his shoulder, and Eugene holds her other hand in his. Lillian is in a long sleeveless sun-dress, head thrown back in laughter. In another photo, Lillian is lying in the grass, her dark hair parted to the side, sweeping past her shoulders, her hands behind her, propping her up. She's in a swimsuit of the era with a belt across her hips, and trunks that hit her thighs. She has my mother's long legs and large bust and she's smiling for the camera. Other photos show them at the beach, playing in the water. In another, Lillian is with a girlfriend, and they are teasingly sitting on the hood of a Model T car in bathing suits with their feet pressed against the spare tire. In another, Eugene is in his bathing suit with a crop of dark wavy hair, looking as blissful as I've ever seen him, sitting on the grass. Lillian is playfully straddling his shoulders with her bare legs swung in front of his upper body and he's holding each one in his hands.

———

DURING THE LONG afternoons, while Eugene works at the bank, little Iris and her mother bake sugar and orange cookies in the warmth of the yellow and green tiled kitchen. Iris takes in her mother's slender hand as she stirs the cookie dough, follows her mother's every move, breathes in her lavender scent, and the sight of the wave of her dark hair that shines when it catches the light. She feels as if she possesses her mother's warm and kind heart. She's the center of Iris's world. Before she starts school, Iris has her mother all to herself when her father is at work. Her mother greets her when she comes home from school with a glass of milk and two cookies on a small plate. Lillian calls her daughter her little helper, her darling Iris. Iris follows her mother around the table to set it for dinner. Lillian instructs that the knife's blade angles toward the plate and that the soup spoon belongs next to the knife. Iris trails after her when Lillian loads the washing machine and then hands her mother the clothespins from a little basket, helping her hang the laundry on the line to dry. Lillian is a talented seamstress. She sews draperies and slipcovers, and stitches pillows for their home's modest rooms, as well as makes dresses and blouses for herself and her daughter. Iris likes to sit next to her mother as she embroiders a pillowcase, watching in awe as one stitch goes into the fabric and then out the other side of the cloth. She marvels at all the things her mother can do. How she's always there when Iris needs her. How she wakes her up in the mornings with a smile and a kiss, calls her darling, braids her hair, helps her choose what dress she wants to wear. Sometimes she chants "Pop Goes the Weasel" or "Hey Diddle Diddle the Cat and the Fiddle" and little Iris laughs and sings along with her.

Every day is nearly the same, breakfast at the little aluminum table in the kitchen, always warm oatmeal or cream of wheat with hot milk and honey, fresh orange juice, toast with her mother's preserved jams. Lillian packs a lunch of whatever is left over from dinner the night before, brisket or chicken sandwiches for Eugene to take to the bank. They tease each other, and sometimes Eugene pats Lillian's tuchus playfully when she's by the sink or leans over to kiss her neck. Once Eugene leaves the house for the bank, Lillian turns to Iris and teases her that they can do whatever they want now that Poppa's gone. Iris laughs at her mother's subterfuge. Iris plays with the rag doll her mother made for her while Lillian cleans the breakfast dishes, vacuums the house, and does all her chores. Afterward they go out the back door to have a spot of fresh air. If it is a nice day, they'll go to the backyard, where there is a small swing set for Iris. Before nap time, Lillian reads her a chapter from *The Little House on the Prairie*. It's like being wrapped in a soft blanket all day.

————

HOME FROM A long day at work, Eugene retreats into the den, lights his pipe with its cherry-smelling tobacco, relaxes on his cushioned armchair, reads the Cleveland *Plain Dealer* and then *The Jewish News*, and listens intently to the reports on the radio. He hears Franklin Roosevelt's first inaugural address, "the only thing we have to fear is fear itself—nameless, unreasoning, unjustified terror." And indeed, Eugene is terrified. There's little money and anti-Semitism is growing. For a time, they take in Max, a boarder who has a room on the third floor of their side of the house to help with expenses. Eugene grasps Lillian by the hand and sweeps her onto his lap, and they embrace. As long as they are together, as long as they are happy, it's enough.

Eugene's tired from being on his feet all day at the bank. Sometimes, he grows irritable, worrying about money and supporting his family on a bank teller's salary. He's the oldest of six siblings and feels its weight on his back. So many of his cohort are unemployed. If he snaps, Lillian bites her tongue. "Men don't like to be criticized," she whispers to Iris. "They like to be pampered. You'll see." Lillian enters the den, kissing her husband's cheek, and Eugene softens. He is crazy about his wife and will do anything she asks, even though he hides his feelings because if he lets them out, he's afraid he'll never be able to stuff them back. He doesn't know how he got so lucky. Every

Friday, he brings home a bouquet of flowers for his wife, and Lillian gets up on her tiptoes to kiss him. Lillian leads him to the supper table. She's dressed it in a white lace tablecloth with cloth napkins, always their best china, and then calls Iris from her bedroom to join them. During the week, the three dine alone, happy to have a break from Eugene's overbearing sisters and mother. Lillian's family is far away in San Antonio. Lillian buys her groceries at the kosher butchers and delicatessens along the strip on Woodland Avenue. She bakes challah for Sabbath and Iris helps her roll out the dough. There is always a pot of chicken soup on one of the burners of her stove. After dinner, they may listen to one of the children's programs on the radio, *Little Orphan Annie* or *Hit Parade*.

Lillian squeezes into Iris's twin bed every night before bed and kisses her forehead. Iris takes in her lavender scent, and they whisper *Now I lay me down to sleep, I pray the Lord my soul to keep. For if I die before I wake, I pray the Lord my soul to take.*

Sometimes, Iris doesn't want her mother to leave and pretends she's afraid of the dark. Her mother tells her there is nothing to fear and snuggles her daughter close, telling her she'll keep the little light on in the hallway. Her mother's love is so big that it is as if they share the same soul.

On Shabbat, it's off to Eugene's mother's house for dinner, where the entire Greenbaum family gathers. Gizella Greenbaum, called Gizzie, is the matriarch of the family. Iris calls her Grandma Cookie because she always bakes cookies for her granddaughter. Her husband, Jerome, was born in Hungary in 1870 and immigrated to the United States in 1883. He witnessed the May Day Riots, a series of violent demonstrations against the city leaders after the unemployment rate in

Cleveland shot up, causing the Panic of 1893. He struggles to make ends meet with a family of six children. Grandma Cookie is always stooped over a pot in the kitchen, she, too, has bags underneath her eyes, worrying about her six grown children—because what mother doesn't worry—wearing an apron around her thin waist, serving matzoh ball soup, noodle kugel, and baked chicken to the family but never sitting down herself even though her children scold her.

———

ON THE WEEKENDS, you can find Eugene, an avid gardener, in the backyard. He boasts a vegetable garden abundant with tomatoes, cucumbers, and peppers in the summer for Lillian to add to her repertoire and bring to the table. He mows the lawn, trims the shrubs, tends to his prized rose bush. He feels most at home with his hands in the dirt, enjoying the bounty that springs forth from his hard work. In the backyard is a splash pool for Iris to play in while Lillian sits beside her on a garden chair, her sewing on her lap. In the rear of the house is a screened-in porch that overlooks the backyard. Eugene likes to sit there at night to feel the cool breeze, smoking his pipe and staring at his darkened garden.

As the Nazis begin to take over Europe, Jewish refugees are looking to escape. Still, most Americans are opposed to taking in Jews out of worries that the immigrants might strain the slowly recovering US economy. Anti-Semitism is spreading, fueled by fear and mistrust. It is best to stay at home, to be invisible.

Since funds are tight, Lillian wears only the dresses she makes herself. She neatly irons the napkins and tablecloth for

dinner. In photos, I can see she has my same wide forehead and
nose. She calls her daughter, *darling Iris*. Iris, the tall purple
flower, is the center of her family's universe; the radius from
which all things seem possible, the center from which everything, all color, and all movement unfolds. She is the darling
of the extended family.

Eugene's two married sisters, Aunt Horty and Aunt Harriet, could never have children. They adore Iris. His third sister, Aunt Florence, is what would then have been known as a
spinster. She works at May Company as a secretary and reads
paperback romance novels at night. She is said to have once
been in love with a married man, but she never wed. A worrier,
she's always asking Iris to put on a sweater because there's a chill
in the house. She worries her niece is too thin, and constantly
examines Iris's plate at dinner urging her to take a second helping. Florence's other heartbreak is her twin sister, also named
Lillian, but referred to as Lily, who has lived in an institution
ever since a breakdown when she was nineteen. The story is
that Lily was in love with a gentile, but her father refused to
let her marry him and this sent her into a psychotic break.
Florence and Lillian are proof it is better to read about love
than suffer a broken heart. (Years later, when Gizella moved
in with her daughter Florence, they slept in the same bedroom
in twin beds, one of which once belonged to Lily.)

Then there's sophisticated Aunt Harriet, who always
dresses elegantly in her sweater and skirts with pearl clip-on
earrings and a string of pearls, hair in a perfect bun, married
to Uncle Joe, a dentist, and veteran of World War I. Harriet
is a homemaker, an excellent cook, and Iris's favorite aunt.
She has mementos in her small, immaculate apartment from

when Uncle Joe was in the service and they traveled to foreign countries. A miniature shoe from Denmark. A fan from Asia. A beautiful porcelain bell she acquired when Uncle Joe was stationed in England that now sits on a shelf in my New York apartment.

Aunt Horty, with her skin wrinkled and permanently tanned from the Florida sun, her voice hoarse from chain-smoking, and her hair always in a French twist, is the family's glamorous sister. She lives in Daytona Beach with grumpy, handsome Uncle Charlie. When she comes home for a visit, the whole family gathers. Uncle Jimmy is Eugene's brother. In the fashion business, he's the wealthiest of the family, with a big house in Gates Mills and a German shepherd named Duke.

There are at least twenty or more relatives seated across long, immaculately set tables to read from the Haggadah on Passover. Jimmy is married to Aunt Margaret, and they have two children, Iris's cousins, Francie and Mark. On the table are cut-up radishes in the shape of roses, dill pickles, scallions, long slivers of carrots, and celery. Aunt Harriet brings over her famous homemade chopped liver she serves on mini rye bread. As I write this, I'm proud of my humble, hardworking, devoted family who held each other together when times were tough. I feel its deep roots when the matzoh is broken and passed around the Pesach table, symbolizing brokenness and freedom.

Lillian and Eugene want to have another child. Lillian is pregnant again when Iris is seven. Eugene works overtime at the bank to put away more money, expecting a new mouth to feed. The house reverberates with anticipation. After Lillian gives birth, congratulatory telegrams come through the wire; phone calls are made from one relative to another, cigars are passed. But the baby—a boy—catches a fever and dies two days later in the hospital. Lillian is beside herself with grief. Unable to sleep at night, she comes into Iris's room and scoots in next to her to ensure her only daughter's heart is beating. That is what losing a baby does to you. It makes you crazy with grief.

Within the year, Lillian is pregnant again. Eugene hopes the new baby will help to take away some of his wife's grief. Iris is excited to have a baby brother or sister, but truth be told, she still wants her mother all to herself. The pregnancy is difficult. Lillian lies down most afternoons; often she's too tired to put supper on the table. Grandma Cookie comes over to help care for Iris and Eugene and cook for them. Lillian falls sick with scarlet fever. It's rampant in the community. Her fever spikes, she has a terrible rash and an unbearably sore throat, and aspirin can't seem to control the fever. The danger is that the infection can spread to other parts of the body. This is before antibiotics. The disease is so infectious that families were told to quarantine. In some households, physicians or public health officials put a note on people's doors to protect others from the fever. The mortality rate for scarlet fever in the 1930s and 1940s was 20 percent, and hundreds of thousands of cases occurred in the United States, though mostly in children. Little Iris must be quarantined from her mother.

Lillian's water breaks when she is still sick with the fever. In terrible pain, she goes into labor at home on March 16, 1943. She is thirty-two years old. Eugene rushes her to the hospital. He paces the linoleum floor of the hospital waiting room under its too bright lights, praying for his wife.

Lillian dies giving birth. It is a tragedy beyond comprehension, the first time in Cleveland history that a baby is born after the mother has died, and the news is written up in the local paper and *The Jewish News*. The entire family is in shock. It's like a Greek tragedy. The closest I can recall is Rhea, wife of Cronus. He made Rhea swallow her children out of fear that they would take over his kingdom. After the fifth child died, Rhea tricked Cronus and swallowed a rock to save her son. But must a mother die to save her child? The motherless baby is named Lawrence, a name too old for a baby. Iris is crushed by grief. Who knows if she howled when she learned her mother died or whether her tears were shed in private, weeping into the chest of the rag doll her mother made for her. Poor little Iris, a loss so improbable it will shape the rest of her life. She can't believe she will only see her mother again in her dreams and memories. In the short and impactful length of childhood, which feels endless to a child, this is the day Iris will always remember. And poor Eugene. His grief makes him flail about in his garden, sometimes cursing his shovel, pulling out weeds from his flower beds. And poor baby Larry who will never know his mother.

Even as I write this, the story takes on a life of its own. I cannot fathom what this loss has done to Iris. Whenever I try to imagine it my fingers refuse the keyboard, but I must press on. Of course, the irony does not escape me; it is the death of my father at the age of two that has informed every facet of my own life. This is something my mother and I share: the loss of a parent. Iris was emboldened by nine loving years with her mother. Losing my father at two years old, he was more a phantom. Still, these losses mark us in ways often hidden from us.

But let's return to darling Iris. It is the moment, just nine years old, when her idyllic world cracks. For isn't a mother's doting love a luxury and balm? The longing to have her mother back to braid her hair, comfort her, and tell her she is the most darling of daughters creates a cavern in Iris's young heart. You'll find her sitting by the window in her nightgown and robe; perhaps it is snowing, and the air is heavy with absence as the lawn fills. Perhaps she is chasing the snowdrops on her window with a finger. There's an ache inside her that will always be there. Every child keeps her mother within herself. I think of Iris, seventy-nine years later, looking out the care home window for a fraction of a second, perhaps remembering her mother and the smell of her lavender perfume when she put her to sleep at night.

———

WHAT DOES NINE-YEAR-OLD Iris make of her baby brother? Will she unconsciously blame him for her mother's death? Would Lillian have survived scarlet fever if she hadn't been pregnant? What is death to a child but longing. *Nothing is ever the same again.* Nobody speaks about Iris's mother after she dies. "That's just the way the Greenbaums were. Perhaps they thought it would upset me," my mother told me. But Lillian's beautiful ghost forever reigns in the Greenbaums' tight-knit family. The dead never leave us is Iris's mantra. Lillian lived on in Iris, and now Iris lives in me, and in the stories we tell about them.

———

MARCH IS COLD in Cleveland and the snow is black with dirt, frozen and ugly, piled along the streets. Icicles drop from the roof of the house and crack. The sky is gray and low and spits out a drizzle of rain. On a Saturday or Sunday, even if it's bitterly cold, Iris likes to be outside, to escape the silent drama inside her house. Some days, she's furious; other days, sadness seeps into her bones like a deep chill. Suddenly, every day is longer than it was the last. In her mind, she hears her mother's voice say to make sure she brushes her teeth, washes her hair once a week, and sits up straight at the dinner table. In bed, she hears her mother softly recite the same prayer they said together every night of Iris's young life, that will be passed down to me by my mother. Now, it's her aunt or grandmother that offers her cookies and milk when she comes home from school. But she's lost her appetite. Sometimes, she laughs to herself when she hears her grandmother say something in Yiddish, chiding one of her daughters because if her mother was alive, she'd have looked at Iris and playfully rolled her eyes and said not to bother. Sometimes she wants to block her ears against the gaggle of her relatives always at her feet, telling her not to forget her hat or gloves, scolding her to finish the food on her plate. Why won't they talk about or even mention her mother? Then, there's motherless baby Larry crying in his crib, and Iris must comfort him.

———

AFTER LILLIAN DIES, Eugene's sister Horty moves in temporarily from Florida to take care of Iris and her baby brother. Aunt Horty's husband, Charlie, is in the navy. When he returns from duty, it's Harriet's turn. Her husband, Joe, is also in the service. Then it's Grandma Cookie's turn. Grandma

Cookie and Iris's aunts dote on her, dress her up in pretty dresses, braid her hair too tight, sometimes pinning the braids on top of her head in a wreath, making sure she's wearing a hat and gloves when it's cold outside, worry she's not eating enough, bringing her a sweater when she's playing with her dolls, so she will not catch a draft. Grandma Cookie's the one who watches the refrigerator and calculates all the meals while keeping to a strict budget because they are poor. On Shabbas, the aunts are on top of Iris to eat more, passing her whipped mashed potatoes, slices of brisket, and more kugel on her plate. She doesn't have a big appetite. And her mother is not here to tell them to stop. Iris is nine years old in 1942 and World War II is raging. This explains why her relatives are always so nervous and afraid when Iris goes to school, waiting by the door for her to come home, but she doesn't fully comprehend what is happening. She doesn't want to always be near her aunts and grandmother, with their sour breath she smells hovering over her, their thoughts inside her, eagle eyes on her, watching her every move. All she wants is her own space where she can remember her dead mother. Her father is so devoted to his only daughter, Iris, that he decides he won't wed again until Iris is married. He doesn't want his daughter to feel he'd taken a new wife to replace his beloved Lillian.

———

AUNT FLORENCE, IN a button-down cardigan in a pretty color from the May Company where she works, once wanted to be a vaudeville star. She sings Iris vaudeville tunes to entertain her.

My Momma told me she would buy me a rubber dolly,
if I be good, but don't you tell her I got a fella,
she won't buy me a rubber dolly.

Aunt Florence dances and points her index finger back and forth while she sings, her thinning white hair parted to the side with a bow attached to a bobby pin to hold the strands back. Iris giggles and claps her hands, forever devoted to making her family happy. Even if she's annoyed, she still claps; her mother told her to never hurt anyone's feelings.

———

IN SEVERAL PHOTOS of Eugene and Iris, Eugene carries Iris in his arms or holds her hand as if he's afraid to let go. One weekend, he takes her to New York City for a diversion and hence a photo of the two of them with the Statue of Liberty in the background. Eugene's world crumbled once his beloved died. He doesn't know what to make of it, or how to fill the blankness. How to stop himself from thinking of his wife's warm, soft body pressed up against him at night, her wide grin.

———

EVERY SUNDAY, THE Greenbaum family pack themselves in their car and go on a family outing to see Lily at the institution. Iris waits in the backseat with her baby brother while the rest of the family visits. Iris looks out the car window at the brown brick of the institutional walls in wonder and bewilderment, her aunt Lily locked in the attic like the mad woman in *Jane Eyre*. Her brother, Larry, blows on the car's windowpane to write his name in the steamy fog. Years later, in early March of

1949, Jerome Greenbaum, Iris's grandfather, Eugene's father, will take his own life. The cause, we were later told, was heavy financial burdens that had never ceased to stop vexing him, but who really knows? I think of this legacy of mental pain in my family, my great-grandfather's suicide, Lily's institutionalization, which was rarely talked about in her family's life, my mother's bouts with depression, and Kim's suicide. When I became an adult and was struggling to stay afloat, I feared, too, that the disease would catch me. I eventually learned that working, reading, writing help to keep an anxious mind at bay.

———

POOR IRIS NEVER has a moment to herself. Her aunts and uncles press shiny coins in Iris's palms on holidays. They dress her up like a doll in velvet dresses with a thick bow at the neck, matching gloves, and a hat when they go to the temple or to another relative's house, at a loss as to how they can make up for what she's lost. Iris feels suffocated by all the attention. They dote, coddle, tell her how pretty she looks, *isn't she the spitting image of her mother?* They instill in her that a woman's role is to run the house and take care of the family and that a husband's role is to be the breadwinner. As Iris grows into a woman, she receives positive attention from the boys she dates, and her classmates for how pretty and kind she is, for her knockout figure. She knows what her relatives expect of her: that she'll find a good man to marry who will always take care of her. What was supposed to happen, and what happened instead? I wish I could intercede. Pull her by the arm, tell her there is more to her than being an accouterment to a man. More than her beauty. Allow her to grieve for her mother, to talk about her loss, to expand her horizons. There she is, in my mind, pressed up against the bathroom mirror in her dressing room in our house on Lytle Road, putting on her lipstick and mascara, pinching her cheeks, spraying perfume on that little spot on the back of her wrists, just as she taught me to do.

Epilogue

It is October 2022, a year and a half since my mother died. The days go by so quickly but writing slows them down. We forget what we want to hold on to, and we remember what we long to forget. I know I'll never get it all and so I must find a way to the end. I'm taking my first trip back to Cleveland for the setting of the headstone. In the Jewish religion, it's customary for the stone setting to take place a year after the Kaddish mourning period, typically eleven to twelve months. But once again, the pandemic does not permit us to return the following April. Still, in October, the leaves on the trees, before they shed their summer burdens, are in all their colorful glory to greet us. There is a cool breeze in the air and dampness that predicts a rain shower.

Endings are always sad—and somehow knowing I will see the headstone for the first time marks for me an ending, but perhaps also a beginning. It is a time to acknowledge how deeply the choices and accidents of life—my mother's— informed my own choices, decisions, and direction. We are all part of the history of our families. As I prepare the short eulogy I will say at the graveside, I find myself writing about the heroism with which my mother approached her losses and misfortunes, even if, during certain moments in my life, I didn't see her as heroic. "In the end is my beginning," wrote T. S. Eliot in the section of the *Four Quartets*, called *East Coker*. In those lines, he alludes to the circuity of his life and his own spiritual journey. "What we call the beginning is often the end/And to make an end is to make a beginning./The end is where we start from," he writes in Little Gidding. "We shall not cease from exploration/And the end of all our exploring/Will be to arrive where we started/And know the place for the first time."

Inherent is the notion that parts of ourselves are concealed from us but always known to ourselves, hidden because we are not always able to deal with the torment and suffering that make us want to forget. We are each an entity, no matter the beginning or the end. The end is my mother's beginning, too, and my beginning. And in the end is the beginning of who we are. The end and the beginning are in each one of us.

———

THE ENDING OF a book for its writer is bittersweet. It means letting go of the preoccupation with the book's subject. Letting go is like slowly watching the autumn leaves change color before they die off, as if in their bright reds and oranges, they are asking us not to look away until they are finished with their dying. Somehow an equilibrium has settled in. For to write is to know and to bear witness.

———

THE PURPOSE OF the stone setting is to let mourners see where the grave is and to honor the deceased, to remind people of the lost one's deeds. Months earlier in New York, I worked by phone with a small memorial mason company in Cleveland to design Iris's headstone. I shared color options with my sisters by text. The sympathetic employee at the company—how many grievers had she counseled in her years—told me not to worry that we couldn't set the stone exactly a year after Iris died, as is the Jewish practice. The ground has been too cold anyway, she reassured me. We selected a grayish-pink granite stone our mother would have chosen; it will glitter in the light. To compose the engraving involved more back and forth with my sisters. We finally settled on a short phrase and a drawing of an iris, my mother's namesake flower:

Iris Yvonne Bialosky
December 31, 1933–March 29, 2020
May her beautiful soul rest.

On the Fourth of Nisan, a month in the Jewish calendar, before the stone is set, Laura visits our mother's grave without its headstone. The ground on top of where she's buried is filled with cracked mud but there are beautiful small stones everywhere over it and small fistfuls of grass sprouting, she reports via text.

"Death exists, not as the opposite but as a part of life," the novelist Haruki Murakami says in *Norwegian Wood*, and on this day, it feels true. I am released only in the physical sense. I no longer must travel to see my mother; I no longer must worry about how she is being cared for, whether she is in pain, lonely, or neglected. I want to remember her before the disease took hold. But I am not released from grief.

I've passed through something though it is impossible to

articulate exactly. I'm happy to no longer shoulder worry and the need to care for my mother. I know and I wish I could have done more.

I hear my mother's voice when I put on a sweater and feel an itch because the label is still attached. When I scold our puppy who is barking, I hear myself say "sha," something my mother used to say when she wanted quiet. When I set the table for a dinner party, I remember how carefully she set her own table, choosing the right tablecloth, linen napkins, never paper. I boil noodles, and when draining them remember always to run cold water over the noodles to stop them from continuing to cook, as she taught me. Never wash your face with soap, she told me; it will dry your skin. Wash your underclothes by hand, never put them in the washing machine. When I drive in the car and hold up my hands to view my nails, I remember my mother doing the same gesture to admire her manicure. When I brake suddenly, and a passenger is in the seat next to me, I shoot my arm out, the same way my mother used to, to protect me from hitting the dashboard. I call my son "honey," as my mother used to call me. I remember to smile, even when I'm sad. I choose kindness, as my mother always did. And I imagine, too, that some of what she had taught me, she may have learned from her own mother, those precious nine years of her early life she had with her, and reflect upon what I now bequeath to my own son, and marvel over how we are shaped by those we love.

———

AS IN MANY families, any kind of family event tends to elicit old emotions, anxieties, and behavior. One sister wants the date of the unveiling one weekend, another wants it another weekend and suddenly it's *why are you so controlling? Why do you get to decide which weekend? Are you telling me or asking me?* and before you know it, no one is speaking to each other. And so, by October's arrival, one sister isn't coming to the luncheon we planned after the stone setting. She stands on one side of the wide green lawn underneath a black umbrella because, of course, it is raining. It seems as if it is always raining in Cleveland. I don't like to see her alone, but I can't yet find it in me to intercede. I want only to be focused on my mother. You would think that feelings would mend between sisters when mourning our mother, but inexplicably, it only causes more emotional distance; our guards are up. Feelings tucked away. Each of us needing to preserve our emotional fuel. Eventually, we will give in and let go of our differences. We are forever intertwined.

The rain comes down in buckets and then slowly subsides. It is as if the dampness is in our bones, the gray skies part of the inner layer of our consciousness. We drive through the winding roads of the cemetery, the gravestones awash in rain so that they are like shiny little soldiers lined up, ready to defend the spirit of the afterlife. I look at these rows and rows of gravestones. So many relatives, so many families, and suddenly it seems a safe place to go to rest. We follow the line of cars pulled over, looking for section 108, row P, grave 47. My mother is supposed to be buried next to my sister Kim, but there was a mix-up at the funeral home. After Kim died, Aunt Harriet bought the plot next to Kim's for my mother. I had vaguely remembered that Aunt Harriet had reserved the plot in 2000, but it turned out that the grave deed was under the last name Iris took when she remarried. In 2015 when we did the paperwork for our mother before she could be admitted to Menorah Park, Iris had changed her name back to Bialosky. She didn't reclaim her first husband's name after her divorce when Kim was alive, not wanting her to be the only one in the family with a different surname, but once Kim was gone there was no reason for her to continue to use her second husband's last name. The funeral home did not connect the names, and hence, unknowingly, two plots were saved for Iris—one next to my sister's grave and the other under Bialosky a few rows above. By the time the mystery is solved, the funeral home has already buried my mother. To unearth her would cost more money. Too, we worried that moving her might be spiritually negative or harmful. The rabbi did not like the idea either, after Laura called to ask. Hence, my sister is buried a few rows above her mother in the same section of the cemetery. One of us will claim the other plot.

I think about my father and Iris's wish to be with him in the afterlife. Their union formed the sustenance and courage which allowed my mother to endure. It was the foundation of the staircase she climbed, bolstered by the hope that her spirit would be reunited with his and the two will be lovers again in heaven. In a strange way, I understand because despite never truly knowing my father, I've always felt his essence and his love for me. That was undeniable. I know, too, that I chose to marry the kind of husband my father was to my mother—sturdy, loving, responsible. And that is my mitzvah, intuitively passed down to me by my parents' union.

———

IRIS YVONNE BIALOSKY'S unveiling ceremony consists of the recitation of psalms, a brief eulogy from the rabbi encapsulating characteristics of the deceased collected from his conversations with her daughters, removing the cloth covering the headstone, the El Maleh Rahami prayer, which asks that the departed be granted proper rest, and the Mourners Kaddish. After the rabbi says a few words about Iris and her life and recites the prayers, we three sisters each give short eulogies. I speak about the losses my mother suffered and how she endured, and as I say the words aloud, I feel enormously proud of her heroism in the face of loss, so much so that for a minute, I can't breathe. The rabbi asks us to remove the thin cheesecloth-like fabric from the headstone. It stops raining for a moment, and the light catches the glitter of the granite, and it sparkles.

The tradition is for mourners to place a stone on top of the headstone. There are many interpretations of the meaning of this ritual. Some believe that putting a stone on a grave keeps the soul in this world. The Talmud mentions that after a person has died, the soul continues to live in the grave for a time. Another says that it will protect golems from entering the grave. Flowers die, whereas stones are eternal and symbolize permanence. The rabbi asks us to pray silently.

One by one, we each place a stone on the headstone. We embrace friends and relatives, maybe twenty of us, and then people return to their cars. Morning has turned to afternoon. Before leaving, we seek out our youngest sister Kim's, headstone. I ask the rabbi to say a blessing, and we pile her headstone with stones muddied from the ground. Let them be together, I pray. Give my mother this last gift. Why not believe she is where she always imagined she would be, with my father locked in his arms and my sister by her side? The rain has turned to a drizzle. There is dampness on my skin. A cluster of blackbirds swoop down, peck at a haven in the grass, and then fly upward into the crack in the sky where daylight peaks.

The leaves have turned orange, red, and brown and carpet the ground. Nearby, a row of cars pull up. Another unveiling is taking place. I watch a woman get out of the car and then what looks like her young daughter. The woman opens a big black umbrella, and the young girl looks up at her mother and leans into her. I think of all the times I leaned into my mother as a child and all the times we were together when there were no words to be said because you don't need words when you have come out of a mother's body and as a daughter you have been her forever witness. I am not sad. I look up at the sky, and it feels like a flock of birds resting on my shoulders, weighing me down for so long, suddenly fly upward. And swiftly and unequivocally, I am released. And then I look up again at the sky, and truly a flock of birds fly upward and fold into a pocket of sky, and a slant of light comes between two clouds, and it is as if my mother is silently winking at me. *You're always so dramatic*, I can hear her say. *Mom*, I say to myself, looking at the headstone. *You led an extraordinary life. You survived more losses than most. You were always your own person, kind, warm, willful, exacerbating, and true. Your children live in you.* I look up, and now the sliver of light coming through the two clouds forms a smile. And I smile, too. And it's true. Though I miss my mother, I am free.

Acknowledgments

Thank you to my editor, Peter Borland, for his faith, care, and editorial brilliance and to my agent, Sarah Chalfant, whose steadfast support has been a sustaining miracle in my life. Thank you to my wonderful teams at Atria, especially Hannah Frankel, Debbie Norflus, Erin Kibby, Lisa Sciambra; and The Wylie Agency, hats off to the wonderful and steadfast Jacqueline Ko.

Thank you to my early readers. This book would never be completed without the care, attention, acumen, brilliance, and love of my dear friend, Diane Goodman, who read and commented on numerous drafts. Her scrupulous eye is reflected on every page of this book. Alix Kates Shulman's novel, *Memoirs of an Ex–Prom Queen*, set in the same community where my parents came of age, helped me to imagine the era. Thank you, Alix, for reading an early draft and illuminating what I hadn't understood. Thank you, dear friends Helen Schulman and Bill Clegg for your insights, support, and love. I'm so lucky.

I'm grateful to residencies at the T. S. Eliot House, The Betsy Hotel Writer's Room, and the Civitella Ranieri Foundation for giving me a room of my own in which to write, good fellowship, and amazing hospitality.

Thank you to my family, especially my two sisters, Laura and Cindy. I couldn't have written this book without your love, faith, and support. Thank you to my aunts, Irene Kretch and Rita Montlack for sharing memories of my father.

All love to David, Lucas, and Sophia (my beautiful pup).

Notes

10 "The Lord is My Shepherd," Psalm 23, The Book of Psalms, King James Version

10 "A funeral is not death, any more than baptism is birth or marriage union. All three are the clumsy devices," *Howards End* by E.M. Forster, pg. 12

13 "I heard a Fly buzz—when I died," by Emily Dickinson, *The Complete Poems of Emily Dickinson*, Little Brown & Company, 1960, pg. 223

26 "No tortured wailing," *Inferno* by Dante Alighieri, translated by John Ciardi, Modern Library Series October 15, 1996, pg. 39

The Magic Mountain by Thomas Mann, translated by John E. Wood, first vintage international edition, November 1996 Copyright © 1995 by Alfred A. Knopf, https://books.apple.com/us/book/the-magic -mountain/id6451349099:

26 "A silent sister," pg. 161

27 "Life is desire," pg. 1122

27 "we measure time," pg. 626

28 "how fast and loose they play with time," pg. 17

49 "When one day is like every other," pg. 17

49 "Habit arises," pg. 190

60 "There were pots of marmalade," pg. 80

37 "the eight activities of Daily Living required to be independent," *Being Mortal: Medicine and What Matters in the End*, Atul Gawande, Picador, USA, https://books.apple.com/us/book /being-mortal/id852965204

38 "The poet Yusef Komunyakaa, in his poem 'Blue Dementia,' *The Chameleon Couch* by Yusef Komunyakaa, Farrar, Straus and Giroux, 2011

38 "I thought they'd quit doing that," "The Bear Came Over the

Mountain," https://www.newyorker.com/magazine/1999/12/27
/the-bear-came-over-the-mountain

43 *"What good is sitting alone in your room? Come hear the music play.
Life is a cabaret, old chum, come to the cabaret,"* from the song "Life
is a Cabaret," from the musical *Cabaret*

46 "There's a sad sort of clanging," from the song "So Long, Farewell,"
from the musical *The Sound of Music*

48 *"New York Times* called 'The Last Thing Mom Asked,'"
https://www.nytimes.com/2018/08/31/sunday-review/mother
-death-euthanasia.html

54 "down virtually to the last detail," *This Little Art*, Kate Briggs, Fitzcarraldo Editions, 2017, pg. 15

63 "Piazza has a free wine bar," https://www.cleveland
-jewishnews.com/features/health/menorah-park-piazza
-pleases-and-grows/article_0a4788a4-4536-11e6-8def
-43313936dde6.html

65 "was the deception, the lie," *The Death of Ivan Ilyich* by Leo Tolstoy,
OPU, 2018, 98 https://books.apple.com/us/book/the-death
-of-ivan-ilych/id1357711298, pg. 64

66 "People don't just live for pleasure . . . they also want to preserve their dignity," "The Comforting Fictions of Dementia
Care" https://www.newyorker.com/magazine/2018/10/08
/the-comforting-fictions-of-dementia-care

67 "the failure of those around Ivan Ilyich to offer comfort," *Being
Mortal: Medicine and What Matters in the End,* Atul Gawande, Picador USA, https://books.apple.com/us/book/being
-mortal/id852965204, pg. 5

69 "Time past and time future," " *East Cocker, Four Quartets,*
T. S. Eliot

72 "It is designed with profound respect," https://jewishcareguide
.com/stone-gardens-assisted-living/166

76 "Elie was fifty-eight years old when she began to lose language,"
Dogs at the Perimeter by Madeleine Thien, W. W. Norton & Company, pg. 10

82 "The features settle into," Elegy for Iris, https://www.newyorker
.com/magazine/1998/07/27/elegy-for-iris

86 "According to the Cleveland Clinic," https://my.cleveland
clinic.org/health/diseases/24991-treatment-resistant-depression

87   "Jane Kenyon in her poem," "Having it out with Melancholy," *Constance* by Jane Kenyon, published by Graywolf Press, 1993

96   "What place this is," act four, scene seven, *King Lear* by William Shakespeare

99   "The Man all tattered and torn," from the nursery rhyme, "The House that Jack Built"

103 "The experiencing self," "Understanding the Self of People with Dementia," Fabian Hutmacher, *Zeitschrift für Gerontologie und Geriatrie*, 2020, https://doi.org/10.1007/s00391-020 -01718-1

104 "refers to a range of symptoms," medschool.ucla.edu/news -article/alzheimers-vs-dementia-what-is-the-difference

111 "idea of God feels more present or more essential," Nick Cave interview: https://www.theosthinktank.co.uk/comment /2023/02/16/nick-cave-and-the-christian-understanding-of -suffering#:~:text=What%20meaning%20is%20there%20to , entangled%20in%20one%20mystical%20experience

112 "The edges eventually wear away," *The Limits of My Language: Meditations on Depression* by Eva Meijer, p. 34

115 "more an absence than a presence," *The Limits of My Language*

115 "Depression is the flaw," *The Noonday Demon: An Atlas of Depression*, Andrew Solomon, Scribner, 2001, pg. 15

127 "Over and over women," *The Feminine Mystique* by Betty Friedan, A Norton Critical Edition edited by Kirsten Fermaglich and Lisa M. Fine, W. W. Norton & Company, 2013, pg. 9

131 "We have made woman a sex creature," *The Feminine Mystique* by Betty Friedan, pg. 21

137 "No one can make you feel inferior," Eleanor Roosevelt, quote is widely attributed to this author

137 "Trust your dreams," *The Prophet*, Kahlil Gibran, Knopf, 1923

157 "one flew off, and then," adapted from the nursery rhyme, "Five Little Butterflies"

165 "Rock a bye, baby," a nursery rhyme and lullaby

171 "Fee Fi Fo Fum," from "Jack and the Beanstalk"

173 "Because I could not stop for Death," *The Complete Poems of Emily Dickinson*, pg. 194

180 "Star light, star bright," nursery rhyme

191 "I am my beloved's and my beloved is mine," Song of Solomon, 6.3

191 "In the name of God," traditional Jewish wedding vows

195 blessing over the wine, *Baruch Atah Adonai Eloheinu Melech Ha-Olam, boreh p'ri ha-gafen, Blessed are you, eternal one, our God, ruler of the universe, Creator of the vine,* traditional Jewish blessing

229 "A rush of young Americans," https://scalar.usc.edu/works/con structing-a-culture/life-through-the-camera-lens-analyzing -post-world-war-ii-teenage-social-norms-in-life-magazine.38

233 "The only thing we have to fear is fear itself," Roosevelt's first inaugural address

234 "Now I lay me down to sleep," bedtime prayer

243 Lines from "My Rubber Dolly," old handclap song

248 "What we call the beginning," *East Cocker, Four Quartets,* T. S. Eliot

249 "Death exists, not as the opposite but as a part of life," *Norwegian Wood,* by Haruki Murakami, *Murakami: Vintage,* 2000, pg. 25

Bibliography

Works Cited

"Because I could not stop for Death," from *The Complete Poems of Emily Dickinson*, Little Brown & Company, 1960.

Being Mortal: Medicine and What Matters in the End, Atul Gawande, Metropolitan Books, 2014.

"Blue Dementia," from *The Chameleon Couch*, Yusef Komunyakaa, Farrar, Straus and Giroux, 2011.

The Death of Ivan Ilyich, Leo Tolstoy, Bantam Classics, 2024.

Dogs at the Perimeter, Madeleine Thien, reprint edition, W. W. Norton & Company, October 3, 2017.

Four Quartets, T. S. Eliot, Faber & Faber, main edition, May 16, 2019.

The Feminine Mystique, Betty Friedan, W. W. Norton & Company, 2013.

"Having it Out with Melancholy," from *Constance* by Jane Kenyon, Graywolf Press, 1993.

Howards End, E. M. Forster, Penguin Twentieth Century Classic, 2000.

"I heard a Fly buzz—when I died," from *The Complete Poems of Emily Dickinson*, Little Brown & Company, 1960.

Inferno, Dante, translated by John Ciardi, Modern Library Series, 1996.

The Limits of My Language: Meditations on Depression, Eva Meijer, translated by Antionette Fawcett, Pushkin Press, 2023.

The Magic Mountain, Thomas Mann, Vintage, 1996.

The Noonday Demon: An Atlas of Depression, Andrew Solomon, Scribner, 2001.

Norwegian Wood, Haruki Murakami, translated by Jay Rubin, Vintage International, 2000.

This Little Art, Kate Briggs, Fitzcarraldo Editions, 2017.

Articles Consulted

Cleveland Clinic. "Treatment-Resistant Depression." Cleveland Clinic. May 16, 2023. https://my.clevelandclinic.org/health/diseases/24991-treatment-resistant-depression.

"Constructing a Culture: Analyzing Post-World War II Teenage Social Norms in LIFE Magazine." n.d. Constructing a Culture. https://scalar.usc.edu/works/constructing-a-culture/life-through-the-camera-lens-analyzing-post-world-war-ii-teenage-social-norms-in-life-magazine.38.

Hutmacher, Fabian. 2020. "Understanding the Self of People with Dementia." *Zeitschrift Für Gerontologie Und Geriatrie* 54 (2): 161–66. https://doi.org/10.1007/s00391-020-01718-1.

"Jewish Care Guide." Jewishcareguide.com. 2025. https://jewishcareguide.com/stone-gardens-assited-living/166.

Bayley, John. "Elegy for Iris." *The New Yorker*, July 19, 1998. https://www.newyorker.com/magazine/1998/07/27/elegy-for-iris.

Lyall, Sarah. "The Last Thing Mom Asked." *The New York Times*, August 31, 2018, sec. Sunday Review. https://www.nytimes.com/2018/08/31/sunday-review/mother-death-euthanasia.html.

MacFarquahar, Larissa. "The Comforting Fictions of Dementia Care." *The New Yorker*, October 1, 2018. https://www.newyorker.com/magazine/2018/10/08/the-comforting-fictions-of-dementia-care.

Munro, Alice. "The Bear Came over the Mountain." *The New Yorker*, December 19, 1999. https://www.newyorker.com/magazine/1999/12/27/the-bear-came-over-the-mountain.

"Nick Cave and a Christian Understanding of Suffering." Theos Think Tank. 2023. https://www.theosthinktank.co.uk/comment/2023/02/16/nick-cave-and-the-christian-understanding-of-suffering.

Rosenblum, Jonah L. "Menorah Park Piazza Pleases and Grows." Cleveland Jewish News. July 8, 2016. https://www.clevelandjewishnews.com/features/health/menorah-park-piazza-pleases-and-grows/article_0a4788a4-4536-11e6-8def-43313936dde6.html.

Sievert, Diane. "Alzheimer's vs Dementia - What's the Difference?" UCLA Med School. July 5, 2023. https://medschool.ucla.edu/news-article/alzheimers-vs-dementia-what-is-the-difference.

About the Author

Jill Bialosky is the author of the *New York Times* bestselling memoir *History of a Suicide: My Sister's Unfinished Life*, a finalist for the Books for a Better Life Award and the Ohioana Award, and the memoir *Poetry Will Save Your Life*. She is the author of five acclaimed collections of poetry. Her newest volume of poetry, *Asylum: A Personal, Historical, Natural Inquiry in 103 Lyric Sections*, was a finalist for the National Jewish Book Award. She is also the author of four critically acclaimed novels, most recently *The Deceptions*, a finalist for the Gotham Prize. Her poems and essays have appeared in *The New Yorker, The Atlantic Monthly, Harper's, O Magazine, The Kenyon Review, Harvard Review, Paris Review,* and *Best American Poetry*, among others. She co-edited with Helen Schulman the anthology *Wanting a Child*. She is an executive editor and vice president at W. W. Norton & Company. In 2014, she was honored by the Poetry Society of America for her distinguished contribution to poetry.